Dear Old Rebel

A *Priest's Battle for Social Justice*

Harvey Steele

Pottersfield Press, Lawrencetown Beach,
Nova Scotia, Canada
1993

Canadian Cataloguing in Publication

Steele, Harvey, 1911 -

Dear Old Rebel

ISBN 0-919002-80-7

1. Steele, Harvey, 1911- 2. Missionaries — Canada — Biography. 3. Scarboro Foreign Mission Society — Biography. 4. Catholic Church — Canada — Clergy — Biography. I. Title.

BV3705.S75A3 1993   266'.2'092   C93-098603-2

Cover photos: Lesley Choyce and Canamedia

Pottersfield Press gratefully acknowledges the ongoing support of the Nova Scotia Department of Tourism and Culture, the Department of Communications and the Canada Council.

Pottersfield Press
Lawrencetown Beach
R.R. 2, Porters Lake
Nova Scotia B0J 2S0

Printed in Canada

Contents

Dedication

To my favourite SFM priests, the first SFMers to depart this world, the only two buried in China. Their graves and bones have disappeared outside the walls of Lishui.

Jim McGillivray from Glace Bay, N.S. 1897-1935. For his wisdom, wit and more.

Aaron Gignac from Ridgetown, Ont. 1902-1940. For his beautiful, even saintly person.

I owe them both so much.

Their deaths were like Christ's. No person ever had so little to show for his life's work as Christ when he died on the cross. All was useless—a failure, as far as human eyes could see. To the eyes of faith, it was another story.

Author's Note

Three years ago several publishing houses asked me to write my memoirs. My talent as a writer did not measure up.
Patrick Donohue came to the rescue. He not only polished the manuscript but helped me to find a publisher. This book owes more to Pat than to me.

Harvey Steele, 1989. (Photo courtesy CANAMEDIA)

Preface

Dear Old Rebel is a book which looks back on an extraordinary life. Because the author is highly literate and reflective, it is a thoughtful retrospective. This alone would claim our interest and add more necessary documentation on the struggles of missionary priests in the middle of the twentieth century, but Harvey Steele's engrossing account in the pages ahead does much more. Inadvertently and in embryonic form, Steele's life and his musings bring us face to face with several important themes which the Roman Catholic Church and indeed all of the Christian churches must deal with in the coming century. Among these I would list in no particular order the following: the compatibility of Christianity and capitalism; Christian socialism; the desperately needed rethinking of sacramental theology in ways that are accessible to ordinary people; the role of celibacy in the Catholic priesthood; the Church as authoritarian, hierarchical and centralized vs. the Church as democratic, declericalized and indigenous; the role of the Church in a post-Christian era. Readers will be stimulated by these questions as they get swept up in the narrative.

As much as Dear Old Rebel is a document of the universal Church and its worldwide mission, it is a distinctively Canadian tale. The early chapters remind us once again of the phenomenal gift of Cape Breton Island to the Canadian Church. If it were not for this rugged patch of Nova Scotian real estate, the Canadian Catholic Church would long ago have lost much of its soul.

The hardiness of the Scots' settlers, the ruggedness of the land, the poverty that they endured and the Catholic faith they so tenaciously clung to created a critical mass which when it exploded warmed the Canadian Catholic Church into an institution which had to face the spat-upon face of its founder. Once again, and we need to hear it again, we see the rise of the co-op movement and credit unions, institutions which favoured cooperation over competition, solidarity over individualism. We hear the neglected voices of Mike Gillis, Jimmy Tompkins and Moses Coady demanding, "a full and abundant life for everyone in the community." Contrast the Antigonish Movement founded at St. Francis Xavier University with the terribly destructive policies and rugged individualism of the university's famous graduate, Brian Mulroney. *Dear Old Rebel* retrieves the more authentic Antigonish for us.

Steele's recounting of his painful years in the seminary and his marginalization because of his powerful justice leanings remind us how out of touch seminary life was at that time, how absolutely middle class it was, how terribly conservative, locked as it was in its rigid counter-Reformation stance and theology. Yet, somehow Harvey persevered.

Steele's missionary tales of China and Latin America raise profound questions about the enculturation of the gospel, about effective evangelization. Harvey, it would appear, was light years ahead of his contemporaries whose seminary training ill equipped them to meet people at the depth of their humanity. So caught up were they with rigid institutional concerns and a sacramental theology which bordered on the magical that they missed the one great sacrament, Jesus in the marginalized.

Harvey intuitively understood that for the gospel to be good news to the poor it must address felt, material needs. Instilling in farmers — *campesinos* — the great commandment of sharing and co-operation rather than competition and greed, he proved to them that religion was not simply consolation, but it was liberation as well. Because Harvey stood with the poor over against their oppressors and over against the societal forces which stole their dignity, he made enemies of the wealthy.

Harder to stomach were the blind guides of organized religion, many in his own society, whose silence legitimated the unjust and exploitative nature of the capitalist economy. Because Harvey saw and understood the economic and cultural milieu of the humans he had sworn to serve, he quickly came into deep conflict with these enemies of life. His negative reputation was sealed: he was labelled irreligious, communist, loner, radical.

Fortunately, this book is redeemed by Harvey Steele's absolute candour and his great sense of humour, qualities which have both brought him much isolation but also much enjoyment. While candid about his own faults and those of his Scarboro Foreign Mission Society, he is never cruel. Readers for whom this book is an introduction to Harvey "Pablo" Steele will find out for themselves why he really is a dear old rebel.

Ted Schmidt
Catholic New Times Editorial Group
June 1993

Introduction

On a radio show here in Toronto, the host was asking me how it was that I, a young man from Cape Breton became a radical priest, went to China and Latin America, got in trouble in several countries, then got myself kicked out of them. "You're eighty years old now," the host said. "Usually older people become mellow. Are you still a radical?"

I am. True, most people mellow as they become older. But there are always exceptions to rules. The fact that few of my peers agree with my ideas doesn't bother me. I am only trying to follow my model—the man from Galilee. Wasn't He a great radical, the person who, in many ways, turned the world upside down?

Here's an incident (among many) which turned me into a radical.

It happened in 1923, when I was twelve years old. Our family was living in the coal-mining town of Dominion (about 2,000 people). We had moved there two years earlier from my grandparents' farm. Most of my rustic features had worn off by now and I fitted into the miners' culture.

I was one of a mob of several hundred men, women and children lined up in front of the big company-owned store on a hot day in Cape Breton's short summer. Among us were many miners from nearby towns who had appeared on the streets that afternoon. The wind was spraying us with salt water from the Atlantic, only a few yards away. Everybody knew what we were there for.

Another miners' strike was on, the third in four years. All of the coal mines in the area, about ten of them, were on strike. While coal was the only wealth the Creator put on the little island of Cape Breton, the owners of the mines were British and

American. They admitted making some $9 million in profits the previous year.

All the miners wanted was an increase in their wages at a time of inflation. People were hungry. There had been violence between the miners and the company's police. The company had the backing of the provincial and federal governments, as well as the silent backing of most professional and commercial people in the area. Even most church people, not speaking up for the miners, supported the owners by a tacit silence.

But the mood of the people gathered that afternoon was almost festive. Some were singing popular songs, others laughing and talking. Of course, some had been drinking. Yet, there was an undertone of sadness, even fear.

Then the first stones were thrown, smashing the big plate glass windows of the store. The mob moved in and looting began. People grabbed whatever was in their reach: food, clothing, hardware. I saw a small boy wobble away with a bag of flour that weighed more than he did. Hours later, when the three floors of the store were pretty well emptied, gasoline was sprayed and the big fire began. It lasted through the night. No fire engines came.

Soon after, Ottawa and Halifax sent in the militia. I can still see the train slowly coming our way down the tracks into town. In front of the engine was a flatcar piled four feet high with sand bags, the mouths of cannons poking out. We were living under martial law.

The fury of that summer played on my mind a long time. Why should such an easy-going, conservative people, mostly Scots, hold so much pent-up anger? Later, I discovered that the rage was fuelled by the inhuman conditions miners worked under, conditions that killed many men. As a priest, I saw the conditions for myself when called to a mine accident. This time, an Italian had been killed by a fall of stone. To get to the site of the accident, I had to ride on a small electric train about five miles under the Atlantic Ocean. Then I crawled the rest of the way through a small hole to anoint the part of his cold head that was not blown away.

That showed me something of the horror of the miners' lot. Miners dug coal with pick and shovel on their knees. Salt water constantly dripped in from the ocean overhead. Some miners, descending into the mine before dawn and not emerging until dark, went as many as six months without seeing the sun. Among them were boys only twelve years old.

Only years later did I fully understand how much these poor people had suffered at the hands of the foreign owners of the mines. It wasn't just physical hardship. There was a kind of spiritual slavery involved. The foreigners were the owners of just about everything in town. In a way, they owned the miners' souls.

It was simple injustice. My sense of outrage, although not leading directly to the priesthood, did make me the kind of priest I am—a fighter, a radical. Yet, priests are supposed to be obedient, conservative people. My kind of priesthood would turn out to be one that was constantly battling the establishment to get a fair deal for poor people. Through the building of Co-ops, largely in Latin America, I was to spend my life helping people to control their own destinies in spite of the opposition of vested interests.

Recently, as a result of a television documentary on my life, several people have urged me to write my autobiography. What good will such a book do? The market is filled with biographies of public figures. There are, however, few about priests. Maybe, a century from now, when the celibate priest has disappeared, people will wonder what kind of rare birds we were.

Certain questions come to mind: should I tell all the truth or just part of it? If I tell the whole truth, some people are probably going to be hurt — priests, some members of my family, maybe others. What should I say about my parents, now long dead? Is it possible to hurt the dead?

Well, I don't know the answers to all of those questions, but I'm going to start writing. At least it will keep me busy. At my age, that's a boon. I'll look on the process as an examination of conscience regarding my past life. It will be a kind of spiritual retreat.

It might be fitting to quote the wise and witty Mark Twain who once said, "When I was young, I could remember things happening, whether they happened or not. Now...well...I forget what I was going to say." Some experts claim that a person's memory reaches its peak at age twenty and that, from there on, it's downhill all the way. As far as I can judge, my memory isn't

13

too bad, though I admit there are some foggy patches here and there. So the reader must make allowances for the odd inaccuracy.

Chapter One

Growing Up in Cape Breton

All my life, I have been asking questions. One of the first ones was: where did my mother get the name she pinned on me? I've never much liked it. Whenever I asked where it came from, my mother would only smile enigmatically. So, as with many of the questions in my life, I had to make do without a satisfactory answer.

When I was born on Wednesday, May 3, 1911, at Sydney, Nova Scotia, my parents, Michael Steele and Mary Sutherland, were both twenty-two years old. Thirteen more children were born to them, four dying in infancy. Nine of us still live as I write — five sons and four daughters. Both parents passed into their nineties before departing this world, after celebrating seventy-two years of married life. To say they were years of bliss would be less than truthful.

Writing about one's parents is not easy. It is hard to be totally honest, to tell the truth with the warts and all. Like the mules in the German proverb, we all want to claim that our ancestors were horses.

My view of my ancestors is that they were ordinary people, sinners all, few saints, but good humans. They were not very ambitious. Undemanding of life, they were content with a simple life, even with poverty. Greed, so common among people today, was less prevalent then.

Both my parents were Scots, their ancestors having arrived in Cape Breton early in the nineteenth century. Gaelic was the first language of my grandparents on both sides. My parents understood it but could speak little. As a child living with my grandparents, I could understand a little of the household Gaelic.

The Catholic Scots who settled in Cape Breton were highlanders driven out of the Hebrides by greedy landowners wanting more land for their sheep. I have often wondered why, forced off those bleak islands, the highlanders would want to settle on rocky Cape Breton with its even harsher climate. It has been said that they fell in love with the island's rugged beauty because it reminded them of their homeland. Maybe that tells us they were more romantics than realists.

Perhaps they were also attracted to the isolation of Cape Breton. Thanks to the remoteness of the Hebrides, they had held on to their Gaelic language despite the edicts of Henry VIII in favour of English. This linguistic uniqueness, combined with the isolation, also accounted for their retaining their Catholic religion, some have said.

In Nova Scotia, the settlers met with the same kind of discrimination and language barriers as in their former homeland. Again, they were second-class citizens. It wasn't until 1829 that the elimination of the oath against "Popery", a pre-condition of voting, emancipated Catholics. The sense of separateness, born of resentment, still shows in the fact that many natives of the island call themselves Cape Bretoners rather than Nova Scotians, even though the island was assigned to the jurisdiction of Nova Scotia more than 100 years ago.

In the book *Beyond the Atlantic Roar*, by D. Campbell and R. MacLean, the characteristics of the Highland Scots who settled Cape Breton are described as follows: "Their wants are comparatively few, and their ambition is chiefly limited to the acquirement of the mere necessities of life." Thanks to the insular lives of Cape Bretoners, these cultural traits have lasted longer than those of many people. On the island, time is something to enjoy, an opportunity to be neighbourly, to chat. Making money and working hard are not very important. A gentleman is never in a hurry. The slow pace of life and the hospitality are impressive to outsiders.

My mother's temperament, however, was more like that of the Protestants among her people a few generations back. Serious, quiet, even taciturn, she was opposite to my father in most ways. She was thrifty. Alcohol was abhorrent to her. To say she was a hard worker would be an understatement. She enjoyed few pleasures and even fewer luxuries.

My mother was an only child in so far as her brother died when she was only eight (I think he was younger than she). Her mother died the same year. I've heard two versions of the story: it was typhoid or tuberculosis that killed them. As my mother was not much inclined to talk about her past, I don't know which is the true story. She was brought up by her father who didn't marry a second time until many years later. Since most of my mother's aunts and uncles lived in the US, she saw them rarely. Her father was a carpenter and lived much of his life in Sydney. Just recently, one of my brothers told me that, since mother was able to attend Holy Angels School run by the Notre Dame sisters in Sydney, she got a good education — probably grade eleven, far more than the average in rural areas.

Given the scarcity of relatives on my mother's side, combined with her reticence when it came to family memories, to speak of my family background is to speak largely of the Steeles. My dad was the youngest of nine children, three brothers and six sisters. His father was John Steele and his mother Catherine McInnis. All nine children were born on the farm at Beechmont. The three sons left home in their teens. The eldest went to Western Canada and worked as a carpenter. The second went to work in a coal mine in Sydney Mines. He volunteered in the Great War, fought four years in the trenches, returned to the coal mine and, a year or so later, was killed instantly by a fall of stone. The youngest brother, my dad, started work at age thirteen at the Sydney steel plant. The six sisters all married, raised large families and lived in urban areas.

When my father was growing up, education for rural people in Cape Breton was minimal. Typically, a student completed about three grades of school. My father earned his grade three diploma in a little red school house at Beechmont where he was born. Some twenty years later, while living with my grandparents, I spent four years in the same school.

The Steeles were faithful to their religion (often with some Gaelic superstition thrown in) but it was not a big deal for them. In terms of parish boundaries, Beechmont was just a mission of Boisdale, several miles away. A priest came to the Beechmont chapel several times in the summer months but never in winter when the roads were blocked with snow for seven months.

One indication of how religion rated in their lives is the scarcity of religious vocations among the Steeles. From more than fifty of us grandchildren came only three religious vocations: a nun (my sister Florence) and two priests (my cousin Joe MacDonald and myself). There have been no vocations to religious life among some forty of my nieces and nephews. There was, perhaps, one really saintly person in my background — my dad's mother. If prayer helps bring on a religious vocation, I credit her prayers with mine.

My dad, as the youngest of nine, was by all accounts the favourite of his family, spoiled first of all by his mother, who doted on him, and then by his sisters. My older brothers and sisters who lived at Beechmont with our grandparents agree with me on this. But they all loved him for his sense of humour. Besides, he was a handsome six-footer. One day, shortly after my ordination, I dropped in on Aunt May, his sister. She quipped, "You look great in that roman collar, Harvey, but you can't hold a candle to your good-looking father."

Like his two brothers, he was addicted to alcohol. (Some of his sisters were overly fond of it too, as I recall.) This weakness, once condemned as sin, is now considered a disease by some medical people. Considering how many of the family had it, it must have been in the genes of the Steeles. In the six years I lived with my grandfather, however, I never saw him intoxicated. That may be because he was too poor to buy liquor. Besides, my grandmother, like my mother, was strongly against liquor. That didn't affect their love for my dad because, for many years, they knew nothing about his drinking.

When the First World War broke out, the Sydney steel plant, the largest in Canada, started working around the clock to produce more steel, a vital ingredient in fighting a war. Men often worked twelve hours a day, seven days a week. This gruelling work took its toll on my dad. In 1915, when he was in his early twenties he had a nervous breakdown and was ordered to take a complete rest.

So we moved to the farm to live with my dad's parents. I remember driving there in a horse and buggy, with my mother and a younger brother and sister, to join our dad. It turned out, though, that farm life didn't suit him. After a couple of years, he went back to work at the steel plant in Sydney. He lived with our Aunt May, his married sister, while the rest of us stayed on at the farm.

The Beechmont farm was twelve miles from Sydney and bordered on a copper mine that had operated for a few years at the beginning of the century. A dirt road leading to Sydney passed a few yards in front of the house. No neighbours' houses were visible though they were less than a mile distant. The hills around us on all sides were covered with forests of spruce and hardwood.

The farm house was typical of the area — wooden, a storey and a half, with a small cellar. On the ground floor were: a kitchen where we spent most of our time; a pantry; a dining room seldom used; a visitors' parlour or "front room", hardly ever used; my grandparents' bedroom; and a small porch. The only heat came from the wood-burning stove in the kitchen. Upstairs were three bedrooms. Even though the storm windows were never removed, the bedrooms were freezing cold half the time. Two or three kerosene lamps provided light. Water came from an outside well. Plumbing was a two-holer a few yards from the house.

Beyond that were the carpenter shop and the barn. Our livestock consisted of a horse, three cows, a few pigs and some sheep and hens. The farm was small, only twelve acres of the poorest soil. With slightly more than three months of growing weather, it was a meagre living but my grandfather's work as a carpenter helped to put food on the table.

The cellar kept our food supplies for the long, cold winters: potatoes, turnips, carrots, beets, apples, salt codfish. Barrels were filled with corned beef, pork and herring in brine. Flour, corn meal, salt, sugar and other cooking needs were kept in the pantry.

Beginning in November or earlier and lasting till May, the road was piled with snow, drifts ten feet high. Sometimes even horses and sleighs couldn't move. I can see myself pressing my hand to the frosted windows of the kitchen to see if anything was moving on the road. All was quiet, covered with snow, not even birds could be seen. More than a month would pass without a visitor. There was little to talk about. Diversions were scarce.

Radio wasn't yet a household item. There was no telephone, nor were there magazines and newspapers. There was no music and there were few books — just the bible and the farmers' almanac.

One neighbour, Alec MacSween, who did come once in a while, filled us with ghost stories. They were fascinating but scary. After hearing them, I was always afraid to go upstairs to bed. After one session, Alec was heading out with his lantern for his house about a mile away. My grandfather must have sensed some hesitation in Alec's step.

"If you're afraid, you can sleep here," Grandfather said.

"Oh, that'd be great," Alec answered, and he gratefully bedded down on the kitchen floor. He had frightened himself with his stories.

Alec's mother, being double-sighted, saw funerals of people before they died — including her own. How to explain these preternatural events, I don't know. To a child, they were impressive. Even my grandfather sometimes experienced them. As the local coffin maker, he often knew when business was coming his way: he would hear sawing and hammering in his carpenter shop at night. But, on investigation, it would turn out that only the ghosts were there.

It was the end of May or later before any planting could begin. Summer was the delightful time of the year. There were trout to be caught in a nearby brook, wild strawberries and raspberries to be picked and, near the end of the season, sweet apples on our trees. Neighbours came to visit, especially relatives from Sydney. It was a chance to meet kids my own age. There were only two things wrong with summer: having to pick potato bugs and removing stones from the ploughed fields. I was convinced that stones grew like other things because each year the thin soil produced just as many as the previous year.

Since my dad was only with us at intervals, grandfather was the one who taught me the things a farm boy should learn: to milk cows, to harness a horse, to plough and harrow the fields. Trips to Sydney with him were always exciting — a chance to see crowds of people, cars, stores, that wonderful taste of candy and the first ice cream cone.

One highlight of every summer was the annual parish picnic at the country school. It was the only time of the year when neighbours came together. Kegs of beer, wine and rum were the staples of the party. Women brought cakes and pies to be auctioned off. When the spirits hit their mark, the fiddler and organist began the music and square dancing started. The sweat began to flow, then it was time for the men to show their machismo.

As the fighting began, women huddled together and cried. Some of the fights may have been over a woman, title to land, an old family feud or just for the sheer love of having a fight. Years later in Latin America, I was to see farmers getting together for similar celebrations that turned into brawls. The big difference in the two scenarios was that the Latins carried knives. Often people were wounded, even killed, during parties there.

If I close my eyes, I can still conjure up the atmosphere of those parish picnics in my youth. One year on the morning after the party, my grandfather took us up to the school house which was the site of the festivities. As the man who looked after the building, he had to begin to see about clearing up the mess. Windows and doors had been closed all night. That pungent smell of beer, wine, sweat and blood stayed in my mind a long time.

Shortly after coming to the farm, when I was just past four years old, I came near death with a burst appendix. Among farm people at that time, not too much was known about the inflamed appendix. It was called the big stomach pain. Even though people often died of it, doctors were seldom called in. A general suspicion of doctors and medical intervention was widespread. I doubt that my grandfather ever consulted a doctor about his health. (Perhaps a bit of his attitude has rubbed off on me. So much of medical practice nowadays seems a waste of time — being shuffled from one specialist to another. When you're a little kid, you have growing pains; when you're old, you have dying pains. They come and go and there's not much anybody can do about them.)

But my grandfather could see that my condition called for quick action. Vomiting and in obvious pain, I was clearly on the point of death. Luckily for me, the attack happened in summer so my grandfather was able to drive me with his horse and buggy to the nearest hospital, in North Sydney. The doctor who saved my life was M.T. McLean, the grandfather of the Hollywood star Shirley McLean.

At some point during the hospital stay, a nurse was trying to make me do something or was trying to inflict some medical procedure on me. As usual, I balked, stubborn as a mule. She barked at me, "If you don't do as I say...(then she grabbed my toe)...I'm going to cut this off." I bawled, but yielded.

The remedy for the severe constipation following the operation was Epsom salts in orange juice. I had to hold my nose to get it down. It cleaned me out all right, but for years after, I couldn't drink orange juice.

The only punishment I can recall from those years was being locked in a closet. Usually, my cries and tears brought my grandmother to the rescue. I have no memory of my dad ever "laying his hand" on me, to use that old expression.

My grandfather, however, taught me one unforgettable lesson. One winter morning when it was still dark, he called me to get out of bed. Later, when he called a second time, I got up and trudged downstairs. Grandfather was sitting in a rocking chair with my one-year-old baby brother in his lap. The baby was dead. Grandfather said, "If you had got out of bed when I first called you, you would have seen your brother alive. Now he is dead. Kiss him." I bent over and kissed the baby's forehead. It was already turning cold in the unheated living room. This was the first time I ever saw a dead person.

Other memories of my grandparents show how much times have changed. For instance, this advice from grandfather sounds strange in today's world: "Always tip your cap to the priest, to the medical doctor and to your school teachers." Another vivid recollection concerns a visitor to the house. Probably a relative from the big city (Sydney), this young woman sat in our parlour with crossed legs and smoked a cigarette. Both behaviours, being taboo to my grandparents, labelled her a hooker in their eyes, as was apparent from their comments after her departure.

Usually visits from the Sydney relatives were lots of fun. In the summer months, they often stayed a night or two. Most of these uncles and aunts enjoyed their rum. After a few belts, their Scottish blood would come to the surface; they sat in a circle, holding hands and singing old Gaelic songs. Perhaps somebody would get up and do some step dancing.

My mother never joined in these parties. One time, she was down on her knees in the kitchen, scrubbing the hardwood floor, while the aunts and uncles were getting ready, after two days of partying, to move the revels to another relative's farm. When the three buggies were ready to depart, Dad came into the kitchen and asked Mother to go with them. She refused. He kicked over the bucket of dirty water and left.

An hour or so later, Mother came downstairs with a beat-up suitcase. "I want each of you to kiss me goodbye," she told us children. "I'm going away and I'm not coming back. I can't stand any more of this."

My sister, six years old, kissed her, then my five-year-old brother did.

"I'm not going to kiss you," I said. "You can't leave. You're my mother."

But she did leave, striking out on foot for North Sydney, five miles away. I sat the rest of the day under the poplar tree beside the house, sobbing and looking down the road. Near sundown, mother came walking up the road towards us.

I have no doubt my mother was fully intent on leaving. Quite apart from her temperamental incompatibility with the Steeles, living under another woman's roof could not have been pleasant for her; it rarely is for any woman. At the time, my mother would have been just under thirty years of age. She was separated from her husband much of the time. My brothers and sisters near me in age agree with me that our dad seemed to love his mother more than he loved us and our mother. He was strong on the fourth commandment! One time, after we had moved back into town, he took a taxi loaded with groceries and went to his mother's farm, leaving us without money or food. Luckily for us, a local merchant gave us groceries on credit.

While I was still a little boy, mother came to me more than once, with tears in her eyes, to tell me her troubles. She had nobody else to tell them to. Often, I could not understand. Even so, exposure to my mother's worries made me something of an adult while still a child. Aunts and uncles often said I was too serious. Similar comments were made to me years later as a seminarian. Even today, some of my fellow priests think I'm too concerned about what's going in the church in every part of the world.

In later life, my brothers and sisters often told me stories about how I was more trouble to my mother than any of the other children. Mother never said so but it's probably true. After all, it's a new experience for a mother to have her first child. The fact that my grandmother spoiled me probably didn't help matters. Moreover, boys are often more difficult to handle than girls. There is little doubt but that I was a strong-willed little boy. (I haven't changed much through the years.) In the case of my refusing to accept our mother's leaving us, you might say my stubbornness paid off. Stubbornness — a gift or a curse? Or might it better be called perseverance? Whatever it is, I still have more than a good share of it.

Some of these traits may have to do with being the oldest child. The firstborn is often described by psychologists as overly serious, responsible, a leader, conscientious, strict. If I can judge, it seems I have many of these traits to this day. Being the oldest in a family can also have a marked effect on one's relationships. One basic fact of existence, for example, was that I didn't have to wear hand-me-down clothing while my younger brother did; this didn't help my relations with him.

Another quality did not endear me to my brothers and sisters — I loved to work, even when not asked to. At eight years old, I gladly chopped all the wood to keep fires burning in our home. Later, when we lived in town, two tons of coal would be delivered and my brother would just sit there but I'd go out and move it without being asked. This willingness to work has, to some extent, stayed with me through life. This trait seemed to cause some envy in my brothers and sisters, perhaps because my work habits made me look good in the eyes of the grown-ups.

Studies have shown that if there is a big gap between the oldest and youngest in a large family like ours (my youngest sibling is twenty-two years my junior), the younger members often see the older ones more as aunts or uncles than as siblings. This is true of my family. In a way, our family is split into two groups — the older ones born in Sydney and Beechmont and the younger five born in Dominion. The younger group mostly lived in affluence but the older members of the family endured meagre years on the farm. The differences between poverty and affluence have left their marks on us and have separated us, our ways of thinking, our ways of looking at life.

In September 1921, we set off in a double-seated buggy from Beechmont. My mother, my two brothers and two sisters were the passengers. I, at the age of ten, was the driver. We were bidding farewell to farm life because the little farm house was running out of room for us. Moreover, my dad naturally wanted to have his family with him. So we were going to join him in a coal mining town called Dominion.

Like a dozen other towns in the area, Dominion, with its population then of 2,000, was built around a coal mine. Mining on Cape Breton goes back as far as 1758 when it began at Sydney Mines. In 1893, the Dominion Coal Company began opening up coal mines and at one point they operated some twenty mines, producing more than a third of all the coal mined in Canada. Through the years, scores of miners as young as thirteen years old died in mine accidents.

The company not only owned the mines but virtually everything else in town — the houses the miners lived in as well as the large department store where people bought the necessities of life. The stores were called "Pluck-Me's". All purchases were deducted, along with other fees, from the miner's pay. Here's a sample of the kind of accounting that used to appear on the miner's pay envelope:

House rent	$1.50
Doctor	0.50
School Tax	1.10
Church	0.90
Poll Tax	1.10
Coal Haulage	1.10
Oil for lamp	0.95
Powder	3.10 (for blasting)
Hospital	1.00
Union Fee	1.00
Store Account	24.55

Only a few dollars remained from the man's total pay.

The company houses were small, two units in one (semi-detached). Only minimal repairs were made on them. They did not have indoor plumbing or central heating. People lived for the most part in the kitchen where one stove provided all the heat for the house.

In Dominion it wasn't easy to find a place to live because the mining company had not built houses in years. We were lucky to find small quarters on the first floor of a two-storey building owned by the Salvation Army — three small bedrooms, kitchen and dining room. There was no bathroom. The Salvation Army used part of the lower floor; the upstairs was rented to the coal miners' labour union. We had lights and indoor water, two luxuries we did not have on the farm.

A marvel almost beyond belief was the primitive radio in the house. I remember standing with a bunch of kids straining to hear something through the crackling static. Sure enough, there were voices — barely discernible but real. "Do you mean to tell me," I asked, "that this thing can pick up what somebody's saying and people miles away can hear it?" When the answer was in the affirmative, I announced, "I'm never going to confession again!" A similar shudder of fear comes back to me today when I think about the potential for invasion of our privacy by state-of-the-art technology.

Dominion's one school, a public one, was near our house. The church was just over a mile away. Entering a new school in grade five wasn't easy. Not only was I timid but, given the isolation of farm life, I hadn't mixed much with other kids. Of course, I took some razzing and was called a country bumpkin. The recess games were new to me as I had never played ball of any kind.

There were about thirty boys and ten girls in our class. I took top honours each year and skipped grade seven. Grades nine, ten and eleven were all in the same room, with only one teacher, the principal of the school. I think I was the youngest student in the high school. Most, including myself, didn't finish grade eleven. Boys in their teens usually went to work in the mines.

As the great majority of the town was Catholic, on holy days school was closed. In some other urban areas Catholics had their own schools, usually run by nuns. I often think how lucky I was not to have them as teachers. Judging from the reports of other people who did, I'd say there's a good chance that nuns would have turned me off religion.

We had arrived in one of the roughest times for mining communities. Demand for coal and steel had dropped at the end of the war. Often men worked only a few days a week. Strikes were frequent in both industries. Some of the strikes lasted as long as nine months and usually all the mines went out on strike at the same time. This meant several thousand men in the area would be idle.

The company had made millions and, although we did not know it at the time, was preparing to pull up stakes. The burning of their store did not come as a surprise to them. Inventory had been reduced and maximum insurance was taken out. Later, we learned that the watchman of the company store was told not to be on duty at the time of the raid.

The anger, frustration and hunger of the people led not just to violence. Radicalism also surfaced. Propaganda from the recent revolution in the Soviet Union reached our little island. Devout Catholics stopped going to church. Communism seemed the best hope for many. Tim Buck, the head of the Canadian Communist party, came from Toronto to visit the area.

Ironically, at a time of such suffering for many, our family fortunes took an unexpected turn for the better. Since a new baby was arriving every eighteen months or so, our tiny living space in the Army hall was becoming more crowded. When another family moved to Boston, we were able to rent their house, a larger one, right on the main street. To try to keep up with the surging appetites of the growing family, mother bought two cows. It was my job, helped by a younger brother, to look after them. We carried the milk in tin cans to sell to neighbours. I kept half of the proceeds. Around the same time an older boy next door gave me his paper route. With my fee from looking after the cows and the money from the papers, I was making almost as much as some of the miners.

That gave mother an idea: would I like to join her in running a little candy store? I agreed. Dad had no objection. Mother and I put up the money, about $75, and sent an order to a Sydney wholesaler for candy, tobacco, ice cream and some other items. All was sold in a day or two. Our next order was for double that amount. Soon, we were selling small groceries as well. Today, people think my strong grip comes from milking cows but it's from scooping rock hard ice cream out of those five-gallon tins packed in ice and salt. My hands would be numb sometimes.

With all these jobs to look after, my school days seemed to be ending. At the end of grade nine, I passed the local test but failed the provincial one. However, I was allowed to enter grade ten, and then grade eleven, but missed classes most of the time. Another business opportunity came when a store owner moved to Boston and we were able to move into his much larger place. It grew into the largest general store in town. By now, my dad was running the business. He never returned to the mines. He was the boss in the store and all the older children were helpers.

It was a credit business. The miners had never learned to handle cash since the coal company did that for them. To my mind, that checkoff system made miners irresponsible and helped to make them dishonest about their debts. So running a credit business wasn't easy.

Saturday was payday. In the afternoon, kids would arrive with a long list of a family's needs for the week. We made up the orders and put them in boxes. Often the mother of the family would come later with a story to the effect that she could not pay her bill or could pay only part of it. The following week the same story; eventually the credit would have to be stopped. Then came the tough job of going to the homes to try to collect. Nobody would answer the door, or the woman would give you 50 cents on $100 debt. In hopeless cases, we would put the account in the hands of a lawyer who took forty percent of what he collected. The threat of going to jail made some pay up.

So the Steeles had enemies in town. I recall one angry woman coming into the store one day and telling me, "All you merchants will go to hell." I knew her quite well. She was a devout Catholic and one of the town's most rabid poker players.

The other side of the story was that if people did not pay their debts to us we would not be able to pay the wholesalers and our credit would be cut off. When I was a bit older, my dad pretty much left me in charge of the business during the three months I was home from school. For the summer, I was the one who dealt with customers, wholesalers and travelling salesmen. I was tougher on customers than my dad was. He found it hard to refuse people even when he knew they were dishonest or unable to pay their debts.

Looking back on those experiences, it seems to me that the Protestants were more honest in paying their debts than the Catholics. Since becoming a priest and working among these same Catholics, I often wonder how much good it did them to be going to confession. Did this sacrament help people to form a better conscience? Or did confession merely mask their consciences? I'm reminded of the old L.O.C. (League of the Cross), a temperance society that had its roots in Ireland. As teenagers, we could join it for the sake of playing basketball. Every week, the fellows would take the oath: "I'm not going to take a drink of liquor for one month." Next week, they'd be back, taking the oath all over again. It was just a joke. Well, confession was somewhat the same.

Chapter Two

My Years in Antigonish

One day in the summer of 1927, while I was cutting meat in our store, my uncle Rod MacDonald came to talk to me. As the Grand Knight of the Knights of Columbus in Sydney, he suggested that I write the exams for the K. of C. scholarship that paid most college costs at St. Francis Xavier University for four years. The exams would be held in Glace Bay in just a week. I hadn't given much thought to continuing my education but had no objection to trying the exams. What with working in the store, there was little time to prepare for them. Twelve of us from grades eleven and twelve wrote the two-day exams on eleven subjects.

A month later, *The Glace Bay Gazette* reported that a Glace Bay boy had won the scholarship. I was not disappointed. A few weeks later, however, my uncle came to see me again. Curious about my performance on the exams, he had found out that while I had scored 894 points, the Glace Bay boy who received the scholarship had scored only 791 points. The priest in charge of the competition had given him the scholarship because his dad was a pillar of the parish. My uncle raised such a ruckus that the Glace Bay priest was forced to give me a scholarship while the other boy retained his.

Understandably, my winning the scholarship was not good news for my dad because it meant I would be leaving the store. For me, it was a liberation from drudgery. What a great feeling when I arrived at St. F.X., as it is popularly known, in the fall of 1927 — to be free from the slavery of the store, to be with young men from all over, to be able to play games I never had a chance to play before. Back home, I never had time to learn to swim even though there was an excellent beach 100 yards from our house. At St. F.X., I tried my luck at football (English rugger), hockey and basketball, even though I wasn't much of an athlete. Eventually, I would get my varsity letter in football. I was elected manager of the academy hockey team and was on the staff of the varsity monthly paper.

I had enroled in grade eleven in what was called the academy, consisting of grades eleven and twelve, associated with the university. My sports activities meant considerable travelling and time lost from my studies but I was getting passes in all subjects. Near the end of the year, however, I received a letter from the Glace Bay priest saying that I would lose the scholarship if my final marks did not improve. By hard work, I did upgrade my marks in those final months.

A month after my return home, the Glace Bay priest informed me that my scholarship was revoked. True, my marks had improved, but I was taking too many science subjects, he said. That was considered an unsuitable preparation for the priesthood. The priest claimed that the scholarship was intended only for future priests. This was news to me. I later found out it wasn't true. (The Glace Bay boy continued to enjoy his scholarship for a while but did not finish college and did not become a priest.) It was a great shock to me that a priest could be so dishonest. This added to my radicalism. It also made me a bit anti-Church. Not logical, I admit. Why blame the Church for the wrongs of one priest?

To tell the truth, a feeling that perhaps I should be a priest had been with me ever since I was a little boy. If it could be put in words, they might be something like this — I had a love for God (more, I'm afraid, than I have now) and thought that to be a priest was the best way of showing that love. Where that idea came from, I'm not sure. Perhaps my devout grandmother made remarks to that effect. Or maybe it seemed obvious to a young boy that the priestly state was the closest any human could come to God.

However, the dishonesty of that Glace Bay priest blocked my inclination towards the priesthood. Wanting to work in some profession that would help poor people like those with whom I had grown up, I decided on medicine. Rather than contest the scholarship issue, I simply paid my own way at St. F.X., finishing high school and then taking the two-year pre-med studies.

On the campus there were almost 200 students, most of them from Atlantic Canada, a few from Ontario, Quebec and the Boston area. Although St. F.X. was no longer a diocesan seminary, as when it was originally founded, there was a strongly Catholic atmosphere about the place. We were urged by some staff priests to go to daily mass but attendance was not mandatory. There was a priest prefect on each floor.

Bells told us when to rise and lights were turned off at ten-thirty at night. Young women from the nearby Mount St. Bernard College, run by the Notre Dame sisters, shared classes and laboratory work with us. In the afternoons, we were free to go downtown. After supper, boys learned popular dances, such as the foxtrot, by dancing with each other. As that did not appeal to me, I never learned to dance. Quite often some boys skipped out to take in dances downtown. Drinking was quite common and I took my first drink of rum. I also began smoking, a habit that stays with me.

In my adolescent years, I had become interested in boxing and had attended most local fights. It was a popular sport among the miners. Having little time to play games in those days, I had taken a correspondence course in boxing. Published in New York, it was a thirty-week course by Michael McFadden, an American who had trained several world title holders. Included in the lessons were diagrams on how to throw various punches, rules, and boxing lore.

It so happened during my third year at college that the head of St. F.X., Dr. H.F. McPherson, "the Old Rector" as he was fondly called, went to see a world heavy-weight match in New York's Madison Square Gardens between Jack Sharkey and Jim Maloney. As I recall it, the rector received the ticket from a niece who was married to a nephew of Jim Maloney. The rector had a ringside seat. A big man, he loved all kinds of sports but now boxing topped the list.

He wanted to know if anybody on campus knew anything about boxing. Most of the priests, who made up a large proportion of the faculty, were opposed to boxing. Somehow word got to him that I had taken a course. He insisted that I send home for the lessons. The jumble of papers arrived during Holy Week. On

Thursday morning, the old man and I were in his room on our knees, sorting out the mess. A knock came on the door. A messenger had been sent to inform the rector that Holy Week ceremonies in the cathedral were being held up because the rector was not present. (As well as being head of the college and a monsignor, he was also the vicar general of the diocese.) The bishop, about 100 priests and a cathedral full of lay people were waiting. The incident prompted one of the priests to warn me to "lay off this boxing stuff" with the rector. But he was the one who was pushing it, not I.

Boxing became his obsession. That made me, in his eyes, the most important student on campus. He asked me to pick potential boxers from among the students and start giving them lessons every afternoon in the gym. As far as I could tell, none of the 200 boys on campus had ever boxed. The old rector himself singled out some and invited them to train with me. Often he would call for me to discuss some student who seemed to have potential as a boxer. He got us all the equipment needed for training. Then he ordered the St. Martha's sisters in charge of the kitchen to set up a table with special food, the very best — steaks almost every day — for the boxers.

Once the team's training was well under way, the rector invited other Maritime colleges to get their boxing teams ready. At his urging, the first Maritime inter-collegiate boxing match took place in Halifax. Our team won almost all the titles and continued to do so for several years. When I left the campus, a retired pro-boxer was brought in to train the students.

Had I not been on such good terms with the rector, I might well have been expelled from St. F.X. for my involvement in a protest over the quality of the food — which was worse than normal for Depression times. (This was before the setting up of the special table for boxers.) In a clandestine way, three of us were named to call a food strike. We persuaded everybody to line up and refuse to enter the dining room at meal time.

Along came the rector. "What's going on here?" he asked. No answer. He looked at me, "Steele, are you the leader of this?"

To a great extent I was, but he had picked me out of the crowd because of our boxing connection. A nod from one of my companions told me to speak.

"Doctor," I said, not answering the question about my leadership role, "we are asking for better food. It is impossible to eat the meat (local cows). We cannot even cut it with a knife (which was true)."

The rector, bigger and stronger than any of us, yanked the dining room door open, "Get in there, all of you," he ordered us. "We'll fix this thing up."

We obeyed and the food did improve a little. In a way, this was the beginning of my career as a radical, the first of many instances of sticking my neck out for just causes.

Poverty and hunger have been known from time immemorial in many parts of the world. Our western world, however, except in times of war or revolution, had never experienced poverty and suffering as severe as they were in the 1930s. Millions of people lost all their savings in bank failures. Throngs of people lined the streets to get rationed food to stay alive. People in the millions had no employment. Gloom and despair were everywhere. Nova Scotians hadn't been unfamiliar with economic hard times before the 1929 crash but this was worse than ever. Local politicians and the clergy, being in favour of the status quo, did little to help the most afflicted people.

Behind the scenes at St. F.X., unknown to most students, something was being brought to birth which was going to address this injustice. It was also to prove one of the most important influences in my life. A special kind of co-operative movement, it would become famous around the world as the Antigonish Movement. Some have said that the best known Canadian place-name among the poor people of the world is that Micmac word "Antigonish", thanks to the fact that the movement bearing that name has had such a beneficial effect on their lives.

I was aware of it, more perhaps than any student on campus, because of a family friendship with one of its founders — Father Michael Gillis, a priest who was born on a farm next door to the one my mother was born on. After war service as a chaplain, he was assigned to his first parish in 1919. As it was near my grandparents' farm, he occasionally dropped in. Apparently, he saw something special in me. One time, when I was about eight, he and I were riding in the buggy with my grandfather. "How many grandchildren do you have, John?" Father Gillis asked.

"Oh, I guess about fifty," grandfather said.

Father Gillis put his hand on my knee and said. "Well, this is the greatest of them all."

That moment — the sense of the priest's belief in me — stayed with me and gave me a kind of strength all my life.

A humble man, Father Gillis was loved and trusted by everyone because of his honesty. There was no doubt about his sympathy for the underdog. When I was at St. F.X., he always had time to say hello to me on his visits to the campus. His dreams for helping the poor appealed to my radicalism and hatred of injustice. To my young mind, Father Michael Gillis was a model priest, in contrast to the one in Glace Bay.

Another key figure in the movement was Father Jimmy Tompkins. Born of Irish parents on Cape Breton, he had been vice-president of St. F.X. early in the 1920s. His ideas about co-ops and adult education for the poor were considered pretty radical. What upset people even more was his campaigning for the amalgamation of all the Maritime universities into one. In his view, that would have been a tremendous saving financially and would have provided better education. An ecumenist before the word was invented, he saw no obstacle in the fact that under amalgamation the Catholic colleges would fall under the influence of Dalhousie University, originally founded as a non-denominational college. But to the Catholic establishment of St. F.X., such a possibility was abhorrent. They threw him out of the college and "exiled" him to the most isolated and poorest parish in the diocese — a small fishing village called Canso.

Some years earlier, he had made a trip to Europe on a cattle boat, searching for ideas on how to help the poor. He learned about the Co-op Movement, born in England, in 1844, and the credit unions started in Germany the same year. The idea of credit unions had been brought to Quebec in 1901 by Alfonse Desjardins, a Quebec newspaperman who had studied in Europe. Because of language and cultural barriers the concept hadn't reached other parts of Canada. A co-op consumer store at Sydney mines had no far-reaching effects because it was something of a closed idea, being limited to Presbyterian membership.

Desjardins did successfully start credit unions in New Hampshire, among French-speaking people originally from Quebec. His idea was taken up by Edward Albert Filene of Boston, a Jewish philanthropist, who spent much of his personal fortune promoting credit unions. In 1931 Filene's assistant, Roy Bergengren came to Nova Scotia, at the invitation of Father Tompkins, to explain how to run credit unions successfully.

Tompkins, a little man with a high-pitched voice, was constantly button-holing people to talk up the idea of co-ops. Trying to convince everyone that something should be done to help the poor was his passion. The effect he had on people is well expressed by the comment of a Cape Breton coal miner at Tompkins' burial: "By heavens, he was one hell of a man." A nun who worked with him said, "Father Jimmy was God's greatest nuisance." Years later, a *Readers Digest* article by John Chafe described Tompkins as "The most unforgettable character I've met".

One of the first converts to his ideas was his double first cousin, a priest some ten years younger, Dr. M.M. Coady. While Tompkins was an agitator and a visionary, Coady was an academic. He was a former school teacher and had a doctorate in education. In contrast to his small, cousin, Coady was a big man (over six feet) who resembled the greatest boxer at the time, Jack Dempsey. Coady was indeed the right man to promote the new idea. His size, his totally masculine face, his big hands, his voice, and even his name, Moses, fitted the bill.

Above all, his forceful speaking style challenged people. He even dared to tell the workers and farmers that they themselves were responsible for their poverty. As he was not looking for popularity nor seeking votes as a politician, he spoke with a candour that angered many people who had vested interests in the status quo. Few of the priests of the diocese backed him and fewer were his friends. He was labelled a trouble-maker.

It is strange how some people, and not others, are grabbed by this virtue, justice. Always at the bottom of the Catholic list of virtues, it was never mentioned in the seminary training in my time. Pope Leo XIII, near the end of the nineteenth century, was the first pope to mention it. Ever since, popes have been mentioning it but such pronouncements have been taken seriously by few bishops or priests. How could they understand? They lead affluent lives and were never told in their seminary days that justice is important.

So where did Tompkins and Coady get their radical ideas for justice? They were both born in the Margaree farm area, the only place with good soil on Cape Breton. It's unlikely, then, that they experienced hunger like that suffered by farmers in other areas of Nova Scotia and by urban workers of the province. Coady did his studies at the Urban College in Rome. There never was, nor probably ever will be, any new idea from Rome and its institutions.

The only explanation I can think of is that they were good men and good priests. My impression is that Coady became even more radical as his work evolved and he saw the exploitation, especially of the urban workers. Perhaps his tenaciousness, his indifference to scorn, had something to do with his being Irish. The situation in the old country shows us how most Scots compromised with the conquering English whereas the Irish fought the oppressors.

These two Irishmen in a sea of Scots were joined by a few other priests, including my friend, Father Gillis. A few laymen and a United Church minister, Reverend Nelson MacDonald also took an interest. This handful of men met through several years, working on their plan to help the poor of the area.

These pioneers of the Antigonish Movement had lost faith in the prevailing capitalistic way of life. Yet, at the same time, they were not buying Russian communism, though many people thought of them as communists. Most of the 200 priests in the diocese were opposed to or not interested in the new ideas pouring out of Moscow. After all, people in that area, largely Scots, were conservative by nature.

Undaunted by widespread suspicion, the Antigonish pioneers believed in the economic benefits of co-ops and credit unions as ways of getting people to work together. But they figured something was lacking — education. People had to be shocked and awakened from their apathy and their lack of belief in themselves. Their minds and hearts had to be opened and the key to this was education. Tompkins and Coady, both on the staff of the college, bemoaned the fact that the college, supported largely by workers' donations to parish collections, was educating only the sons of the well-to-do.

Father Mike Gillis and lay Catholics put pressure on the college to open an extension branch to help the poor. The academic priests running the college weren't keen. Father Gillis threatened to raise the money and run an independent program if St. F.X. wouldn't rise to the occasion. Finally, the governors of the college agreed. The extension of the university was launched in 1928 with Dr. Coady in charge.

Farmers, fishermen and miners were brought to the university for all kinds of courses and seminars. Although some deans were not pleased with the fact that nearly illiterate men and women were brought to campus and would be rubbing shoulders with the sons of the elite, the program flourished.

The Antigonish Movement is based on six principles:
1. The primacy of the individual;
2. Social reform through education;
3. Economics as the basis of adult education;
4. Education through group action;
5. Effective social reform involving fundamental changes in social and economic institutions;
6. Full and abundant life for everyone in the community.

A quote from Dr. Coady might be fitting:

> The good society of the future should be a mixed society. This means four kinds of ownership: 1. Individual ownership of homes, farms and vocational equipment; 2. A large measure of co-operative ownership; 3. Some state and municipal ownership of the things that are in the nature of public utilities; and 4. An indefinite and potentially large field for private-profit enterprise.

The federal government asked Dr. Coady to organize the fishermen of the Maritimes who were among the most exploited people in the area. Under his leadership, fishing co-ops by the scores were organized. By doing away with the middlemen and selling their catches directly to the consumers, the fishermen earned three times what they had been receiving.

Credit unions, co-op stores and other types of co-ops slowly began to spring up all over the Maritimes. From Nova Scotia, co-ops spread across the rest of Canada. Today, Ontario has perhaps the most credit unions of any province while in British Columbia, the provincial government employees' credit union is the largest in the world.

Antigonish in the early 1930s, when people were seeking solutions to the Depression's devastation, became a Mecca. Motorcades of Americans wanting to learn about the new movement came in the summer months. Other students came from Asia, Africa and Latin America. Coady was in demand in Canada and the US to give talks. In 1932, he and Gillis were invited by the Archbishop of Toronto, Neil McNeil, a native of Cape Breton, to give talks to the priests of the Toronto area. Father Gillis told me, however, that the three-day talks were a waste of time. The conservative clergy of Toronto, mostly affluent people, had no interest in such wild ideas.

As for western Canada, co-ops other than credit unions had begun there years before the Antigonish Movement. The Co-op Movement is still a powerful force among western farmers. It came to the west with immigrants like the Swedes who had flourishing movements in their homelands. They were not religious leaders. They were hard-nosed business people.

That business sense was sometimes lacking in the Maritime co-ops. Often they were oriented around the parish. In many cases, a priest played a role. Priests, by their training, are about the poorest business people in the world. (Some exceptions, of course.) Often the priest persuaded the people to put a certain man in charge of the co-op because he went to church regularly, or because he had a big family and needed a job. The man may have been a good Catholic (whatever that may mean) but a hopeless manager and perhaps even dishonest. The result — the co-op would die in a short time. Business is a hard game. Mixing it with charity is often fatal.

Despite the inevitable failures, the co-ops in the Maritimes flourished for nearly a decade. Then the Second World War came, bringing all kinds of employment. People were affluent for a time. Co-ops and prosperity don't mix well. There still are co-ops and credit unions in the area but study clubs and adult education are no longer part of the movement as in the early years. To Maritimers, then, the once-famed Antigonish Movement is no longer of much importance.

But the word Antigonish still is very well known by millions of poor people around the world. In 1959, shortly after Dr. Coady died, St. F.X. built the Coady International Institute in his honour. The original function of the institute was to organize the teaching of the program, which had previously been somewhat haphazard. Now the Coady Institute runs a variety of courses almost totally for people from the Third World and a few

Canadian missionaries who work there. The institute also puts on a series of courses in the Third World. Several small Coady institutes, modelled on the parent institute in Antigonish, have been set up by dioceses in Africa and the Philippines.

On the Antigonish campus every year, about fifty students come from several dozen Third World countries to take the five-month course. Most of the students come from Asia and Africa. Being government employees, most of them speak English.

Formerly, there were also some from Latin America. That presented a problem as few of them spoke English, the language in which the courses were given. For some years, Antigonish offered a crash course in English but this did not solve the problem. English, by no means an easy language, can't be mastered in two months. Perhaps it's especially difficult for Latin Americans. In my many years living with Latin people, I never found them very gifted in learning other languages. Even among the highly-educated Spanish priests who worked in Latin America, few spoke a second language, unlike priests from other European countries. Among the Latin American students at the Coady Institute, the result of this linguistic obstacle was that they became frustrated with the Antigonish program. Many quit after a short time and returned home. Those who stayed on longer failed to grasp much of the philosophy of the Antigonish Movement. On more than one occasion, I met with some of these students in their home countries and they were openly critical of the Antigonish program.

In addition to the language barrier, there were other problems. Food, for instance. I remember a Peruvian priest who arrived in Antigonish, having just received a doctorate in Rome. He told me how he hated the Antigonish food, especially the meat and bread. It was difficult for me to suppress a smile at his condemnation of the two products which I thought were the best Canada produced. He had never eaten cold storage meat; he was used to eating meat the day it was killed. The bread he was accustomed to was made of flour and starch, a common bread in Latin America that is quite tasty but hardens within hours after it is baked.

For many Latin American students the weather was also a problem. The majority of them come from tropical areas and there is nothing tropical about Antigonish winters.

I discussed these difficulties with Dr. Coady when I had been working in Latin America for a short time. He agreed that Antigonish was not the place to teach Latin American students. We both believed that the Latin students should be taught in their own language and in an environment they were used to.

Before I leave the Antigonish scene and those pioneers of the movement which had such an influence on my life, two stories about Michael Moses Coady come to mind.

I was heading back to the Dominican Republic after being there a short two years and trying to organize co-ops. Before my departure from Antigonish, Dr. Coady asked me to give a talk to the students on my work. He introduced me as a fighter, who years before introduced boxing to the university but was now fighting for justice. For the talk, some six priests sat on the platform and about 400 students were in the audience.

Around eleven that night, a rap came to my door. I was on my knees saying my prayers. (Apparently I was quite devout at the time.) It was Dr. Coady. He apologized for interrupting and said he would come back later.

Near midnight, he returned. It looked as though he'd had a drink in the meantime. He was not a habitual drinker but, like many older people, did take a drink once in a while. "I'm sorry to bother you..." he started. "I want to congratulate you on your talk. I know you are getting opposition from the men in your society. Few people see the importance of social justice in our religion. A passion for justice is a special gift from God and you are one of those He has favoured. Keep it, treasure it, no matter what. Keep on doing what you have started. Don't leave the missions or your society. You have a glorious chance to do great things for a lot of people."

It seemed to me, as he said these words, that a tear was about to drop from his eye. He put his hand on my shoulder and walked out. His words that night helped me in many lonely hours in the years that were to follow in the Dominican Republic when I was under attack from the dictator, as well as from some of my confreres.

A few years after his midnight visit, I was astonished to receive a letter signed by the president of the St. F.X., Monsignor H.H. Somers. It read: "St. F.X. will be very pleased and honoured if you will accept the honorary degree of Doctor of Laws this year …" Asking me to deliver the baccalaureate address to the graduates, he concluded his letter, "No one is more entitled to recognition by St. F.X. than yourself."

As much as I tried to find out who was responsible for nominating me for the honour, I never could, but my best guess is that it was my friend Dr. Coady.

My talk to the 700 graduating students started with a story about Abraham Lincoln's saying to one of his secretaries, "Every person over forty years of age has the map of his life written on his face, if you can read it." I asked the students to think about what they'd like their faces to show twenty years down the road. Years later, somebody told a young man by the name of Brian Mulroney graduated from St. F.X. that year. Whether or not he was in the audience, I don't know. It would be interesting to know what kind of map he sees when he looks in the mirror.

Chapter Three

Toronto — The China Seminary

It was September, 1931. At the age of twenty, I was beginning another stage in my young life — embarking on medical studies. I was on the train, heading for "Toronto the Good" as it was called — the WASP city of Canada, where Masons and Orangemen ruled, the city known to many Canadians as the snob city of the country.

For me, train travel is a great way to think — seeing parts of the country I have never seen before, watching fields, towns, villages and people go by. On this trip, my thoughts were roaming over my past life, especially the past four years at St. F.X. University. What did I learn? What did I experience? I also wondered about my decision to go to medical school. Was it the right thing to do? Did I really like the idea of becoming a doctor? I could not give solid, honest answers to these questions.

When I looked back at the years in Antigonish, I recalled some positive experiences: the freedom of being on my own, the company of young men my own age, playing games I never had a chance to play before, getting a varsity letter in football. As a student, however, I had nothing specially to be proud of. I merely got by because I gave too much time to extracurricular activities and I left without a sheepskin, so prized by others.

After four years at St. F.X., I felt there were more negatives than pluses on my record. I had tasted liquor for the first time. I began to smoke and now, sixty years later, I still have these two habits.

Another deficit: my ideal of what a priest should be was tarnished. Through the scholarship affair, I knew of the less-than-honest priest of Glace Bay. Also, because of another priest, I heard about homosexuality for the first time. This was a priest who had propositioned a great many students. (He was not one of the priests on the college staff. I looked on them as fine men.) The behaviour of the homosexual priest was a great shock to me and to my companions who, likewise, had never heard of homosexuality. Today, some experts tell us that homosexuality may be attributable to a genetic pre-disposition and that homosexuals are not at fault for their condition. But in my youth, it was an almost unthinkable perversion.

Also, I had less than good feelings for a priest on staff who tried to push me into the priesthood and who shamed me on this score several times. He bombarded me with invitations to join his church choir and other activities. He was well-meaning and recognized as a holy person but he was no diplomat nor was he much of a psychologist. Besides, he was a Scot and should have known how stubborn Scots can be.

Meanwhile, I had learned something about my own sexual nature. I did not seem to relate to girls as most of the students did. Physically, yes, I was attracted to them but something — fear, maybe — kept me away from them. This perhaps was the reason why I did not learn to dance as most students did.

I was accompanied on the train to Toronto by a friend who was also enroling in medical school. Also a native of Sydney, he was one of the few protestants at St. F.X. (He got his medical degree at Toronto and later became the head of the Hamilton hospital in Bermuda.) We passed the time chatting about Antigonish and wondering what Toronto would be like. As the train rolled along, we watched the countryside and saw how different New Brunswick and Quebec were from Cape Breton. Quebec, with its beautiful, lush farms extending for miles, seemed much more prosperous than Nova Scotia. Perhaps that was because the Quebec houses were showing new paint jobs and gayer colours than those in our native province.

We had a one-hour stop-over in Central Station in Montreal. With everyone around us speaking French, it was like being in a foreign country. We understood only some of what they said. Then, on to our destination, the Queen City, as some called it. Arriving in the morning, we walked out of the Toronto station, looked across the street and saw the largest building we had ever seen, the Royal York Hotel (now dwarfed by sky-scrapers). After breakfast at a Murray's restaurant across the street from the station, we took a taxi to our boarding house on Spadina street, not far from the university. Three other students lived there. We soon found that the middle-aged landlady treated us like sons. Her breakfasts were more than generous. We took our other meals in nearby restaurants.

After finding the medical school and registering, the first order of business, apart from classes, was initiation. It was not pleasant. One of the pranks was to show you a bowl of urine with a stool floating in it. Then you would be blindfolded and your head would be pushed into the bowl. In the meantime, the original bowl had been replaced by one with ginger ale and a sausage in it. Another ordeal was having your body painted all over with iodine. Wearing a tie was obligatory but seniors would come along with a scissors and snip off your tie bit by bit. Then you'd be bawled out for not having a tie. All this was meant to humiliate us and it did. Perhaps that was good for some smart-alecs who needed the stuffing taken out of them.

There were over 150 students in my class, five of them women. Later I learned there were only seven Catholics among us. Several of our professors had English accents and from time to time some of them showed their WASP mentalities. One professor, for example, used to say that a human organ had the same shape as the Masonic apron — as if it could be taken for granted that this garment was familiar to all of us.

After a couple of weeks my friend and I received two or three invitations to dine at fraternity houses. To belong to a high-ranking fraternity could mean a lot to a future doctor, although, from what I hear, fraternity membership doesn't mean much to one's career today. At these dinners for potential recruits to the fraternities, one of the leading questions had to do with one's religion. As a result of our answers on that score, my friend was invited back to several of the houses. I was not.

Two months or so later, my companion, with apologies for abandoning me, decided to move into a fraternity house. Then I heard about a vacancy in an apartment nearby where three down-east students lived. The three of them were older than I by a few years (the oldest was finishing his last year of studies) but I was invited to join them.

The small apartment — two double pull-down beds, a kitchen, living room and bath — was on the second floor of a five-storey building on a street near the university. We took turns buying food and preparing our meals. The other fellows had the experience of housekeeping in the years immediately preceding but this was my first attempt to master some of the domestic arts. That practice was to serve me in good stead on the missions when housekeepers were hard to come by. We Maritime students in Toronto were always trying to find fish from the east coast but without much success. As we were used to tasty fish from the cold salt water of the Atlantic, the fresh water fish did not suit our tastes.

Every Saturday afternoon, the four of us went to tea parties at the Newman Club, a centre established to bring Catholic students together. These weekly socials were never much fun for me. Dancing being the major part of the program, I was relegated to wallflower status. It meant that I passed most of my time with two or three other guys who had never learned to dance. A few girls invited me to go to a show, a dinner or perhaps a hockey game, but I never accepted. I wanted to...and yet I didn't. I was, as I was told, anti-social. Even years later as a priest, I have been told that.

A couple of months after I moved into the apartment, one of my companions whistled to a girl walking by. Like many girls in those Depression years, she had turned to prostitution to get money to stay alive. It didn't take much persuading to get her to come up to the apartment. My companions went to bed with her. Being the youngest, I was last on the list. When it came my turn, I refused. I locked myself in the bathroom and sobbed until the girl left. So I cheated her of a dollar or two. In a way, I wanted physically to do as the others had but there was something that kept me from doing it. For a time, my companions teased me about that.

The months passed. I was not a happy person. Something of a misfit, I did not enjoy the social life and things other young men enjoyed. The bigotry against Catholics, a new experience for me, combined with some of the offensive things priests had done, made me somewhat anti-priest. For a time I stopped going to Sunday mass, something I had never done before. Due to boredom and a lack of a sense of direction, I was not doing well in my studies even though a lot of the courses merely repeated biology and organic chemistry I had already learned. In fact, I was losing whatever interest I had in medicine.

Some pleasant cultural events of that year, however, stand out in my mind. I went to the recently-opened Maple Leaf Gardens to hear Winston Churchill speak on the unity of the British Empire. I also went to the Royal Alexandra Theatre to hear the famous Irish tenor John McCormick and, later, the then acclaimed greatest violinist in the world, Fritz Kreisler. This interest in classical music also set me somewhat apart from most young men.

Up to this time, I had never heard of the China Mission Seminary. All I knew was that Jim McGillivray from Glace Bay, a fellow I knew slightly at St. F.X., was studying in an institution some ten miles or more on the outskirts of the city, in a place called Scarborough. Recently ordained a priest, he was soon to depart for China. I found out the name of the place where he lived and phoned him. We met several times.

Jim was almost fifteen years my senior. He had graduated from St. F.X. the year I entered, having worked for the coal company for some years before college. (Jim had been turned down when he enlisted for the First World War because of a heart murmur.) At St. F.X., he was head of the student council and probably the most popular man on campus.

He told me he had once been engaged to a Protestant girl but then decided to become a priest and go to China. Why the change of mind, he never said. The origins of his vocation were largely a mystery. Something equally mysterious must have happened in my chats with Jim. Yet, he never gave the slightest hint that he thought I might become a priest or go to China. After all, I was going to be a doctor, we both thought. I gave Jim no indication that the thought of becoming a priest had ever crossed my mind. And I certainly had no interest whatsoever in that far away place called China.

At the end of the school year, in May, 1932, I was back in the land of the coal mines — back with my family, cutting meat and running a grocery store. None of it made me happy. Nor was I happy about Toronto. It all seemed like a bad dream. I was caught in the same trap I had twice escaped from. My dad was not on the job, due to drink. I was irritable and nervous. Several sleepless nights passed. My mother noticed there was something wrong and suggested seeing a doctor. I wouldn't agree. I knew there was nothing wrong physically.

In fact, the trouble was spiritual. It was as though a voice deep in my soul kept repeating, "Harvey, you are on the wrong track. You must be a priest." Not that I actually did hear such a voice, but the nagging thought wouldn't go away.

Although I had said nothing of this to anyone, my mother may have suspected the drift of my thoughts. Trying every avenue to help me, she phoned a first cousin of mine, Joe Mac-Donald, ordained just two weeks before. He came to see me. Not knowing him very well, I didn't say much, just something to the effect of my not being able to sleep, feeling on the verge of a nervous breakdown. I did mention that the thought of the priesthood kept pestering me. His diagnosis was that I was meant to be a priest and had been fighting the idea.

I acknowledged that as a possibility.

My cousin suggested that an older priest, a so-called expert on vocations, should come to see me. It was the very man who, at St. F.X., had been pushing me into the priesthood. Not feeling very kindly towards the old man, I grudgingly agreed to meet him.

Within days, he appeared at the store. He began by telling me that, from the first time he saw me, five years before, he knew I was cut out to be a priest. (What was it he saw in me? I do not know.)

I had to admit to him that becoming a priest was in my mind when I first went to Antigonish.

He asked me if I still thought of being a priest.

"Yes, to some extent."

Then he asked: "Where would you like to work as a priest?"

My reply came at once: "Anywhere but home." This was because of my dad's drinking.

It happened that the old priest had been a great booster of the China Mission Seminary since the place was founded. His next question was: "How would you like to go to China?"

My reply (as I thought of my friend McGillivray and my dad), "All right — as far as I can get from here."

"Will you agree to apply to the China Seminary if I give you the address?"

"Yes, I will."

He gave me the address. When departing, he said, "I think you should do some special praying, maybe go to mass every day."

The decision was made, the die was cast, all in less than half an hour. It was a great relief. How, after years of waffling, did I make up my mind so fast? I don't know. In any case, experts on the spiritual life tell us that we don't make the choice, rather it is God who calls us to these vocations. Probably the best that can be said is that it is an enigma. Isn't life itself!

I told my parents that night. My mother, taciturn as ever, said nothing. To this day I am not sure whether she was happy or not. My father protested, "Why so far away to China? Why not here?" There was no comment from the other children.

Following the old priest's instructions, I went to daily mass for the rest of the summer. As people in town noticed this behaviour, naturally there was gossip. A few years later I heard some of the comments. One was from an Anglican woman, one of the most honest customers on my paper route. She was telling people, "I always knew that Harvey would be a priest." People know more about us than we know about ourselves!

Regardless of what others thought, I knew in my heart that it was the right decision. I was back to my normal self and continued working in the store. Knowing I would never again be stuck in the store with no prospect of escape, I was happier than in previous summers.

Not that there weren't bad moments. A month or so after the decision, Joe MacDonald, the young priest, came to visit and gave me one of his old soutanes. It gave me a funny feeling of alienation. This damn black robe with all the buttons down the front was a garb for an old woman, I thought. I almost said, "To hell with it!" But this was the only road to the priesthood and I would have to wear the robe the next five years almost all the time.

In spite of my basic contentment with the decision, I had some serious concerns: would I make it as a priest or would I be thrown out of the seminary? Obeying rules, which was the essence of seminary life, would not come naturally. It was not going to be easy for me to subject my rebel nature to others. Another question that gave some worry: could I be chaste for the rest of my life? My sexual desires were strong and girls were mightily attractive. Yet, I felt that other young men who had become priests must have had the same drives as I. Still another concern was my anti-priest feeling. Would I, on closer familiarity with priests, find that many were not really honest people? If this were to happen, I said to myself, then I would quit the seminary.

Looking back through a prism of sixty years, some explanations for my attitudes and feelings come a bit clearer.

Firstly, why was I a rebel and why did I have a strong passion for justice? (The two qualities seem to go together.) Already, I mentioned the coal miners' strikes and the losing of the scholarship. But perhaps the stronger factor was my dad's alcoholism. In all alcoholic families there are grave injustices which the family does its best to keep secret. But sometimes the shame becomes public. It is hurtful when another kid comes up to you and says, "I saw your father drunk again, staggering up the street." Few miners drank, except on weekends, because they lacked the money and their jobs would be in jeopardy if they were too drunk to show up for work. My dad did not have either problem: he had money and his children kept the business running for him.

Nowadays, some experts see alcoholism more as a disease than a sin. But there definitely is a sinful aspect to it when families suffer from the abuse of alcohol. In many cases, they lack the needs of life because so much money goes towards the bottle. There is often violence involved too. In my dad's case, violence towards any of us never went any further than threats but there was lots of violence against the furniture.

Despite his weakness for the bottle, I cannot think of another man in the community whom I would prefer as my dad. Maybe I should even be grateful that his weakness led me to my vocation. In the community, there were other upright, sober men, good church-goers. One outstanding man in this group was even considered a kind of saint, but, as I learned later, he was a miser. There were others who used religion to make people think highly of them. There were others who were externally loyal to their church duties but did not pay their bills. So, although my dad's alcoholism helped make me a rebel, I do not condemn him.

Secondly, why was I afraid of girls and yet sexually attracted to them? The best answer I can give is that I never saw love in our home. I have no memory of seeing my dad and mother kiss or hug. (Younger members of the family say they have such memories.) Both being Scots, they were, of course, not good at showing their emotions. I often think of what Father Ted Hesburg, former president of Notre Dame University, said years ago: "The greatest gift parents can give their children is to show their love for each other in the presence of their children." This I never saw.

I received love from Mother but little from Dad. Maybe this explains why I find it hard to show love for others, even though I feel it inside. Living so much of my later life among emotional Latins was hard to take. They shake hands and hug each other every time they meet, even several times a day.

Apparently, however, I have compassion for people and other living creatures. Otherwise, I would not have done the work I did. Two boyhood incidents show my sensitivity to animals. Once, a snare of mine caught a rabbit by its foot. I ran home crying, unable to kill it. The other incident was when my dad asked me to hold the legs of a lamb to be butchered. As soon as I saw the blood flowing and heard the lamb's cries, I ran out bawling.

Related to my fear to show love is my tendency to hesitate rather than to make the first moves of friendship. Through my life, my close friends have always been people who made the first moves. The feeling of holding back on my part is always stronger if the other person is a woman. Perhaps, I suspect ulterior motives. So, through life, I have been labelled proud, stubborn and macho. I have to admit there is some truth in these charges. These traits have made me a loner with few intimate friends. That's why some call me "Stainless Steele."

These insights into my character, however, were far in the future when, in September, 1932, just past my twenty-first birthday, I found myself in the China Mission Seminary, dressed in that long black robe. With over fifty young men enroled, the seminary was filled to the hatches, most students doubled up in small rooms. An annex was built a year later, giving us all private rooms.

Our class of eleven students was the largest since the founding of the seminary fourteen years earlier. In my class, there were two students from Newfoundland, three from Nova Scotia, one from Quebec, and the rest were from Ontario. Like the other new students, I did not know anybody. Almost all newcomers were just out of high school. Only one had graduated from university. He had attended as a day student; another fellow also spent a few years at university as a day student. Having rubbed shoulders with so many different types of fellows while living on campus at St. F.X., I felt more worldly-wise than the other newcomers to the seminary.

The staff of the seminary consisted of three priests: the superior, a man older than the fathers of most of us, and two younger men. They handled our spiritual formation (instruction in prayer, etc.) as well as our training in discipline. The preparation of a priest in those days was much like that of a military person: blind obedience to many rules and regulations. Bells ruled our lives from 5.30 a.m. till lights out at 10.15 p.m. Students were strictly forbidden to enter each others' rooms. Meals were meagre. Money was scarce. It was the Great Depression. Financial support for the seminary came daily in small donations, as it still does.

Our academic life took place across the field, about 100 yards away, at St. Augustine's, a large seminary, established about 1912, with more than 200 students from all parts of Canada and some American dioceses. The teaching staff of St. Augustine's was comprised of some dozen or more priests mostly from Toronto. Some lectures were given in Latin, a subject I never liked. Away from it a few years, I had forgotten much of it. Though we shared classes with the St. Augustine's students, there was relatively little communication between us and them, except for some athletic events. Few of them, came to our place during recreations and we rarely mixed socially with them.

The seminary course would take six years: two of philosophy and four of theology. I was given credit for a year of philosophy in Antigonish, so I had five years of seminary studies ahead of me.

All went well the first month. I was happy and mixed well with the students. Three of them, along with the youngest priest on staff, latched on to me and tried to get me to share their free time. But then things changed and the rest of my seminary years were, to say the least, not much fun. Many priests treasure memories of seminary days as the happiest of their lives. Not I.

What turned things sour for me was a very forceful lecture by the rector on the subject of particular friendships — something strictly forbidden in the seminary. This concept of particular friendships (PF's) would not be familiar to anyone who has not lived in a religious community. The principle was that it was extremely dangerous and inappropriate for anyone to form a strong and exclusive friendship with anyone else. No explanation was given but, no doubt, the fear was homosexuality.

This injunction on friendship was a marked departure from my recent way of life. At St. F.X., the general camaraderie had overcome my natural hesitancy when it came to socializing. For five years I had enjoyed belonging to a small circle of friends. However, I took the rector's lecture with all seriousness, perhaps because it was so unexpected, so different from my previous notions. In any case, I had decided to obey all rules as well as I could. Others did not see it that way and told me I was taking the rule too seriously. The same three who had monopolized me now turned against me for refusing to share my recreations with them. So I had enemies.

A short time after, I was on the carpet in the rector's office. One of the group of three, piqued at my stand-offishness, had spread the word that I was accusing them of forming a clique.

The gruff old superior almost barked at me, "Is it true, Harvey, that there is a clique of students here who plan their recreations and so on together?"

"Yes, Doctor, it is true."

"Will you tell me who they are?"

I gave the names.

"Is it true that Father X is one of the group?"

"Yes, Doctor."

The superior pushed a buzzer, calling for the priest to come to his room. He asked the priest in my presence, was it true he largely shared his recreations with certain individuals? The priest admitted it was. I was then asked to leave the room.

I didn't know whether to begin packing my bags or not. To my surprise, though, nothing more came of it from the rector's quarter, although the resentment of the other students continued. I felt sorry for embarrassing the young priest. He was, as I learned later in life, one of the most wholesome of people. A beautiful person, he never held a grudge.

Less than a month later, the second bomb fell. While out walking, a young man from Ontario peppered me with questions about the coal miners, the many strikes and the violence in Cape Breton. I gave straightforward answers. It amazed me how little the Ontario people knew about eastern Canada, less, I thought, than Americans know about our country. In the course of our conversation, the other student elicited my favourable opinion on John L. Lewis, the head of the United Mine Workers of America. Without malice, my walking companion told other students about our talk. Again, I was on the carpet in the superior's room.

"Is it true Harvey, that you talked with a certain student and said that you are in favour of labour unions, credit unions and co-ops?"

"Yes, Doctor, I firmly believe in those things."

"Is it true that you spoke highly of this Mr. John L. Lewis?"

"Yes, Doctor, I did. He kept us alive during the long coal miners' strikes."

After taking a deep breath and pausing to think, he bellowed at me, "Harvey, if I ever hear you speak of things like that here, you will pack your bags and get out. There is no room in the priesthood for communists."

I lived in gloom and sadness for the next weeks, expecting that any day the order would come kicking me out. In trouble with the authorities twice within two months — not because I disobeyed — but because I was trying to obey orders and to be honest and truthful. The only course from then on was to keep my mouth shut, not to be intimate with anybody, not to share my opinions with others. It did not pay to be frank, to be sincere, to be serious.

Most students knew of the two incidents. I became something of a pariah. Although the next five years were unpleasant, I somehow managed to survive. I was learning about types of future priests. Even to this day, when I pass the room where the old superior lived, a shadow of fear surges in my mind.

Because of my medical studies, I was appointed infirmarian during my second year and held the job until my last year. The duties were not onerous, except when colds and 'flu hit the place. Then a lot of food trays had to be carried. At such times, I had permission to enter other students' rooms. Also, students who felt ill could come to my room for aspirins, or whatever. My responsibilities included treating the superior when he was bedridden with a cold. So my job gave me an inside track on what was going on in the place. It was a surprise to me to learn how little respect some students had for the rules. Some even had ways of smuggling in forbidden newspapers.

We were supposed to be segregated as much as possible from the world. In addition to the ban on newspapers and magazines, radios were taboo. Every so often, though, we were allowed to hear a hockey game or listen to the popular radio talks of Father Charles Coughlan from Detroit. Families of students were allowed to visit for a couple of hours one Sunday a month. We had a record player in our smoky recreation room where mostly classical records were played. The pool table was the other important item in the room. We were permitted to go to a variety store a few hundred yards away to make needed purchases. A stint of two hours' manual labour once a week, pick and shovel, was part of the routine some months of the year. In winter we took turns flooding and putting the ice rink in shape. Hockey, handball, baseball and climbing the Scarborough bluffs were the popular sports.

After barely surviving the first year — having expected twice that I would be kicked out — I ended up back in Cape Breton for the summer. Within days of my return home, my dad, unable to be on the job, expected me to replace him. I had to make a hard decision: whether to be trapped in the store for the next four summers or to make the break now. I told mother I was going to return to Toronto, get a summer job there, get ordained and go to China.

I told the same to my dad. On his knees, he promised he would never drink again. There were lots of tears flowing — from both of us. I did open the store for a few days, and then he was on the job. He kept his promise; as far as I know, that was the longest dry period of his life. He built a new house, the largest in town, with seven bedrooms. In my China years, I hoped that he had continued dry but, as I learned after getting home, he "fell off the water wagon", as the saying went, a year after I was in China. His dry spell ended on a visit to the 1939 World's Fair in New York.

In August, 1935, while I was at home in Dominion, the year before my ordination, my superior in Toronto phoned with the news that my friend Jim McGillivray, the one who had introduced me to Scarboro, had just died in China. The superior asked me to break the news to Jim's elderly parents, whom I had never met. I felt like a boy doing a man's job. There was so little to say except that Jim was dead after fighting malaria for only a few days.

On my return to the seminary, I suggested to the superior that all students should have complete medical examinations. He bought the idea and I made contact with a young doctor. The upshot was that two men were dismissed because they had active tuberculosis; two others were borderline cases.

There were seven steps to the priesthood: four minor orders and three major orders. After receiving the four minors, we were asked to take the serious oath to give our whole lives to working in China. Then came the first major order — ordination as a subdeacon, followed by the diaconate and finally the priesthood. The promise to lead a celibate life was made at the time of ordination to the subdiaconate. Looking back, I often think that the oath to spend all my life in China affected me more than the promise of celibacy.

In May 1936, we were ordained subdeacons in Toronto. There were eleven in my class (none had dropped out). After receiving the necessary canonical papers, we returned to our homes to find a bishop to ordain us to the priesthood. My friendship with the old rector of St. F.X. gave me an in with the bishop of Antigonish, James Morrison. On August 9, 1936, he ordained three of us in Bridgeport, the parish that included my home in Dominion. (I had been ordained to the diaconate at Holy Heart Seminary in Halifax, about two months earlier.)

After ordination, there was a festive mass in the chapel at Beechmont. My family had all arrived and we were standing around out front, chatting with the farmers and assembled community. Father Gillis came up and whispered to me, "Harvey, you're needed in the sacristy."

"What for?" I asked.

He said, "Your grandmother wants you to hear her confession."

He was as embarrassed as I. But I had to go through with it. I went in and heard her confession.

In the fall, we newly ordained priests returned to the seminary to finish the last year of studies, on the understanding that we would depart for China in the fall of 1937. By then, however, the battle of Shanghai was raging. Since that ruled out travel to China, we were told to find work in our home dioceses for a year or so.

Strange how fate works. The old pastor of Bridgeport went immediately to the bishop and asked that I be appointed to my home parish — the one place in the world I didn't want to be, the place I ran away from. But I had no choice. I had to obey. God was going to use the same tactic later on to bring me back to something I ran away from.

This reminds me of a famous poem written a century ago by an Englishman, a convert to Catholicism, Francis Thompson. It is called "The Hound of Heaven", and was first published by A.R. Mombrays & Co., Oxford, U.K.

I fled Him, down the nights and down the days;
I fled Him, down the arches of the years;
I fled Him, down the labyrinthine ways
 Of my own mind; and in the midst of tears.
I hid from Him, and under running laughter.
        Up vistaed hopes, I sped;
        And shot precipitated,
Adown Titanic glooms of chasmed fears.

From those strong Feet that followed, followed after.
        But with unhurrying chase,
        And unperturbed pace,
Deliberate speed, majestic instancy,
        They beat—and a Voice beat
        More instant than the Feet—
"All things betray thee, who betrayest Me."…

        .....

"All which I took from thee I did but take,
        Not for thy harms,
But just that thou might'st seek it in My arms.
        All which thy child's mistake
Fancies as lost, I have stored for thee at home:
        Rise, clasp My hand, and come."

There is no doubt in my mind but that the Hound of Heaven was trailing me (and no doubt still does) and I was trying to get away from Him.

The parish of Bridgeport extended about four miles along the road, including a section of Glace Bay, the town of Dominion and a rural section. The pastor, Father Charles W. MacDonald, was a few years older than my father. A jovial man and a hard worker for his age, he apparently took a shine to me. An unpleasant aspect of the situation, however, was the fact that he was providing a home in the rectory for his widowed niece and her three young sons. So I was, in effect, living in a family setting again. Not the ideal situation for a young priest.

Having worked in our store, I knew most people in Dominion but few in the other areas. I suggested to the pastor that a visitation of the homes was in order. Although he thought that unnecessary, because of a census taken a couple of years before, he didn't object to my proposal. There were many people who hadn't been going to church since the big strike in 1909 and I wanted to get them back. People blamed the pastor, "the old man," as they called him, for allowing cannons to be placed on the church steps in that big strike, although he probably had nothing to do with it.

When visiting parishioners, I tried to arrive when the men were home. I always entered the back door, stepping directly into the kitchen. (At home, miners lived in the kitchen as it was the only heated room of the house.) Invariably, the first reaction was, "Why are you here, Father? What's wrong?" My reply was, "There is nothing wrong. I just want to get to know you." Then, often the answer would come, "But this never happened before. A priest only comes when somebody is dying."

It soon became the talk in the mines how this young priest was visiting all the homes. The men loved it. Many a man commented, "I never saw my house so clean before." But the women hated it. Just for the hell of it, I would jump from one street to another, in a zig-zag manner, so the women never knew when I was coming. In spite of their attempts to keep ahead of me, it amazed me to find how dirty some of the homes were.

Still, the visits were nearly always pleasant and the results were gratifying. Having sold the old pastor on the idea of a parish mission, I asked each family I visited if they would attend.

Nearly all said they would. Then I wrote their names in a little black book by way of making the promise seem more formal. Most kept their word. Many hadn't been in church for thirty years or more. A third mass had to be said on Sundays to accommodate the crowd.

There were only two exceptions to the general welcome I received in miners' homes. Two Catholics were bitter against the Church. An Irishman and a Belgian, they let it be known that they would shoot me if I entered their homes. With the Belgian, my efforts met total failure. He would never open the door to me. Once when I visited him in hospital, he simply turned his face to the wall.

But the Irishman at least let me into his shack. We sat there for a few minutes, he in his rocking chair. "How're you doing, Paddy?" I asked. "How many days do you work?" He met every one of my attempts at conversation with stony silence. His wife sat there trembling, worrying about the explosion that looked inevitable. Finally he got up and went upstairs. When he came down a few minutes later, having washed his face, he was astonished to find me still sitting there.

Suddenly, I noticed an old violin up high on a ledge. Amazed to find such a thing in this hovel, I naturally expressed my interest. I said, "Someone gave me a violin as a kid but I never learned to play it."

He took the dusty instrument from the ledge and put it in my lap.

That broke the ice and we had a long talk. He had been holding a grudge against the Church ever since the strike of 1909. By the end of our talk, he agreed to make the upcoming mission. I saw him at church shortly before my departure from the parish. He died while I was in China.

On seeing the untidy shacks these poor men came home to after working in dangerous and inhuman conditions, I said to myself, no wonder they drink. During the hours that the government liquor stores were closed, people wanting booze could always find it in an Italian area known as "Bugrow" and in other joints run by Scots. Most of the miners drank only on the weekends. The few who never drank were Protestant. Alcoholism was the social sin of the miners. Their inhuman work, the victimizing injustice, caused much of it.

The full horror of the conditions came home to me on my first sick call to the mine, described earlier. The poor miners — how I felt for them! I can never forget the story of what happened to one miner whose carbide lamp went out. He was lost in the cold, dark shafts. He was found lying on the ground, half-dead, while rats as big as cats were eating away at his body.

How could I help these poor people in the short time that was available before leaving for China? I came to the conclusion that their most urgent need was decent housing. Dr. Jimmy Tompkins was building a co-op housing group in the neighbouring parish. My interest in that brought me in contact with this little man and his dynamic ideas. About five days a week, I would be in Father Jimmy's house. He had a group of fifteen miners studying the principles of co-ops and the provincial law concerning co-op housing. The government would provide about eighty percent of the materials, plans, etc. The legislation setting this up had been on the provincial government's books for years but it was a well-kept secret until Jimmy Tompkins discovered it.

Back in our parish, I invited a couple of dozen young married men to a meeting and threw the idea at them. They liked it. So we started meeting every Monday night. The group grew to forty.

After a year of studies, the group was down to fourteen and we were ready for action. Since the men were working in the mine, I had to do much of the leg work. I was able to get a cheap piece of land in town, considered a swamp. We drained it, then dug basements with bulldozers. We applied to the provincial government which gave us free technical help in the construction — supervising the electrical work and the engineering done by the men in their spare time.

The houses were made of wood, two storeys, with central heating and indoor plumbing, luxuries miners never had in the company-owned shacks. When my call came for China, the construction was almost finished. Tompkins' houses were finished a few months earlier. These were the first co-op housing developments in Canada. Today, there are thousands of co-op houses.

After housing, my next priority was to do something for the young people. In the long cold winters, they had no place to go for recreation. Instead of working with the usual parish societies

(Catholic Women's League, the League of the Cross, the Ancient Order of Hibernians) which, to my mind, were not very relevant, I picked a dozen middle-aged men and started to raise money for an outdoor skating rink by holding weekly dances and bingo games. I arranged to buy the land. The men, with help from some youths, built a clubhouse to hold seventy or more, levelled the land, put up the lights and hired the only live skating band in the area. We were able to pay all our expenses with a few thousand dollars to spare. My next project, had I remained longer in the area, was to build a social centre for the young. On the land we had acquired for it, the St. Martha's sisters built their convent. Now they are gone and the building is the town hall.

All these "non-spiritual" things done to help people in so short a time gave me great satisfaction. It was a hectic but satisfying time. I spent as little time as I could in the rectory. Come summer, I was expecting the call from China any day. Then, in August, I landed in the hospital with pneumonia. The pastor and my family doctor argued that I was unfit for the overseas mission.

To me, that looked like a ploy to keep me at home. I was afraid that if I didn't get to China soon I would lose interest in going there. So my brother and I drove to the Lahey Clinic in Boston to get an unbiased checkup. They said that my lungs were clearing and that, with rest, I would be okay. They recommended drinking a bottle of Guinness daily. I did not mind that.

The call came from Toronto to report in October. In sum, I would say that the most important part of that time in the parish was the inspiration I received from Jimmy Tompkins. When we were parting, he said, "God, I wish I was young as you are and going to China with your ideas. You can spread the idea of co-ops among those poor people. What a great challenge!" Later, it occurred to me that he hadn't said a word about religion. But what is religion if it is not helping people to live as human beings?

Chapter Four

China — Lishui

My departure for our mission had already been delayed a year by the Japanese invasion of China. They had taken over Shanghai and gobbled up most of the northern and central parts of the country. Claiming, however, that this was just a "police action", they were now re-opening Shanghai to the rest of the world. Meanwhile, war clouds were looming in Europe as Hitler took over one country after another.

In spite of this worldwide turmoil, Scarboro's plan was that we would spend ten years in China before being allowed to return home. Obviously, we would be cut off from the world we had known. It felt like we were taking off for the moon. Secretly, I thought it likely we would never see home again.

How was I going to say goodbye to my family? Here I was at last escaping the scene of so much unhappiness. Yet, parting from my family would be the hardest thing I ever did. Undoubtedly, a last meal with them would be too much of an ordeal for everyone. So I said mass that Sunday, bid farewell to the parish, then had a lunch at the rectory, mostly in silence. One of my brothers picked me up in the family car and drove me home. Wanting to cut this torment as short as possible, I told him to keep the engine running. In the kitchen, my parents and eight brothers and sisters (the youngest was only five years old) were waiting around the table.

How hard it is to suppress tears! I was determined not to cry but tears hurt all the more when you keep them in. There was a stoic hug for both parents, a wave and a nod to the eight kids, then I ran out the door. As my brother and I drove away, my tears finally broke. The most difficult step in the 10,000 mile trip was over.

My brother left me at the train station in Truro, about 100 miles from Sydney, and I made the long trip to Toronto alone. Throughout the trip, memories of family, of childhood, of seminary days, of good times and bad welled up in me, accompanied by the occasional sob.

In Toronto, the society held a farewell banquet for us on October 16, 1938. Our group of eight priests, comprising two ordination classes, was the largest ever sent to China. Three bishops were present for the farewell, along with our own staff and students. About an hour before dinner, one of the staff priests asked if I would say a few words at the banquet on behalf of our group. My talk was short — about two minutes. In my eighteen months working at home as a priest, I said, many people asked me, "Why go to China when there is so much work to be done at home?" I particularly remembered one Irish lady in her nineties who was flabbergasted on hearing where I was headed. I can still see her bony hand pounding the arm of her wheelchair. "You mean to tell me there will be Chinese in heaven?" she wailed. "Then I don't want to go there."

Some people looked on us as fools, I said, some saw us as heroes. But we were neither, at least not in the conventional sense. What would be more accurate, I suggested (drawing on Paul's First Epistle to the Corinthians), would be to describe us as fools for Christ. Our intentions might look foolish in the eyes of the world but not in the light of faith. After supper, one of the priests on staff told me that old Archbishop O'Brien of Kingston was so impressed by my words that he turned to our superior and said, "That man should not go to China. We need priests like him here at home." To my mind, the Archbishop's attitude to the missions was no better than the old Irish lady's.

That evening, as we were boarding the train for Vancouver, our superior, Father John E. MacRae took me aside and said, "Harvey, when you get to our mission in China, write and tell me what is really going on over there." As seminarians, we had heard rumours about friction between the men in China and those at the home base. But I was reluctant to be drawn into the crossfire so I promised nothing.

After nearly a week at our mission in Vancouver's Chinatown, where it rained nearly all the time, we boarded the *Empress of Asia*, a Canadian ship. There were over 300 passengers and as many well-wishers on the docks. As our big ship began to pull out, the band on the dock played *O Canada*. Plenty of our tears from our group dropped into the waters of Vancouver harbour. For me, the emotion had a lot to do with my appreciating for the first time that Canada was my home. Strange how we take so much for granted until it begins to slip from our grasp. I had just travelled from coast to coast, a journey that included my first-ever glimpse of the Prairies and the Rockies. And here I was leaving this beautiful country for God-knows-what! Finally, the paper streamers connecting us with the people on the dock broke and fell into the water. We were on our way.

In our group headed for the Scarboro Mission in Chekiang Province there were eight Scarboro priests and two Grey Nuns from Pembroke. Another ten US priests were on board as well as a dozen or more Protestant missioners. Most of the passengers were Jews fleeing Europe to start new lives in the Orient. Also on board were several White Russians who had been living abroad since the 1917 Revolution.

We had been hoping to take the southern route past Hawaii but Scarboro had booked us on the northern route, which was quicker and cheaper. We hit rough water the second day out and it got much rougher on subsequent days throughout the sixteen-day trip. The name "Pacific" seemed a highly ironic description of that body of water. Many of us got seasick; food didn't matter much. After the fog shrouding the Aleutians islands cleared up, we saw nothing but water and clouds for days. As this was late November, the voyage was cold and dreary in the extreme. One of the worst aspects of the trip was taking a shower in salt water. Soap was useless and you felt itchier than before.

But there was one pleasant event on the voyage. A rich Philippino, a devout Catholic who had been studying the stock market in New York, threw a champagne party for our group on one of our last nights on board. All the priests and some of the sisters attended. That helped to make up for the deprivations of the rest of the trip.

Finally, land — the Orient. The big port city of Yokohama was crawling with people. The docks were covered with hundreds of vendors displaying their beautiful silk wares and vying for our attention. There were no fixed prices and the sellers loved haggling to try and get as much money as they could on their sales. This was new to us. Most of us bought some silks to send back home. One of the most unforgettable sights of that landing was watching a hundred or more tiny women loading coal onto our ship. A long chain of human beings, they passed small baskets from one to the other like a human conveyor belt.

We piled into taxis for the forty-mile drive into Tokyo, then the largest city in the world. Almost all of the Japanese were wearing masks over their mouths and noses. We learned that they were very anxious not to catch germs from the dust. To us, though, the atmosphere didn't seem particularly polluted. That night, the Orient had a dazzling display of beauty for us. Even though there was a full moon, the stars seemed brighter and closer to earth than at home.

After stops in Kobe and Nagasaki, our route took us through the inland sea of Japan. A typhoon struck at three o'clock in the afternoon and it became as dark as night. When visibility gradually improved, 100 or more warships of the Japanese navy emerged from the gloom. A young Canadian officer of our ship who was standing by me at the rail scoffed, "What a bunch of old tubs. They'll be useless if war comes." If only the young man had been right! When war did come, the Japanese navy sank the pride of the British and American navies. Those Japanese "tubs" roared up and down the coast, taking everything in sight and, for a time, even threatening Australia.

Our voyage on the *Empress of Asia* was to end at Shanghai, about fourteen miles upstream from the ocean on the Whangpoo river. As the massive ship moved slowly up the river through the yellowish waters, some passengers spotted corpses bobbing in the water. Presumably, they were left over from the battle of Shanghai that had been raging the previous year. We wondered why the sharks hadn't found these bodies. The only conclusion we could come to was that the slaughter had been so bad that the sharks had their fill of bodies.

Shanghai harbour came in sight and what a sight it was — hundreds of ships of all sizes, from sampans and junks to large Japanese war ships and ocean-going vessels of many nations. As a backdrop to the tumultuous waterfront, there was the skyline of the business district, the Bund, as it was called, with its huge, ornate buildings in the Western imperialist style of the nineteenth century: a conglomeration of cupolas, spires, clock towers and domes.

When we docked, two of our older priests met us. Immigration inquiries moved quickly but the customs people grilled us for nearly half a day. Inquisitive officers opened everything we had. Such common things as flashlights mystified them. They even opened our tubes of toothpaste, smelled it, tasted it.

When that process was finally complete, we found a dozen rickshaws waiting for us and our baggage. During the hour's ride to the French Lazarists' compound, we marvelled at the masses of humanity thronging the streets. A conglomeration of weird smells assaulted us and the streets were virtually covered in yellow and brownish spittle, much of it bloody as a result of the tuberculosis that affected some ninety-nine percent of the population.

But what made me even more squeamish was being pulled along the streets by the sweat of another human being. As the man strained to haul the rickshaw up the hills, the blood vessels in his legs swelled up to the size of my finger and seemed ready to burst. All the drivers were young men; yet it was said that the average rickshaw driver lasted only six years before the work killed him.

The Lazarists, who were to be our hosts for a week, were French priests who had been in China for centuries. (Actually "Lazarists" was their name in China; in France, they were known as the Vincentians, after their founder St. Vincent de Paul.) Their Shanghai residence was headquarters for their retired priests and for their many active missionaries when taking a break from work in the hinterland. Most of the twenty-five or more permanent residents were very old, with long white beards. Some of them had been in China more than fifty years, during which they had never returned to their homeland.

Near supper time, a bell summoned us to meet for Happy Hour. The drink was cognac, France's best, and mighty strong. But conversation with these old white-beards wasn't easy as most of them didn't speak English. We had to fall back on a mixture of Latin and French and I, for one, was no expert in either.

Standing near me, trying valiantly to make small talk with one of the old men was Ed Lyons from Calgary. The youngest priest of our group, Ed was even more naïve than the rest of us; he had never even tasted hard liquor.

"Who are you?" the old French priest blurted out in a few of the English words at his command.

"I am a Scarboro priest," Ed answered. "We just arrived here from Canada."

"What for?"

"I came to help the Chinese save their souls."

"Go home," he sneered. "You're crazy. The Chinese don't have souls."

On hearing that, I couldn't help thinking of a lecture back in seminary days. Our rector, just returned from a quick visit to China, told us about meeting these old Lazarists missionaries in retirement. "How beautiful it is," he had enthused, "to see these holy French missionaries who have given their lives to China, playing dominoes now and awaiting their eternal reward!" And now it appeared to me that some of them didn't even believe the fundamentals of our faith! I was only beginning to see how far our superior was from understanding those missionaries or the Chinese.

We sat down to a substantial meal — a mix of Chinese and European. It turned out that the elaborate spread was in honour of the superior's birthday. In front of each of us was a steaming bowl of rice; dozens of bowls of meats and vegetables filled the middle of the table. The meats were covered with a black soya sauce. For implements there were chopsticks as well as knives and forks.

A particularly dark meat tasted like nothing I'd ever eaten before. So I turned to the superior who was sitting next to me and asked what it was.

Although he spoke English well enough, he fell back on French as he spat out, "*Chat*".

He went on to describe in great detail how the cat we were eating had climbed over the wall of the compound that afternoon and had been killed by the Lazarists' German Shepherd guard dogs. I didn't take much notice of the story as I was too busy trying to quell my stomach.

For about a week, we travelled around the city in rickshaws, taking in the fascinating sights. Shanghai had a population of some four or five million people at the time. It was a sordid city — a city of sin and squalor of every kind. It gave an impression that human life was cheap. From time to time, human heads were seen hanging on lamp posts. Mostly they were the heads of people executed for petty crimes like stealing.

Within the city there was an International Settlement with a million and a half people ruled by a board of foreigners and Chinese. Another section known as the French Concession, with about half a million people, was under French jurisdiction. Foreigners who lived in these areas, and most did, were exempt from Chinese law. They had their own police, courts, government and laws. Similar enclaves for foreigners existed throughout China. These concessions had been forced on the Chinese by the foreign intruders in the previous century. Even some wealthy Chinese lived in these privileged areas. Like foreigners, they lived luxuriously, with servants treated virtually as slaves.

Only a little less luxurious — from the point of view of the poor Chinese — were the foreign mission establishments like the one where we were living. Missioners also had large schools, hospitals and universities throughout the city.

After a week in Shanghai, an Italian-owned coastal steamer took us on an overnight trip 300 miles down the coast to our next stop, Wenchow in Chekiang Province, which was still in Chinese hands. Like every means of conveyance of China, the decrepit steamer was vastly overloaded, not only with hundreds of people, all sitting on their haunches, but with their chickens, ducks and pigs. We barely managed to find space to squat on deck. This was my first close-up look at the people whose souls I had come to save. Their animated chatter in their many-toned language fascinated me. Around midnight, there was a yell, then some cheering. A woman in a crowd of people a few yards away from me had given birth to a baby.

In Wenchow, we were welcomed at another Lazarist home. Although it was a French mission, the superior and three other priests were Polish, two were Formosan and one was American. Across the street was a large compound run by the Sisters of Charity, who were mostly French. Because of their wing-like white hats, the Chinese called them the *fiji-momo* ("airplane sisters"). At this mission, the food was all Chinese and we had to eat with chopsticks. I soon learned that to master them you can't sit upright as Emily Post would have it; you lean over the bowl and shovel the food in.

So far, life in China didn't seem too arduous. But a foreshadowing of what was ahead came in a remark from one of the young Polish priests, Father Viachork. *Viachork* means "evening" so we called him Father Evening. He spoke a little English and one day he said to me, "Father it must be a great sacrifice for you people from Canada to come and live under the conditions here in China. For us it isn't such a sacrifice because the conditions here aren't much worse than in Poland."

There was no road from Wenchow to our final destination — Lishui (pronounced "Lee-shway"). The river was the only way of making the 100-mile trip. After a three-day wait in Wenchow, sampans became available. Ten priests and two sisters, with all our baggage, embarked in two 15-foot craft on the last leg of our ten-thousand-mile journey. For five days, the men handling our sampans pushed and pulled against the current of the river. On the first part of the trip the river was deep enough to use oars. After that it was poles, then they pulled with ropes. At rapids everybody got out and walked. There was a sail on board but raising it would have been useless as there was no wind. The late autumn weather was pleasant enough but all of us, including the nuns, wore pith helmets for protection from the heat of the midday sun.

The river varied in width, averaging about one-quarter mile across, and flowed through rice paddies. Bamboo trees lined the banks in many places. Dotted here and there were villages that used the river for transportation, irrigation, sewage and domestic consumption.

That voyage gave us an experience of the lack of privacy that is so common in China. Everybody on the sampans saw everything that everybody else was doing. There was no opportunity to wash along the way. For "bathroom duties", you simply had to find a spot in the bushes along the riverbank. We tied up at night but the sampan was our hotel. You had to make yourself a bed as best you could, finding a place among the bags and other paraphernalia for your *mienbi,* the stuffed cotton bedroll that's standard equipment for any traveller in China.

***

Lishui — home at last!

Nearly 100 Christian converts were there to welcome us with broad smiles and firecrackers. We were the first Canadians to arrive since before the start of the Battle of Shanghai in 1936. Also on hand were our ten priests who had come to meet us from their missions scattered in a radius of about 100 miles. First, there was an official welcome in the cathedral. For the occasion, our superior, Monsignor W.C. McGrath, donned the purple robes and pectoral cross which his status as Prefect Apostolic (sort of a substitute bishop) entitled him to wear. With stirring oratory, he hailed each of us as a priceless treasure to the mission, describing us as "God's gift to the Chinese." Then came a banquet prepared by six Grey Nuns from Pembroke, Ontario. Almost miraculously, they managed to serve up a real Canadian meal — much of it from their dwindling stocks of canned goods from Shanghai. Soon all such goodies would disappear when the Japanese closed off the coast.

The next morning about dawn, we woke to the sound of a temple bell tolling furiously. That was the air raid warning. Within minutes, Japanese planes were dropping bombs on the airport a couple of miles from our compound. This would be a way of life for the next four years — the temple bell sounding its warning, the drone of enemy planes, bombs falling.

About nine o'clock, there was a rap on my door. Monsignor McGrath, the superior, wanted to speak to me privately. "Tell me, Harvey," he started in, "what is going on over there in Toronto?" He wanted me to pass on any gossip that might pertain to the legendary conflict between headquarters and the men in the field.

My thoughts raced back to the moment when we were boarding the train in Toronto and the rector had asked me to inform him about what was going on here in Lishui. And now, not twenty-four hours on the job, I was caught in the crossfire between the two factions. What was it about me that made these superiors look to me for guidance? Maybe my years at university had made me seen more worldly-wise than of some of my fellow priests, even though some of them were older than I. And perhaps my experience in the family business added to an impression of maturity. I can't think of anything else.

In any case, my heart sank. I had looked on my superiors with awe and yet here they were, each asking me to inform on the other. Was this what working for the Church was about: intrigue and politics? It is often said that every young priest aspires to be a bishop or a superior. Now that I had seen what power did to people, I didn't want any part of it. In fact, I felt like chucking the priesthood itself right there.

When my mind cleared enough to give an answer, it was simply, "Well, Monsignor, as you know I have not been living at our headquarters for the past eighteen months, except for a few days. I really don't know what's going on there."

This, of course, wasn't the answer he wanted. He took me to his office and I was closeted with him for almost three hours. He peppered me with questions about all kinds of things I knew nothing about. He showed me secret letters and cables, documents from the archives — things I had no right to see and wasn't interested in. Most of the time, I just listened and said nothing.

Finally, the call to lunch brought the tête-à-tête to an end. As I walked into the dining room with my new boss, twenty priests, including the ones who had crossed the ocean with me, were staring at me. I wanted to drop through the earth. I knew what they were thinking: "There's that S.O.B Steele, here less than a day, and already he's the superior's golden-haired boy."

For several nights, sleep was hard to come by. My heart was telling me to keep away from all superiors, all people with authority and power. But that wasn't easy to manage while still being an obedient priest. I decided that the wisest thing would be not to write to the superior in Canada. I would do my best to forget the role of undercover agent that had been forced on me. The best thing would be to throw myself into life in Lishui.

* * *

One of the most conspicuous features of the town was the odour. Here we got the smell of rural China. Much of it came from the manure deposited in the streets by the free-running dogs, chickens and pigs. Then there were the tubs of human excrement that farmers carried out to the fields on the end of long poles. Some of the tubs' contents, highly prized as fertilizer, inevitably splashed on the streets. The assault of this pungent conglomeration of odours was so overwhelming that many a young priest, on arrival in the mission field, would gladly have headed straight home, if transportation had been available.

Lying in a valley surrounded by hills, Lishui had more the feeling of an overgrown village than a city. Even though its normal population of 40,000 was swollen with refugees, you could walk the circumference of it in about three hours. There was no industry to speak of, not even a single high chimney. The church steeple was the highest human-built structure in the landscape. There was no particular business section; tiny shops and enterprises were scattered all around. Because of the Japanese blockade, practically nothing arrived from outside and the people made do with the most primitive equipment and materials. Apart from a handful of well-to-do people (small businessmen and artisans) everyone lived a hand-to-mouth existence.

The basis of the town's economy was farming; most people who slept in town spent their days in the fields. There was no grazing land in our area. All land, every inch of it, was used to grow food for humans. The main crop, as throughout the south of China, was rice. In fact, Lishui is situated on the southern edge of the Yangtze Plain, which marks the division between the rice-growing south and the north where the main crop is wheat.

That difference in diet also accounts for certain physical differences among the Chinese. The wheat-fed northerners tend to be tall and strong. The Cantonese Chinese whom one sees overseas tend to be slight and small-boned, so the sight of many strapping six-footers in Lishui surprised me. They turned out to be Yellow River people carried south on the tide of refugees. Most of the Lishui people were neither as tall as the northerners nor as slight as the Cantonese. Another difference between northern and southern Chinese is that most of the northern men have beards, thanks to the plentiful protein in their diets. In Lishui, facial hair was considered ugly.

Living at Lishui when we arrived were five priests: the superior; the pastor of the parish, who was one of our first men to arrive in China in 1926; the pastor's assistant; the procurator in charge of buying for the needs of all priests and sisters; then a young priest who was in charge of the school for about 100 boys. Overall, the Lishui Prefecture had about 12 missions staffed by some 20 Canadian priests, 2 Chinese priests, and 9 Grey Nuns from Canada. From each of the missions there were smaller rural areas for the priests to visit. These trips were only possible a few times a year because travel was by foot, or in a sedan chair (two men carried you on two long poles) or, in a few places, by bicycle. In some places, missioners travelled by small horses. (In Lishui we didn't have horses because of the lack of grazing fields.) Sometimes, a priest would undertake a three-day trek just to visit one family in the hinterland.

Among some 3 million Chinese in our mission area, far less than one percent were Catholics. Before baptism, a candidate received a weekly lesson in doctrine for two years. In Lishui, as throughout China, most people who came to Sunday masses were "Rice Christians". This meant they were attracted to the Church for benefits like free medicine, hospital care, a job, or, in the case of children, an orphanage and free school. Even so, converts were few. In the average mission post, a priest might have one or two adults entering the Church each year.

The main source of our "harvest for heaven" was the dying babies we found and baptized when they had been thrown into rivers or left on the streets. Most of these babies were female. The sole reason for their being abandoned was poverty. No people showed more love for their children than the Chinese did. With a new baby arriving every year in most families, however, there often was not enough food to go around. In such families, male babies could be sold into another family where they could eventually work in the fields and carry water or perform other chores. But there was no such option for dealing with female babies that the family couldn't support.

Our primary task as new arrivals was to learn the language. And the first item of business in this respect was to choose a Chinese name. An attempt was made to find one of the hundred

Chinese names that sounded like our own. However, nothing in Chinese remotely like Steele could be found. So I was given the family name *Chen*. Added to that were two words: *Shen*, meaning spiritual, and *Fu*, meaning Father. So I was *Chen Shen Fu*.

Language studies took about seven hours a day for six months. Our teacher, Mr. Li, was a native of Pekin (as we called Beijing then). He taught us Mandarin which, although the official language of China, was spoken only by people in the north, around Pekin. Unable to speak a word of English, Mr. Li would draw an ideogram (the written form of a word) on the board and then, in pantomime, would tell us its meaning. His buck teeth bared in a perpetual, good-natured smile, he would spray spittle all around the room as he acted out his funny and creative mime routines. The memory work was tough going as Mandarin resembled no language familiar to us. But the trickier part was mastering the four different tones that change the meaning of a word.

Mr. Li's instruction was supposed to bring us to the point where we could recognize, draw and pronounce some 3,000 ideograms. In our writing, we may not have achieved the beautiful balance of freedom and control typical of classic Chinese calligraphy, but we could make do. Our reading knowledge was enough to get the gist of a letter or a newspaper article.

Although ideograms are the common written language for all Chinese, our Mandarin was useless for speaking with local people. They used a very particular dialect. Language experts claimed there were some 500 distinct dialects throughout the country. People from towns separated by only a few miles couldn't communicate with each other except by writing down ideograms. But very few had the education for that. As Mr. Li didn't speak the local dialect, we had to pick it up from our contact with people living around us.

Even though we lived like kings compared to most of the Chinese, our new home took some getting used to. Our priests' residence was a two-storey building built by the Lazarist priests who preceded us. Each of us had his own room with a bed that was more or less western-style: a mattress on boards, perhaps a spring. There was glass in the windows but you had to have mosquito nets to cover the bed or sleep was impossible.

Of course, there was no plumbing. The toilet was a two-holer in the yard. We had electric lights in the evening only, usually for about four hours. Our water, coming from the river where all human refuse was dumped, was totally polluted. Water for consumption had to be boiled and filtered. Controlling our body odours wasn't easy. We used a basin of water and a sponge.

Our recreations were few: playing cards, bicycle riding, classical records played on an old gramophone. When we were playing cards after supper, we sat with our legs encased in pillow cases up to the knees to protect them from mosquitoes. We had one tiny short-wave radio, not much more than a basic crystal set. It gave us world news from the BBC and music from Berlin. North America did not reach us. News from local papers was useless as they always reported that the Chinese were winning the war on all fronts. The opposite was true — the Japanese were taking over.

Slowly we were getting used to the many difficult features of our new life: the dirt, the constant stench, the mosquitoes, the bombings, the lack of diversions and the loneliness. Not least of the hardships was the heat. It could soar higher than 90 degrees Fahrenheit, but it was the humidity, more than the temperature, that made for so much discomfort in the valley where Lishui lay. There was nothing cold to drink, no ice. We drank hot yellow tea, our best cooling device. In terms of material comforts, things reached their lowest ebb when the local supply of Golden Dragon cigarettes dried up. Like mischievous boys, we tried without much success to make smokes from the leaves of trees and bushes,

All this would have been easier to bear if we hadn't had such a monotonous diet: rice, beans, vegetables, pork, chicken, and a few fruits like mandarin oranges and small bananas when they were in season. Most of the vegetables were strange to us and utterly tasteless. The root of the bamboo when cooked tasted vaguely like turnip. The little meat available was usually over-cooked. Still, we ate it with fear and nausea when we saw the pigs and chickens eating the excrement lying everywhere. The story was told of one religious superior who, on a visit to his troops in rural China, nearly starved. Unable to eat even eggs when he saw what the hens were eating on the streets, he survived the trip on Scotch whiskey.

We had no milk. But some Chinese had sources of it. One day I asked Mr. Wong, our catechist, about a mysterious woman who visited him each day. Embarrassed at first, he eventually explained that she was a mother who had got rid of her female baby. She was selling him her milk as a supposed cure for his tuberculosis. Some women who had thrown their babies away sold their milk on the streets to people who suffered from rheumatism and arthritis. Rubbed on aching joints, the milk was thought to relieve suffering.

With the arrival of winter, the temperature hovered around the freezing mark until the sun came up. To stave off the cold, we had tiny charcoal stoves. Because of the dampness, I suffered more from the cold in China than in Canada. We could never quite bring ourselves to cope with it the way the Chinese did. They used to scurry about the streets holding tiny pots of burning charcoal at their groins. It made sense medically — the best places to heat the body are the groin and the armpits.

In the cold weather, you heated up water to wash yourself about once every two weeks. Avoiding lice and fleas wasn't easy. They abounded in the layers of filthy clothing that most people wore. I was fascinated by a weird ritual that our gate man performed in April when the sun started to get stronger. He would begin to peel off the layers of rags, one by one. As each layer came off, he paused to make strange plucking motions: he was killing the thousands of lice that clung to that layer.

In our first months at Lishui, however, the worst blow had nothing to do with physical hardship. We woke up one morning and found that our genial superior had deserted. A city boy at heart, he couldn't stand life in Lishui any more. What hurt most was that he hadn't bothered to say goodbye. We found that he went to Shanghai where he broadcast a religious program on an English radio station for a while. Then he returned to Canada for good.

Appointed to replace him was Father Leo Curtin, an elderly priest who had worked in Ottawa for a long time. His deafness, unfortunately, made it impossible for him to learn the language. During the first few bombings after his arrival, he was strolling up and down reading his breviary. While everybody was scurrying for cover, he would look up with mild surprise and ask "What's going on?"

After completion of the language course came our appointments to our missions. I had been worried that my colleagues might view me as the superior's pet on arrival in Lishui; now there were further grounds for envy. I was appointed to Lishui. As our headquarters and the only town in our area, it was considered a relatively cushy assignment. Probably the main reason for my being appointed to Lishui was that I was expected to use my medical training in a small hospital for men that had just been opened by the Grey Nuns.

Many of these poor men were dying of leprosy, cancer or tuberculosis when picked up on the streets by the sisters. It was the duty of my helper, a young Chinese who had a little experience in a sisters' hospital further north, to inform me when a patient was near death. At that point, the patient had to be moved to an outer room of the hospital. Otherwise, the other patients would run away for fear that the spirit of the dead person would come back to haunt them.

Although our catechist routinely gave all patients instructions in Catholicism, we never proposed baptizing them until they were dying. Usually they would agree. To them, baptism was another mysterious foreign medicine that might cure them. Why didn't we baptize them until death was imminent? Because we knew that they would never practice their new religion if they lived. And yet it might get them into heaven if they died! It seems incongruous but that was the sacramental thinking of the day.

For burial, we purchased a small, cheap box, then called the undertaker who took the body to be buried at any spot outside the city's walls. Even our two priests who died in Lishui, my friends to whom this book is dedicated, were buried on a nondescript hill outside the city. It was forbidden by law to bury anybody within the city walls. Burial was not in the ground but on top of it. The box was covered with clay and stones that were often washed away by the rains after a few months. Scavenging dogs — there seemed to be thousands of them — often made a feast on the remains of the dead, no matter how rotten.

This method of burial was simply due to the fact that our area was one of the poorest in China. It in no way indicated a lack of respect among the Chinese for their dead. No people have more respect for the deceased. Indeed, ancestral worship kept a family together in spirit long beyond the normal span of life. Ancestral worship, dear to the Chinese heart, is at the core of their religious thinking. That's why graveyards are quite ornate in more prosperous parts of the China. Every year on the anniversary of a person's death, the surviving relatives visit the deceased's grave, placing on it food and flowers and burning josh sticks. Such ceremony is very similar to the Catholic observance of All Souls' Day as it was kept when I was young.

I'll never forget one particular demonstration of the Chinese sensitivity to matters of life and death. I had acquired a used movie camera and was showing some of my films taken at the mission and developed in Shanghai. One of the women workers spotted her recently deceased husband smiling and waving up there on the screen. To her, he was suddenly alive again. The shock was so great that the woman passed out dead cold. The sisters had to take her home to revive her.

In truth, there was not a lot for us priests to do, given the lack of interest in Catholicism among the Chinese. I witnessed only one marriage in all my time in Lishui. When the ceremony ended, the groom, a soldier from another province, clicked his heels, saluted me and marched off to his barracks in the other province. He would be coming back in a few weeks for the bride but she broke into floods of tears. With a veil covering her face, she hadn't seen the groom very clearly and feared she wouldn't recognize him when he returned. Of course, the marriage had been arranged by her parents years before.

To help fill in my time, I took up a pursuit that would have amazed my seminary professors. The procurator, or business manager of the mission at that time, was Father Aaron Gignac. A son of a French-speaking family from near Windsor, Ontario, he was one the kindest of men, with a good sense of humour and a ready smile. Although his health was poor after ten years in China, his mind was keen. He owned twenty or more volumes of the works of St. Thomas Aquinas translated into English. The two of us conceived the bright idea to work our way through them. Each of us would take a turn preparing a lesson for the other. The study turned out to be pure delight. In the seminary, theology had been a chore. Now I devoured it. In eighteen months studying with Father Gignac, I learned more than in all my formal studies.

In 1940, however, Father Gignac's health had deteriorated to the point that he had to enter hospital in Wenchow. Besides a weak heart, he had been afflicted with a seriously enlarged appendix for some time. After an appendectomy in the Wenchow hospital, pneumonia set in. As his weak heart was unable to fight it, he died shortly after. He was just thirty-nine, the second of our priests to die in China. Father McGillivray, the first of our priests to die there and a man whose profound influence on me has already been described, was also thirty-nine when he died of malaria.

I fell heir to Father Gignac's job as procurator. Probably my experience in the family business had something to do with this appointment. What a job it was. Inflation was raging so wildly that eventually our money, the yuan, was worthless. The government bank had frozen the bank rate at twelve yuan to one American dollar. Those twelve yuan wouldn't have bought a toothpick. You would have needed a suitcase full of money to buy a package of cigarettes. The actual value of the paper and ink on a 1,000 yuan note was worth more than its buying power.

This meant that I had to keep begging Scarboro to send more money. During my first year in Lishui we had received mail from Canada but when the Japanese blockaded the coast, we were cut off with no contact other than telegrams. My cabled pleas to Canada fell on deaf ears. I remember so vividly the answer coming back one time, "You have ample money." To keep us alive, I was able to borrow some money from the Salt Commission, the group that controlled the vital supply of salt for the town. As Canada did not then have its own embassies in foreign countries, I negotiated with the Swiss embassy to arrange a loan from the federal government in Ottawa which was eventually repaid by Scarboro.

Apart from the constant struggle to find money, my job involved buying food for our two kitchens — one in the priests' residence and the other in the school where the students and employees ate. To some extent, I helped the sisters with their buying for their compound across the street. Another part of my job was making candles and mass wine (from raisins). The only money I brought in was from selling the contents of our two-hole outdoor toilet. What the five of us produced, with assorted visitors, made enough money to pay the salaries of a couple of catechists — perhaps fifty cents a week.

Surviving in business wasn't easy because stealing is a way of life in China, as it is wherever there are poor people. If you gave an employee a dollar to buy something, it was taken for granted that he would pocket ten percent. The problem was when he took more. I knew food was being stolen by my twelve employees constantly but it was a delicate matter to accuse anyone, even when you knew who the thief was. If you fired him, he would lose face, which was just about the worst thing that could happen to a Chinese. In fact, sometimes when a person lost face badly, he would take his life. So the only way to handle the stealing problem was to pile more work on the culprit until he finally quit. In an emotional farewell, the employee would say how sorry he was to leave and how nicely you had treated him. And you, the employer, would praise the culprit, saying how sorry you were to lose him. Everybody saved face.

The most important part of my job — as far as the general wellbeing of our group was concerned — was brewing beer. The Polish priest in Wenchow, Father Viachork, taught me how to brew beer and sold me the hops along with bottles and caps. I made over 200 quart-sized bottles in each batch. Lowering the bottles into a dried-up well dug by our predecessors cooled the beer a bit. When the first two batches were consumed in a few weeks, I raised the alcohol content to about ten percent to make it last longer. That meant adding more sugar. What a hot job — boiling that sugar!

The beer turned out to be a life-saver for us during the summer. Even some of our strict temperance priests enjoyed it. Once I came downstairs and found Father Leo Curtin sitting at the table. Having just arrived home after a tough two-week bicycle trip to perform confirmations in the country, he was exhausted. But the relaxation was unmistakable on his flushed red face, thanks to a couple of glasses of my beer. "Harvey," he said happily, "I think I'm drunk."

Soon, however, even such simple pleasures would be memories.

Chapter Five

Exodus from Lishui

Pearl Harbour, December 7, 1941. That was a day none of us will ever forget. It changed our lives. (It was December 6 in the West but December 7 in China.) We heard the news of the Japanese attack from the BBC. At first we were elated that now the Americans were joining the war. They'd mop up the Japanese, for sure. But the opposite happened. Soon, the Japanese blockade was complete as they took control of the entire coast south to Hong Kong. More than one of our men said to himself, "Now we are indeed the Legion of the Damned. Canada refuses to give us money and we are trapped on all sides."

But the worst was yet to come. One night, shortly after Pearl Harbour, the BBC radio news announced, "Today planes of unknown origin dropped bombs at midday on Tokyo and other cities as thousands of people filled the streets." The Americans had hit Japan's homeland — a catastrophe the Japanese had deemed impossible. We all cheered. At least, we felt, the Japanese were getting a taste of their own medicine after years of slaughtering millions of Chinese, most of them innocent civilians.

But a minute after the BBC report, our lights went out. I went to walk in our yard and heard a plane. Why hadn't the warning bell sounded? The plane circled the sky and then disappeared into the darkness. It hadn't dropped any bombs. Having noticed that it sounded different from the Japanese planes we were used to, I was mystified.

Fifteen minutes passed. Then the temple bell sounded an urgent alarm. Suddenly, the sky was filled with planes dropping bombs all over the city. It was our first night-time bombing and the vivid flares added a fantastic aspect to the terror. It lasted all night. Thousands of people died. In the morning, bodies lay in the streets, draped over electric wires, impaled on posts. That horrible night broke the nerves of one of the sisters. A young woman from the Ottawa Valley, she was one of the bravest ones but, for weeks after that, she cried inconsolably every night.

In a few days, the news reports gave us the explanation for the intensified attack on Lishui. The planes that had hit Japan came from the *Hornet*, a small US plane carrier some 600 miles off the Japanese coast. They were B-25s, light bombers carrying extra fuel strapped to their bellies. Captain Jimmy Doolittle (later a general) was in charge of the operation. The plan was that, after hitting Japan, the planes would land at the airport in Lishui as well as at another one to the north. The lone plane that I heard in the sky was one of them.

Its crew hadn't been able to find the airport, however, because the airport employees, sensing that Japan's victory was inevitable, co-operated with the Japanese by turning off the airport lights. As a result, all of the US planes crashed or made emergency landings, mostly in Japanese-controlled China. When the local government discovered what the airport employees had done, the hapless men were paraded through the streets as traitors before being shot dead.

The Japanese, enraged that Lishui had been part of the plot to bomb their homeland, wreaked vengeance on the poor town. The closer the bombers approached, the faster the temple bell tolled. We prayed for rainy weather; that would mean a day without bombs. When we had advance warning, we crossed the river and headed for the mountains where we had a ringside view of the Japanese bombers spilling out death on the defence-less city. Clearly, our church steeple, the highest structure for miles around, was used as a landmark. It was all dive-bombing, a deadly technique the Japanese used on the Philippines, Hong Kong and other places.

When there wasn't time to flee to the mountains, we missionaries gathered in the shelter under the sisters' house which was built on poles above wet ground. The rest of our group would cower there during an attack but I preferred to stroll the perimeter of the enclosure, scanning the sky for planes. My theory was that it was better to see death coming than to wait and wonder. Often, I could see the faces of the pilots in their gas masks as they dived to bomb places not 100 yards away. If I lost sight of a plane, that meant it might be directly overhead. Only then would I fall to my belly under the shelter. The group told me that my walking around that way was a great morale booster. As long as they saw me upright, they knew they were safe.

In one attack when most of us had managed to escape to the hills, the building housing the priests' kitchen was hit and totally demolished. One employee, a poor man from the country, was killed in the attack. The force of the bomb blew his body around a corner and into another building.

One morning at the height of the Japanese onslaught, I was surprised to see meat on the table in the boys' dining room. When I asked the ten-year-old boys at the table where the meat came from, they just stared at me. Finally, one of them confessed: it was rat. With so many buildings destroyed by bombs, the city was overrun with rats. The night before, the boys had had a spree killing rats.

Then one boy spoke up: "Why don't foreigners eat rats?" Then another chimed in, "The meat is tastier than chicken." Later, I learned that our cooks fed the rats until they were fat for the kill. A boy claimed to have seen one of our priests eating a rat in a village; according to the boy, the priest liked it, not knowing what it was. One of our men lost a dog that used to follow him when he was riding around town on his bicycle. We later found out that the local soldiers had caught the dog and feasted on him.

Soon there were rumours that Japanese soldiers were heading in our direction from Hangchow, less than 200 miles north of us. Reportedly, they wanted to occupy our airstrip to make sure the Americans wouldn't use it for another raid on Japan. Then the rumours were confirmed as facts: 80,000 soldiers in three prongs were bearing down on us. You could tell their arrival was imminent when Japanese spies dressed as civilians began appearing in the streets. As terrified local people fled south or into the mountains, Lishui was becoming a ghost town.

Our priests from more northerly missions that had already fallen to the Japanese had joined us in Lishui. One of the spokespersons for missionaries in free China, Father Leo Ferrari, a Franciscan who was in Chungking, had warned us missionaries not to fall into Japanese hands. Their atrocities were well known. The whole world had heard of "The Rape of Nanking" when Japanese soldiers raped some 800,000 women in the first few days of the takeover of that city.

One morning in May, 1942, five months after Pearl Harbour, a Mr. Sen came to our door. "The Japanese are already here," he announced. This merchant, who did a small business in charcoal and salt, was the only one among our supposed friends who risked exposure to the Japanese by warning us of their arrival. As far as I am concerned, he thus showed himself to be the only true Christian in town rather than a Rice Christian. Begging me to get the sisters and ourselves out of town, he offered to pay for a sampan for us.

Meanwhile, our superior was bedridden with raging malaria. We had enough quinine from the sisters' supply to keep him alive but not to bring down his high temperature. The poor man, utterly out of touch with reality by now, made no reply when I told him the news. I crossed the street to tell the sisters that we were leaving at noon. Refusing to listen to my urging that they join us, their superior insisted on waiting for our superior's advice.

For me, there was no question about what had to be done. Around noon, I crossed the river with my bicycle on a scow. The rest of our priests were fleeing by whatever means they could. Looking back, I saw the sisters and our superior getting into a sampan. That was the last I ever saw of our mission.

For two days, I rode my bike through very mountainous country for 100 miles, with an overnight stop in Powuka, one of our missions. Finally I reached Lungchuan, our southern mission, not far from the border with Fukien province. Within a few days, all our priests and sisters had gathered there. Some of the sisters were carried part of the way on the priests' bicycles and they all arrived muddy and soaking wet from a downpour. We were among the hordes of refugees who had swollen Lungchuan's population of 7,000 to three times that number.

While it was suspected that the Japanese would eventually push on to Lungchuan, we waited there some weeks to try to decide what course of action we missionaries should take. That pause gave me time for thought. Would the war ever end? Would we get back home? Was this the end of our mission in China? As for myself, what had I accomplished? Very little. Much of the time in Lishui had been spent running from bombs.

A more important question: had I grown cynical? The answer was a loud and clear *YES*. Older French priests who preceded us in China had a saying: "Keep your mind and your bowels open." No difficulty about the latter. But it wasn't so easy to keep open-minded and idealistic. I remembered the comment of the old French missionary who told us, "Go home. The Chinese don't have souls." Of course, the old man may have been senile, but I think he was expressing the cynicism common among old missionaries in China. Perhaps they could hardly be blamed for becoming cynical when they saw so little result from their work.

In fact, the Chinese themselves were cynical for the most part. How could they be otherwise? Life for most of them was a struggle to survive, to get a daily bowl of rice. Their hopes for anything better rarely worked out. Naturally, their fatalism rubbed off on the missionaries. Disillusioned missionaries often fell back on the saying, "Everything is hopeless; nothing is serious."

I couldn't help wondering whether the apparent futility of our mission was due, in part, to the lack of harmony among the priests of the Scarboro Society. There were plenty of reasons for the conflict. The beginnings of our society at Lishui were rocky. All those early missionaries of the society, being virtual pioneers in the field, were rugged individuals. It wouldn't have been easy to establish concord among them even in the best of circumstances, and the circumstances were far from easy.

First, there was the political chaos raging in China. Banditry was common all over the country. Moreover, to call China a united country in those years would be an exaggeration. Several provinces were controlled not by Chiang's central government but by warlords who, with their own armies, wielded total control over their people. The Chinese Communists were another unsettling influence. Never mind living harmoniously under those conditions, the early priests of Scarboro deserve credit for staying on the job.

What made their task more difficult, however, was what might be called the problem of governance within our society. When our priests first arrived in Lishui in 1926, they were put under the authority of the bishop of Ningpo, a Frenchman who knew little about Canada or Canadians. In Lishui, a Spaniard, equally ignorant of Canada was put in charge as their local superior.

Meanwhile, the boss back in Canada was Monsignor John E. MacRae. A man older than my father, he had been vicar general of Alexandria Diocese (its main city is Cornwall, Ontario). He probably would have been made a bishop but for the fact that the Ontario bishops asked him to take over the running of our society from its founder, Monsignor John Mary Fraser. Credit must be given to Fraser, a visionary with one idea: to bring the Gospel to China. Like all idealists, however, he lacked the administrative skills to run the organization effectively on a day-to-day basis. Realizing how chaotic conditions were under Fraser, the Ontario bishops stepped in and asked Dr. MacRae to take over.

I often wonder if he regretted taking the job. He never gave up on us, though. It was he who kept the thing going. He made two very brief visits to China. Obviously, he couldn't learn much about China in a couple of days. No doubt, he listened to what each man had to say. They likely had conflicting ideas about our work in China. When he returned from a short trip in 1932, it was a stormy winter day in Toronto and we seminarians met him at the front door. In his big furry coat, he reminded me of a bear shaking the snow off. He seemed to be breathing heavily as though still recuperating from the shock of China. "Boys," he said, "China is a man's job."

It was obvious to MacRae that something had to be done to improve the morale of our men in Lishui. They were restive under the Spanish superior. Still, MacRae had few Canadians from whom to choose a boss. While the priests in Lishui were good men, MacRae probably thought that naming one of them superior would make matters worse, given the natural rivalries. Besides, a superior needs special qualities that aren't in ready supply. So he named Father W.C.McGrath, a man on his way to China, as the new boss. Poor McGrath didn't find out about this fate until he received a cable while on the high seas en route to China.

Father McGrath was a priest from St. John's, Newfoundland and had been working in his home diocese when he decided to enter our society. His first duties with us involved editing our magazine and acting as assistant to MacRae. At the time of his appointment as superior in China, he was about thirty-five years of age, the average age of the men in Lishui. A fine man with a genial personality, a talented speaker and writer, McGrath was, however, a city man. He had never lived among rural people or the very poor. It wouldn't surprise me if he hadn't really wanted to take the superior's job in China, but being obedient, he took it. Almost inevitably, the welcome from the men in Lishui was not unanimously enthusiastic. Some of the men there must have felt they had been passed over for this newcomer.

After a couple of years in China, McGrath wrote to MacRae back in Toronto saying he wanted to come home. He suggested that by lecturing and writing in Canada he could do something helpful for the mission. He did go home but had returned to give it another try in China when we arrived. When he departed the second time, this time for good, he was replaced by the elderly and sickly Father Curtin.

Over and above these problems of finding a suitable superior for the mission, there was the broader issue that is perhaps summed up by Rudyard Kipling in the words, "East is east and west is west and never the twain shall meet." For us, it was never easy to understand the Chinese. While they were constantly smiling, you could never tell whether they were smiling with you or at you. Even today, when there have been so many advances in communication, westerners and Asians often reach an impasse in their efforts at understanding each other.

It should also be remembered that none of the foreign missionaries was invited to come by the Chinese. To a great extent, all foreign missionaries came into China on the coat tails of the Europeans and Americans who forced their way in by gunboats. These foreigners demanded large areas where they lived independent of all Chinese law. The foreigners were exploiters, quite simply. One of their most lucrative operations was bringing opium into China, contrary to the laws of the country. As the Chinese saw it, the missionaries weren't much better: they were selling a product the Chinese had never heard of and didn't want. They had their own religions.

We Westerners often forget that at the time of our first contact with the Chinese, their culture was advanced far beyond ours. In 1263, the two brothers Maffeo and Nicolo Polo, Venetian merchants, received a warm welcome from the Great Khan, the

Emperor of China. They couldn't believe what they saw: a vast empire with laws and government and a civilization far surpassing anything in Europe. All kinds of innovations and cultural advances dazzled them: printing, paper money, spices to preserve meats, ink, sculpture, paintings, porcelain, gunpowder, dogs and falcons as trained hunters, wheelbarrows, coal-burning stoves, and, above all, that precious stuff called silk. When the brothers returned home, nobody would believe their story.

Setting out again in 1271, the two merchants took with them Nicolo's seventeen-year-old son Marco. For twenty-four years, young Marco remained in China, travelling much of the vast country, as guest of the Great Khan. Once again, the people of Europe dismissed reports of the fantastic civilization of China. To Europeans, mention of China stirred up memories of invasions by Genghis Khan, father of the Great Khan, Marco Polo's host. Hence, all Chinese were "barbarians" in Europeans' eyes. But a comparison of the two cultures at the time shows that the Chinese had grounds to look down on Europe's so-called civilization.

In our own time, the lifestyle of the missionaries did little to bridge the cultural gap. Usually, the first action of missionaries on arriving in a new city was to buy land, a piece of the "good earth" so precious to the Chinese. On this land, the missionaries built a compound, surrounded by high walls for protection. Often, the walls were topped with broken glass. In many places, the compound was the most lavish operation in town.

So the priests often got off on the wrong foot with the people they sought to convert. The Chinese well knew that the elaborate compound was only possible because of the backing of the foreign military and money. To the foreigner, accustomed to concepts of open spaces and private ownership, the land acquired for the mission wasn't much. In the eyes of the starving people who had no land at all, it was just another unjust act of foreigners exempt from Chinese law.

In my opinion, the Chinese perception of Christianity as irretrievably foreign had much to do with the Vatican's handling of what was called the Rites Controversy. One of the strangest aspects of our arrival in Lishui was that each of us had to take an oath not to discuss the Rites Controversy. It wasn't hard to take an oath not to discuss it — I'd never heard of it! Only later, from my reading of Father Gignac's library, did I learn of the battle that raged in the sixteenth century when the Father Matheo Ricci, a Jesuit, was trying to get the Vatican to relax its policy against incorporating any Chinese cultural and religious ideas within Catholicism. Ricci felt it would do no harm to adapt some Chinese practices to a Christian context. But the Vatican said *no*. The cause of the Christian religion in China suffered a great deal from that decision. Because of the cultural and religious superiority complex of the Vatican, we were taught nothing in the seminary about the history and culture of China, the country where we had promised to spend our lives.

Although the ordinary Chinese were very hospitable to us, our foreign status was strikingly brought home to us at least once. One day when we were riding our bikes on the outskirts of Lishui, three little boys threw stones at us and hollered *wai-go-jen* (foreign devils). Perhaps the boys' intentions weren't as hostile as their words sounded, given the fact that they were laughing. Likely, they didn't mean to hit us. But the prejudice was real.

It reminded me of how in my home town of Dominion, when I was a teenager, boys threw snow balls at the lonely Chinese laundry man. We probably didn't mean to harm him. Like the old lady who told me she didn't want to go to heaven if Chinese would be there, we were victims of bigotry and propaganda. A comic strip in our local papers at that time depicted a Chinese man with a malicious grin, both his hands hidden in his sleeves where he stored, supposedly, a cache of knives. We were brainwashed to think Chinese were evil personified. So, in a way, it seemed only fair that the Chinese boys would respond to us in a similar way.

It almost seemed that nature detected and resented foreignness in its midst. As foreigners had more protein in their diet, their body odour was very different from that of the Chinese. This put us at some physical risk from animals. The water buffalo tended by small Chinese boys could detect a foreigner's body odour at several hundred yards and could charge unpredictably. Some of us priests had, at one time or another, been chased by wild dogs because of our unfamiliar body odour.

I remember one time, though, when the barriers between our eastern and western cultures were literally stripped away. It was a hot, muggy day and three of us were biking outside the city. We stopped for a rest by the side of the dirt road, only a few yards from the river outside Lishui. The thought of immersing our tired, sweaty bodies in the water, polluted or not, was too much to resist. As there were apparently no people around, we peeled down to Adam's swim suit and left our clothes behind some bushes. As we had hoped, the water was cooling but we had enough sense not to put our heads under.

Suddenly, we heard something moving in the bushes. We swam stealthily nearer to shore. Three boys ran off laughing and yelling *"I-yanga"* ("the same"). We were probably the first foreigners those boys saw naked. It's easy to guess why they were exclaiming "the same". They had probably thought we were another species altogether. Discovering that we had male bodies like theirs, they were delighted. We were too.

So what to make of the four and a half years? I remembered a conversation with one of our priests shortly after my arrival in Lishui. A man a couple of years younger than I, he had been in China two years before me. His assignment was to look after the boys' school. It looked to me as though there wasn't much for him to do except line the kids up in the morning. The Chinese teachers did the real work.

One day, as he was sitting in the rocking chair on the porch, I teased him, "You don't do a tap of work. Do you think you're going to get to heaven?"

"Of course," he answered smugly. "I have left family and home to come here and witness for the Catholic faith. I don't have to do any more than sit here in my rocking chair. I will certainly get to heaven because this is hell!"

That wasn't my theology. I believed our witness for the faith had to be backed up with some effort to help people in a tangible way. The man who convinced me of that was Mr. Li, a sixty-year-old carpenter who lived next to us. A very friendly man, his face always radiated a smile just under the surface. Unlike most Chinese whose hair remains black until they go bald, he had a full head of grey hair. Living in his house with his wife and children, was a "second wife", as the expression went. There was no moral stigma attached to that arrangement. Anybody who could afford one did. And Mr. Li certainly could. His carpenter shop was always busy.

From my upstairs window, I watched him in his patio. Several times a day, he lighted josh sticks and got down on his knees in front of the little wooden Buddha (probably carved by himself). He was a good man, obviously religious. I wondered what he thought of the catechism lessons coming over the wall from our compound in the bellowing voice of Mr. Wong, our catechist. Surely, among all the people of China, Mr. Li must have been the man who was best informed of the truths of the Catholic faith. What kind of an impression had they made on him?

Curious as I was, it took me a long time to put the question. It isn't easy to be intimate with a Chinese. Even among themselves, candour is rare. One day, however, after many visits to him for repairs of furniture, I got up the nerve to broach the subject of our religion.

"Mr. Li," I said, "You must know our teachings as well as I do. Did you ever think of becoming a Christian?"

There was a pause; then he lifted his head. His gentle features broke into a startled smile. "You know, Shen Fu," he said, "I am one of the well-to-do people in town. Almost all the people are very poor. But you live in the best house, surrounded by many servants. You have the best food, even a radio. [He hadn't missed much.] So you don't know what life is like for most Chinese. Even if you went to live in a hovel as most people do, and even if you ate the same food as the poorest do, you would not understand poverty. You can get up and leave any time. You can take a holiday. If you are sick, you go to the best hospital. But these people have no hope of ever escaping their poverty. If you could give them some hope of relief from their misery, then perhaps they might accept your teachings."

He went on to explain: "Your religion does not fit our people. They can afford only two pleasures in life: food, which is often scarce, and sex — which costs nothing and there is always lots of it available. But you condemn sex except in marriage. You say sex does not exist in your heaven." With a look of amazement, he asked, "Why would any sane person want to go to such a heaven?"

What a great insight into the Chinese mind! It brought me back to the teachings of Coady, Tompkins and others. Even if I stayed the rest of my life in China, what good would it do the people if I couldn't show them some way out of their poverty? I would probably end up as cynical as some of the old French priests.

After four centuries of work by thousands of missionaries, only half of one percent of the Chinese population had come to the Church. It was obvious to me that our approach — sitting on our butts on rocking chairs — wasn't the one God wanted.

So why didn't I try to start some co-ops in China? In the first place, our chaotic living conditions under the constant bombings weren't conducive to organizing structures of any kind. But the turmoil in the country as a whole — the banditry and the fighting among the warlords — was the more basic factor militating against any kind of co-operative movement. Furthermore, since Chinese weren't much interested in the religion we were selling, the idea of co-ops, coming from the same foreign source, wasn't likely to meet with much enthusiasm.

There was one foreigner who did try something in the co-op line. Rewey Alley, a New Zealander, spent much of his life as a businessman in China, first in Shanghai. When the Chinese on the coast began fleeing inland from the Japanese, Alley headed with them for Chungking. Thousands of them carried on their backs parts of dismantled machines from factories. In Szechuan province, Alley helped these people put together factories to produce a variety of their needs. In so doing, he organized them into co-ops. Chiang's government, instead of appreciating his efforts, saw his work as a form of communism and jailed him in Chungking for several years.

No, it was not that my belief in co-ops died in China. There was simply no hope that any foreigner could succeed in this kind of work. Later, in Chungking, I got to know Bishop Paul Yu Pin (the future cardinal) and, at his request, I prepared a small pamphlet on co-ops which he translated into Chinese. He wanted me to stay with him in the hope that the war would end and I could help to introduce co-ops in his program of Catholic Action but as further political developments showed, that would have been impossible.

During our two months in Lungchuan, my review of the Lishui years had given me a clearer perspective on the problems of our mission but, at the moment, survival was the issue. Food was getting scarce in the crowded town. Our superior still would not make a decision about what we should do. Mindful of the warning not to fall into Japanese hands, our group met and decided that the only thing to do was to push south into Fukien province in the hope of staying ahead of the Japanese. I divided the little money we had, everybody getting a mere pittance. Not knowing whether we would ever be together again as a group, we took to the road.

Some men set out on their bicycles. I departed, along with five sisters and four priests, on a charcoal-burning government truck that was carrying the provincial mint's equipment for making money. Myself and another priest sat at the back of the truck with our legs dangling but the others crouched on top of the crates under tarpaulins. For several days we would travel this way though very mountainous terrain, rice paddies everywhere, tiny villages here and there. From time to time, Japanese planes strafed the escape route. For that reason, most of the Chinese fleeing on foot travelled at night.

As for our itinerary, we were completely at the mercy of the driver as we weren't paying him anything. When he decreed that we should stop for food, we used our fingers to eat rice that the sisters cooked on a little stove in two large metal wash basins. At night we slept by the roadside in the truck.

On August 15 we entered a flat area called Kutien ("Bitter Fields"). The sister superior said, "I know this is going to be a good day because it's the feast of Our Lady's Assumption." Soon, however, a fight broke out in the cab of the truck where a Chinese woman and man were riding with our driver. In the heat of the argument, the driver lost control and the truck toppled over into a culvert.

The two of us who were sitting at the back of the truck were able to jump clear, landing in a watery ditch in a sort of burial ground. At that moment, a Japanese plane swooped down, dropping some small bombs and strafing our escape route with machine gun fire. Submerging myself as far as possible under the water, I reached under me and pulled out a flat rock to protect my head. The middle finger of my hand holding the rock started spurting blood into the water when hit by a piece of shrapnel. Another piece tore a hole through my pith helmet.

Our travelling companions had been trapped under the tarpaulin when the truck fell. Amazingly, their injuries were not as severe as might have been expected. The sister superior's wrist was broken and I was able to put a splint on it, thanks to my medical training. I also re-set the dislocated shoulder of a priest.

Back when I was infirmarian at the seminary, a doctor had shown me how to do that for one of my classmates who often suffered from a dislocated shoulder as a result of an old football injury.

The accident stranded us in a tiny village for a few days until the truck could be put back on the road with the help of oxen. Throughout that time, we never saw our driver. Eventually, he showed up to tell us we were ready to roll again. In the accident, the sisters had lost their medical kit. So we had nothing to purify the water that we collected from ditches to boil our daily rice. Soon, we all had dysentery. There was nothing to do but let it flow. There were no washroom stops, no opportunities for washing. As we were all in the same predicament, there was no shame involved. I lost my voice from sheer weakness.

Finally, we human wrecks arrived at the American Dominican's mission in Fukien province where we spent two or three days recuperating. Our host was Father Luke Devine, a very kind and hospitable young man from New York State. We hadn't seen real liquor for years and he put at our disposal a plentiful store of Scotch. That did a lot to improve my outlook, at least temporarily. We later found out, to our great sadness, that Father Devine was captured by Chinese bandits a week or so after our visit. He was never heard of again.

We forged ahead, stopping for rest whenever our driver felt like it. During those pauses, we missionaries would stay at the mission of whatever national group served that town. In all of them, we received the finest hospitality. What struck me was that the US missions were much more luxurious than ours. That's of course because American Catholics are so generous to their missions. Mind you, they have lots to be generous with! For most of the missionaries, though, this was the last of the good times. In the months to come, many priests and sisters who welcomed us were to lose their homes to the Japanese.

A number of us met at Kweilin with the American Maryknoll priests who took good care of us. Our group had decided at the meeting in Lungchuan, however, that I was to push on to Chungking. As procurator, I was the person responsible for getting money, and the likeliest place to get it was Chungking, the capital of Chiang's China. Our thirty priests and sisters, although ousted from our own mission territory, still needed cash to live. Some of them had gone to work with US Passionists in Hunan province; others had offered to fill in for German and Italian priests who were held under house arrest in parts of China that were still resisting the Japanese. Still others were trying to reach India in the hope of arranging passage to Canada.

My long trek to Chungking covered a course something like the letter "U". Beginning in Lishui, it took me south to within a few miles of Hong Kong, then directly west to China's most south-west province, Yunan, then north to the biggest province, Szechuan, bordering on Tibet and irrigated by the great Yangtze river. But the day-to-day travel was by no means as direct as that outline makes it seem. For over two thousand miles, through eight of China's eighteen provinces, I was zigzagging to avoid Japanese-held areas.

Thanks to the contacts of the Maryknoll priests, and especially of Monsignor Romaniello (known as the "Jolly Roman"), I wangled a flight on a Flying Tigers plane from Kweilin to Kunming in Yunan. The Flying Tigers were American pilots who had volunteered to help Chiang Kai-Shek under retired US Colonel Claire Chennault. The natural caves at Kweilin formed ideal hiding places for their pursuit planes, the P-40s. It was on a C-47, a type of plane that carried about twenty passengers, that I flew to Kunming. This was my first airplane ride but I was too concerned about escaping from the Japanese to get much of a thrill from flying.

From Kunming, I managed to hitch a ride on another government truck for the long trip north to Chungking. My travelling companions were a young Chinese husband and wife. Huddled together on top of the heavily loaded truck, we passed the two-week journey mostly in silence. My Lishui dialect was unintelligible to them, as was their Shanghai dialect to me.

At one lonely point in the road, we spotted about twenty bandits swarming towards us, armed with bayonetted guns. We had just crested a hill, so the driver gunned it and we sped down that hill as fast as the truck could go. If it hadn't been for the hill, we would have been butchered.

Finally we reached the great Yangtze river, west of Chungking. I somehow turned up a precious ticket for a trip by river steamer into the capital. Once again, the steamer was overcrowded with thousands of people. There was no food, no toilet, not even space to lie down. I spent the wild forty-eight-hour ride down the turbulent river squatting on my haunches.

It was raining and dark when we reached Chungking around seven in the evening on that autumn day. On leaving the ship, I reached in my back pocket and found that my billfold was gone. One of my thousands of travelling companions on the steamer was richer by a few yuan and I was totally broke. Nevertheless I hailed a rickshaw and said to the driver, in Mandarin, *"Tien-chu-tang."* (Catholic Church).

We moved on in the rain for more than an hour. Then he stopped. There was nothing around for miles but the rubble of bombed buildings. I shook my head and told him again, "The Catholic Church". But he stood his ground and pointed doggedly to a street sign sticking up out of the rubble. The sign read "Catholic Church Street."

I tried to tell him that I wanted the church, not the street. Then the moon broke through the clouds just enough for me to spot a steeple a couple of miles away. I pointed at it eagerly, but the poor coolie was exhausted. So was I. It was the low point of my life so far. I had never been so tired, hungry and thirsty. Suppose he left me here as he threatened to? What would I do abandoned here without any money?

I begged him to go on. He asked again for money. Promising him he would get it when we reached the church, I pleaded with him to continue.

He did. We reached the steeple only to find that most of the church was demolished. It was by now about ten o'clock and most people were in bed. Luckily there was a woman standing in the doorway of a building nearby, chatting with some children.

Struggling to come up with my best Mandarin, I asked her, "Do you know a Franciscan, a Father Leo Ferrari? (*Fe Shen Fu).*" I specified that he was "American (*Mei-quo-jen).*"

She smiled beautifully and said, "Yes." (It turned out that she was the wife of Dr. John Wu, a famous convert to Catholicism who later became China's ambassador to the Vatican.) Then she pointed, "He is upstairs."

A window flew open, a head poked out and a man's voice said in English, "Who's that?"

"It's Harvey Steele," I yelled. "Is that you Leo?"

"Where in the name of God have you been?" he scolded. "We've been waiting almost two months for you."

"When I've had something to eat and drink, I'll tell you," I said. "But first, will you please give this poor rickshaw driver some money?"

Chapter Six

Chungking — China's Capital

The dreary weather on the night of my arrival was, I soon learned, typical for Chungking. It has probably the worst climate of any major city in China. In fact, it's fog-bound so much of the time that there is a saying that when the sun shines, the dogs bark at it.

Not that I was complaining, having found a safe haven. Now that the US 14th Air Force had moved in with its anti-aircraft guns, the Japanese had given up on Chungking. Father Ferrari arranged for me to live with the Maryknoll priests in the remains of a large Catholic girls' school where my host was Father Mark Tennien, a Maryknoller. Although the place was half-demolished by the earlier bombing, accommodation here was better than in Lishui; at least we had running water. The food was excellent. Even more important, Father Tennien had brought a good stock of liquor when he came from Hong Kong. Emaciated on arrival (so people said), I soon recuperated from the rigours of my flight from Lishui.

Father Tennien, eighteen years my senior, was from Vermont but had been educated at the Grand Seminary in Quebec. A learned man and a born politician, he was the author of several books about the Church and politics but he was ahead of his time in questioning our approach to missionary work in China. His progressive views were likely the sole the cause of his never becoming a bishop.

Living with him in the school were Ted Bauman, a priest from Youngstown, Ohio, belonging to the Society of the Divine Word. We three we were later joined by Father Ed McManus from Ireland and Jim Smith, a young Maryknoll priest. All of us had the same job — trying to scrape up enough money to keep our colleagues alive in the places where they had landed when scattered by the Japanese.

Our favourite hour of the day was after supper when we tuned in to London's BBC. The constant war news was all-absorbing. While there was no radio contact with North America, dispatches from the US embassy kept us up-to-date on the American version of the war. The fact that it often differed vastly from the British version created sparks in our group. Father McManus, born in Belfast, had served time in a prison as a young Sinn Feiner, so he had his reasons for not being partial to the British view of events. Even more irritating to him, however, was the way the young American priests talked — as though the US were fighting the war alone and the British efforts were irrelevant.

All around us, the city was bursting with refugees seeking to escape the Japanese. Before the war, Chungking's population was 300,000. Now it was more than double that. Among the ranks of refugees was Chiang Kai-Shek's entire government. After losing first Pekin, then Nanking to the Japanese, Chiang had moved the capital to Chungking in Szechuan, China's most western and most populous province. It was hoped that Chungking's distance from Japan would provide some security. Not so. The Japanese found it and hammered it with bombs. During the bombings, tens of thousands of people sheltered in the natural caves at the base of the huge rock on which the city was founded.

That rock at the confluence of the great Yangtze and the Kialing rivers gave Chungking much of its special character. All supplies had to be hauled up the rock from the water by stair-ways or inclined railroad. The slopes of the rock were teeming with a conglomeration of tiny wooden houses and shops, little more than shacks, people moiling up and down among them at all hours like restless ants. Water carriers struggled up the steps with wooden buckets balanced on bamboo poles. Porters carried merchandise or people in sedan chairs.

On top of the rock, the feverish and crowded life of a big city went on. Buses, taxis, rickshaws and sedan chairs clogged the wide main streets and pedestrians thronged the sidewalks. The din was terrific. Practically every vendor had some sort of noise-maker to advertise himself. A barber, for instance, would bang two pieces of metal to attract customers. Many a travelling chef worked his way through the crowd wielding a long bamboo pole. On one end of it were a stove, bowls and serving dishes; at the other were several dishes of food. A hungry pedestrian would strike a bargain with the entrepreneur, then squat on the ground in front of the stove, and proceed to dine on a bowl of rice and the agreed-upon morsels of food. Some people carried high poles loaded with several units of a single item for sale. Coming from Lishui where animals roamed the streets, it amazed me to see cats wearing collars and chained to a post. Someone explained that they were kept to prey on the rats which would otherwise gobble up the silkworms — a source of precious income to everyone.

Most of the allied countries had embassies in the city, making it a hotbed of intrigue. During the Second World War, Chungking and Lisbon had the reputation of being the centres of espionage for the world. Chungking also teemed with crime; it was every bit as sordid as Shanghai. One of our acquaintances once told of hearing a woman in the street who started screaming: "My baby! Where's my baby?" The infant had suddenly been snatched away from her. Likely the wretched child had been sacrificed to the drug trade. Innocent looking women carted around bundled up babies whose insides had been ripped out and stuffed with drugs.

The military aspect of Chungking was fascinating. For some time, it had been the headquarters of the famous Flying Tigers under Colonel Claire Chennault, retired from the US Army Air Corps. Chennault was friendly with Chiang Kai-shek and had married a Chinese. The Flying Tigers, the only opposition to the Japanese, apart from a few old anti-aircraft guns, saved many Chinese lives. But Chennault's prestige was threatened when Chungking also became the headquarters of the US military operations in China under four-star General Joseph ("Vinegar Joe") Stilwell. Eventually, Chennault's Flying Tigers were absorbed under Stilwell. The clashes between Chennault, an easy-going southerner, and Stilwell, a strict Yankee, were legendary.

The big problem for the Allies was keeping China in the war lest it capitulate to Japan. Chiang Kai-shek, as wily a man as could be, used this threat to lever as much help as possible out of Washington. Not that it wasn't needed. His army numbered 12 million soldiers, half-starved, paid a pittance, with one old rifle for every dozen men. From time to time rumours would circulate that Chiang was going to make a deal and capitulate to the Japanese. This would panic the Americans and they'd pour in more money and supplies.

There was little doubt in anyone's mind that, without US help for Chiang, the Japanese would soon take over all China. So the US had air bases scattered all over southern China from which they hit the Japanese in places like Hong Kong and Saigon. All supplies for these bases had to be flown over the Himalayas from India, a very costly operation in terms of money but especially in the loss of men and planes.

Further complicating the situation, there was Mao in his cave at Yenan, in the north-west of China. Sometimes he fought against the Japanese, sometimes against Chiang's troops. As Chiang lost more and more territory, sometimes Mao gained some of it and sometimes the Japanese did.

Then there was Russia's dubious involvement as a supposed ally of Chiang. Russia had the largest embassy in Chungking but it was rumoured that the Russians were counterfeiting the yuan and dropping it over China — further accelerating the yuan's descent into worthlessness. And Russian Communist propaganda was still invading China. But Russia had no use for Mao. Stalin had his own interpretation of Marx's rallying cry, "Workers of the World, Unite!" To Stalin, that meant only urban workers; they, in his opinion, were the only ones capable of pulling off a revolution. But Mao's plan was based on his faith in the peasants of China who made up ninety percent of the population.

Adding to the exotic air of the city was the constant gossip about the goings-on of the three beautiful Soong sisters. Much of the table talk around the city centred on the machinations of these legendary women. The eldest was the widow of Sun Yat-sen, founder of the Chinese Republic in 1911. Ai-ling, the youngest, was married to H.H. Kung, finance minister and master-mind of the black market. Mei-ling, the most beautiful in the opinion of many, had graduated from one of America's most prestigious colleges; she was Chiang's wife, having married him about the time he broke with the Communists in 1927. Besides pulling strings behind the scenes at Chiang's palace, she was constantly travelling to the US to win Congress to his cause.

Power-struggles were raging not only among the military and political personnel in Chungking. In a smaller way, something similar was brewing in Catholic Church circles. The Vatican representative to China, the Apostolic Delegate, was living 2,000 miles away in Pekin. As it was under Japanese control, he could not communicate with Free China. This made him useless to us as the Vatican representative in political matters. The Vatican, however, could not name another representative because that would amount to acknowledging two distinct Chinas. The Archbishop of Chungking, Louis Jantzen, a Frenchman, wasn't able to represent us in dealings with the US military because he spoke no English.

As a result, there was a tussle among three clergymen as to who would speak for the Catholic Church in Free China. One was a Chinese bishop, Paul Yu Pin, who was later to become China's second cardinal and who was a close friend of Chiang. Having taught in Rome after his ordination and having visited the US, Pin spoke English well. Then there were two American priests who were vying for recognition as official spokesman: Father Leo Ferrari, the Franciscan who had first welcomed me to Chungking; and Father Mark Tennien, my host at the Maryknoll house.

Cardinal Spellman, Archbishop of New York and head Catholic chaplain of the US military, was asked by Pope Pius XII to come to China to try to straighten out the situation. But Chiang wouldn't let Spellman in. The cardinal then sent an American chaplain to investigate. After pledging us to secrecy, he grilled each of us about the battle going on among Church leaders. Not having any commitment to either side, I reported my view of the situation as objectively as possible. But I couldn't help feeling somewhat uncomfortable about being immersed in the kind of politicking and power-mongering that was beginning to look like a way of life for many clergy.

There was one event, however, which forced me into a political role that was more a source of amusement than dismay. The Extraterritorial Rights Act imposed by foreigners about 100 years earlier was about to be repealed. It had allowed foreigners to live exempt from Chinese laws in major cities throughout

China. Bishop Paul Yu Pin felt the Church should mark the repeal of the act with a banquet. Father Leo Ferrari was to speak on behalf of the US. But who would represent Britain? The job fell to me, the only priest to be found in Chungking who was a British subject. So I got up at the banquet and extolled the benevolence of England. Imagine me, a stubborn Scot from Cape Breton, a descendant of the highlanders who fled British tyranny, praising Old Blighty!

My job of getting money for our Scarboro group did not come to much at first. Due to inflation, the yuan was worth less and less every day. Given the fixed exchange rate of twelve yuan to the US dollar, funding from Scarboro was hopelessly inadequate. But the bosses at home thought that our financial problems were solely due to my incompetence in business. It was a frustrating situation until Father Tennien explained to me that nobody sold dollars at the official exchange rate any more.

So I learned about the flourishing black market in Kunming. It was understood by everybody to be master-minded by H.H. Kung, the finance minister, believed to be the richest man in China. In Kunming, the closest city to the Indian border, Chinese merchants exchanged their yuan for Indian rupees so that they could buy supplies in India and then smuggle them back into China. What any sensible business person had to do, therefore, was go to India to exchange dollars for rupees, then exchange the rupees for yuan back in China. That transaction produced thousands of yuan per dollar instead of just twelve.

If I'd had any qualms about plunging into the black market, they would have dispelled on discovering that it was sanctioned by the twenty-five or so Catholic bishops who had dioceses in unoccupied China. Most Protestant missionaries, when thwarted by inflation and the Japanese advance, had handed over their schools and hospitals to local groups. But the Catholic bishops decided to try to keep their missionaries on the job as long as possible — even if that meant dealing in the black market like every other major operation in China.

In a sense, we priests staying at the Maryknoll residence became bankers to the rest of the Catholic missionaries in the country. Usually, we flew to India by CNAC (Chinese National Aviation Company) in C-47s and returned on US military planes, with our bundles of rupees in our money belts. Flying "Over The

Hump", as the trip over the Himalayas was called, took us over Japanese-occupied Burma, so these flights weren't exactly joy rides. In fact, on my first trip, we spotted some Japanese Zeros executing their highly skilled manoeuvres in the air some distance off. Fortunately, they didn't come any closer. We'd have been sitting ducks if they had.

On that first trip I was stranded in India by the spring monsoons. It wasn't possible to return to China for two months. For a while I lived with Belgian Jesuits at the Sacred Heart rectory in Calcutta. Never had I seen so much squalor and misery as in that city. It made China look good. It was there that I heard the inspiring story, not well known in the west, about Constant Lievens, the Belgian Jesuit who was reputed to be the greatest missionary since Saint Francis Xavier and who gave his life in the cause of justice for the poor.

After some time in Calcutta, I moved on to Bombay to meet some of our men who were trying to arrange passage to Canada. Worlds away from Calcutta, Bombay was one of the most beautiful cities I'd ever seen. It's built at the site of one of the world's finest harbours. Archbishop Roberts, an English Jesuit, was a wonderful host to me. A fascinating man and something of a radical for his time, he had written a book on the liturgy that anticipated many of the changes that were to come after the Second Vatican Council. He told me how he was strolling down the street in Liverpool one day when he opened the newspaper to find that the Pope had appointed him Archbishop of Bombay. His sole mission there was to resolve the ancient dispute about control of the Archdiocese. Jurisdiction was claimed by both the English and the Portuguese who had colonized Goa, just off Bombay. Once he had named a resident Indian as Archbishop, Roberts was free to retire. He wanted me to stay there since his diocese was so short of priests but I was determined to fulfil my commitment to Scarboro.

That meant returning to Chungking to carry on my banking career. Apart from our quest for money, there wasn't a lot of work for us priests to do. We got invited to a lot of parties and did a lot of entertaining in our turn. One of the fascinating personalities I got to know this way was Theodore White, a journalist for *Time-Life*. Over lunch at the Maryknoll house about once a month, he regaled us with local and international scuttlebutt. A Jew, White was born on the wrong side of the tracks in Boston. He went on to graduate from Harvard, having majored in Chinese history and culture. He spoke Mandarin well, inspite of a slight Boston accent. White had met all the "beautiful" and powerful people in the city and talked with Mao and his cohorts in their hideaway in Yenan. In fact, White had become great friends with Chou En-lai, Mao's right-hand-man.

Like most Americans, however, he wasn't sympathetic to Mao, seeing Communism as the great evil. White's job, as he told us, was to do whatever he could to influence American opinion in favour of helping Chiang to hang in against the Japanese and, ultimately, against Mao. This passage from his book *In Search of History*, explains his mandate when he first was hired in China as an journalist-advisor to Chiang's government:

> I was employed to manipulate American public opinion. The support of America against the Japanese was the Chinese government's one hope for survival; to sway the American press was critical. It was considered necessary to lie to it, to deceive it, to do anything to persuade America that the future of China and the United States ran together against Japan. That was the only strategy of the Chinese government when I came to Chungking in 1939, and my job was to practice whatever deception was needed to implement that strategy.

Henry Luce, who became White's boss when he signed on with *Time*, had been born in China of Protestant missionaries and was a fanatical supporter of Chiang. But White came to see the "Generalissimo" in a less favourable light. In another part of his book, he writes: "He [Chiang] was a man I learned first to respect and admire, then to pity, then to despise." Most North American missionaries, both Catholic and Protestant, would have disagreed with White's perception of Chiang. To North Americans, Chiang was the great and admirable convert to Christianity, but those of us living in Chungking knew White's assessment of Chiang was right. He would never have received much support in the US if his own deceits hadn't been bolstered by the lies and propaganda of the Luce publications.

One day while listening to Ted White at our dinner table, I began to compare his situation and mine. Here was a young man who had come to China the same year I did. He, however, knew

China and its language when he came. I had been given no preparation in terms of study of things Chinese. On the contrary, we seminarians had spent many useless hours learning to sing difficult Gregorian chant when some of us couldn't even carry a tune. Countless hours had been devoted to learning over 400 ritual movements necessary for saying mass, not to mention mastering the breviary with its many rubrics and rules. A large part of our youth was therefore wasted in learning to "pray" in a way that amounted to much turning of pages and shuffling cards and ribbons.

Another thing that I admired about Ted was his intellectualism. It has been said by more than a few Europeans that anti-intellectualism is part of North American culture. We North Americans boast that we are doers, not thinkers. Ted was an exception. I feel that anti-intellectualism is also part of our Scarboro society. Some see intellectualism as a kind of affectation. In a kind of reverse-snobbery, many of our men prided themselves on refusing to read any books about China's history or culture.

One of the most interesting people I met in Chungking was Stanley Smith, an Australian in charge of British propaganda in the effort to keep China in the war. In his early years, he had been a great fan of the Russian Revolution and had, in fact, introduced communism to Australia in the 1920s. He remained one of the leaders of the movement there for some time. But he eventually saw its fallacies. Next, he went to Yale and got a Ph.D. in psychology. Returning to Australia, he tried his hand for a while at journalism.

In this job, he covered a Eucharistic Congress where, for the first time, he met a Catholic bishop. Archbishop Daniel Mannix of Melbourne, an Irishman, was a champion of social justice. Smith compared Mannix with many world leaders he had personally encountered. The first Aussie ever called to a high post in the government of Britain, he had been present when Churchill met Roosevelt in Quebec; he had also attended the conference of Roosevelt and Stalin at Tehran. "You know," Smith told me, "Archbishop Mannix stood head and shoulders above those three men who had so much of the world's destiny in their hands."

I treasured knowing this Aussie. An agnostic, religiously speaking, Stanley Smith was a great humanist. He was convinced that, if we won the war, communism would be the big threat to true human values. One evening at dinner at our place, he told me, "If only you Catholics would get out into the world with your social teachings, communism would disappear in a short time." He tried several times to have the chief propagandist at the Soviet Embassy, reputedly a great intellectual, come and have dinner with us. "There is nothing that I would enjoy more than hearing a Russian communist and a Catholic priest in an argument," he said. He felt the Russian refused the invitation because he couldn't risk the possibility that communism would come off looking second best compared to the social teachings of the Catholic Church.

I never forgot Smith's belief that communism would quickly disappear if the Church pursued social justice. Some years later I repeated the idea to Archbishop Ricardo Pittini of Santo Domingo. Pittini told me later that he passed on the thought to Pope Pius XII, while on a visit to Rome. In due course, the Pope issued an encyclical conveying the very same thought. It would be fun to think that my agnostic friend had a hand in shaping the pontiff's message to the world.

From time to time, one of us priests at the Maryknoll residence would be asked to say mass at the French embassy. One night we were invited there for a party in honour of a French military man who had a distinguished career in Indochina (now Vietnam). He told a story that had special meaning for me. In Hanoi, he had been standing on the docks, looking at the big Japanese navy at anchor just before they took over the country. Turning to the small crowd of people around him, he asked them what they were thinking as they gazed at the huge ships. The answer: they couldn't believe that "yellow men" like themselves could build ships like that; they thought only white people could achieve such marvels. I was to be reminded of this story later in my work among the black people of Latin America. It is astounding how often people of non white cultures feel themselves inferior to whites.

During the year and a half that I spent in Chungking, most of our missionaries had found their way home, so there was little left for me to do. General Joseph Stilwell had, after being forced by the Japanese to retreat into India, quickly re-grouped his forces and was back in the China-Burma area with 250,000 US soldiers. Looking for chaplains for them, Father Joe McNamara of Providence, Rhode Island, the head Catholic chaplain of CBI (China-Burma-India) came to us. It was impossible to get chaplains at home, he said. Would I go to one of the bases? I agreed, provided the base was in range of a city where I could send cables home. Several other missionaries also answered the call to serve as chaplains in the area. We received pay as captains but had no rank. That was a great advantage: it put us on equal footing with the lowest and highest soldiers.

I was sent to a base of the 14th Air Force about a half hour's jeep ride from Kunming in south west China. There were about 7,000 men on the base. Until my arrival there was only one chaplain, a Protestant. The bombers and pursuit planes from our base were hitting the Japanese in places like Hanoi, Saigon and Hong Kong. On almost every raid, planes were lost and boys died, but the spirit on the base was tremendous. The men came from all over the US. Many of them were Texans, a species I had never met before — loud but irresistibly likeable.

Japanese planes dropped a few bombs on us but they were just nuisance raids, nothing like the bombing at tree-top level in Lishui. The different reactions of the men to these bombings fascinated me. Some were stoic and went about their business as usual; others screamed bloody murder and sought shelter under ridiculously flimsy structures. Such blatant expression of fear came as a surprise, after the calm, fatalistic approach that was more common in China. Among Chinese, a violent show of feeling is unforgivable.

In many ways, living with those 7,000 Americans was almost like being back in North America. Occasionally there was a reminder that we were surrounded by a very different world. One Sunday, Joe McNamara and I were out walking in the vicinity of the base. A much older man than I, Joe had no previous experience of China. After a while, we headed into the rice fields to get away from the dust of the road. It was the usual rural scene: some dogs roving about, people working in the distance.

"Pretty soon we're going to come to a dead body," I told Joe.

He was incredulous. "What makes you think so?"

I insisted that we would. He remained sceptical. We continued on for about 100 yards. At that point, the stench of rotting flesh turned us back.

Joe was mystified. "How did you know that body was there?"

It wasn't super-human olfactory powers that had tipped me off, I admitted. It was the behaviour of the dogs. As soon as they had seen us approaching, some of them slunk off with their tails between their legs. By the time we got within smelling range of the rotting body, the rest of the pack had left in the same cowed manner.

"Dogs track down corpses that are buried on top of the earth with just a few stones covering them," I explained. "They feast on the human remains. But, when spotted by humans, the dogs behave as though they feel guilty. That's why those dogs slunk away. And that's how their behaviour warned me of the presence of the body."

Another grim reminder of the way of life in China came one day when a distraught GI called out to me on the way into the mess hall. Crying profusely, he said, "Padre, I just killed a man in the city. I was driving my jeep slowly, trying to get through the crowds, but all of a sudden a man threw himself in front of my jeep. I didn't see him. Are these people nuts?"

"No," I told him. Then I took him aside and tried to explain something that was hard for him to believe. "The Chinese live in a world of spirits, mostly evil spirits, whom they are trying to appease. When a Chinese tells you he has a stomach pain or some other problem, he blames it on the evil spirit (*moi kwei*). He believes that these spirits can only travel in straight lines. Apparently this man believed he was followed by an evil spirit. To get rid of it, he swerved suddenly out of his straight line of movement — right into the path of your jeep."

I offered to hear the GI's confession and give him absolution if that would help restore his peace of mind.

"No, Padre, I'm not a Catholic," he said. "But thanks anyway. You helped."

Chapter Seven

Return to Canada

Early in 1945, word came from Canada ordering me to return home. I had been serving as chaplain some fifteen months. By way of a send-off, the base put on a big dinner and the boys gave me a thousand-dollar purse. I had an offer to fly direct to the US in the private plane of General (Wild) Bill Donovan, a loyal Catholic and the head of American Intelligence, which became known as the CIA in 1947. I declined the offer. In no big hurry to get home, I wanted to see as much of the world as possible. To facilitate that, a colonel arranged passage for me on military planes with stops in the Holy Land and Rome. Since I was in US uniform, the flights were free. At stopovers, I stayed at US military bases.

Because of the war, there were almost no tourists in the Holy Land. I was able to say mass in many of the holy spots: in Bethlehem, on Mount Calvary, and in Nazareth. I was impressed with the Via Dolorosa in Jerusalem. In the narrow, twisting road, much like a road in a Chinese town, I could feel the reality of Christ's painful journey to his death.

Among the interesting spots outside the city, the sight of the mouth of the Jordan as it entered the Dead Sea was unforgettable. Because of the witches' brew of naturally-occurring chemicals in the Dead Sea, fish die instantly on reaching it. Hundreds of seagulls swoop and cry overhead, ready to gorge themselves. (Legend has it that the death-dealing properties of the Sea are due to the fact that the wicked cities of Sodom and Gomorrah were destroyed in it.) And the village of Airen Karen, said to be the birthplace of John the Baptist, particularly fascinated me.

Reputed to have changed very little in two thousand years, it looked to me just like a typical village in China.

Not all the supposedly holy sites were so inspiring. In Jerusalem, I had teamed up with two US chaplains who had spent two weeks visiting the area. They asked me to join them to visit the one holy place left on their itinerary — the spot where Christ ascended into Heaven. An Arab guide solemnly conducted us to a slab of stone supposedly bearing the foot marks where Christ had stood before he disappeared into the sky. Dutifully, the three of us bent down to kiss the slab. As we raised our heads, we eyed one another with a look that said, "What damn fools we are."

Another time, I went into the Basilica of the Holy Sepulchre where a guide was lecturing a group of African soldiers in British uniforms. "This is where Christ was crucified," he said. Then pointing to the well known image of Mary of the Seven Sorrows with seven swords piercing her heart, he went on, "And that is the picture of His mother as she committed suicide."

After the Holy Land came stops in Athens and Naples, then Rome. The Eternal City was under US military control at this point, under General Mark Clark. About half a million US military were swarming the city. The atmosphere was tense because the Germans were still holding on at Florence, less than 100 miles to the north. Conditions were so drastic in Rome that even the rich were hungry. After every meal in our barracks, hundreds of people lined up with buckets to take home leftovers from the mess hall. Among them would be priests and sisters in a variety of religious habits.

After a few days, I moved from the barracks to the Maryknoll residence. A young priest living there was secretary to Cardinal Pietro Fumasoni Biondi, head of the Propagation of the Faith. On hearing that I had just arrived from China, the cardinal invited me to afternoon tea in his office at the Vatican. A very pleasant man, he seemed never to have heard of the Scarboro Foreign Mission Society. This seemed odd to me, since his office was the ultimate headquarters for all missionaries. When he went to a filing cabinet and brought out a file on us, the only thing in it was a slim copy of Scarboro's magazine from 1921. So much for our significance in the eyes of the Vatican!

A few days later, the cardinal's secretary told me that the Pope wanted to see me. Presumably the cardinal had passed on some of my comments about China and the Pope wanted a first-hand report on Church politics there. The assumption was that I, being a Canadian, might be able to give an objective account of what was going on. As Pius XII was in bed with a cold, however, I had to hang around for a couple of weeks for the appointment. Waiting for my encounter face-to-face with my supreme boss on earth, the Vicar of Christ Himself, didn't make me particularly nervous. At this point in my involvement in the Church, I was taking a pretty down-to-earth view of the high and mighty.

Finally, the summons came: I was to present myself on March 2nd at the Vatican at 12.45 p.m. There also arrived an official printed invitation, giving me detailed instructions and specifying that no one was to be admitted to the private audience other than myself. I decided to take with me a wooden box full of cheap religious souvenirs from Bethlehem for the Pope to bless.

On the way to his inner sanctum, we passed through lots of grand halls, and up a winding staircase. Just outside the Pope's apartment, several officious prelates pounced on my box of souvenirs.

"What do you have here?" they demanded.

"Just some things for the Pope to bless."

They tried the lid but it was nailed down. They rattled the box and grilled me further. I made some flippant remark that brought the word "bomb" to their minds.

That did it. The Holy Father had to cool his heels while the Vatican was scoured high and low to produce a hammer. The lid was pulled off my box, revealing the gaudy trinkets inside. I was allowed to proceed.

This was the Holy Father's first day out of bed after a couple of weeks. Thin and ascetic-looking at the best of times, now he looked deathly pale. Of course the obligatory white cassock did nothing to improve his complexion. There was no one else present. We were meeting in a large office adjoining the Pope's simple bedroom which could be seen through an open door. The office was furnished in a massive Victorian style but not any more lavishly than many a bishop's office I've seen. An incongruously modern note was the white telephone on the desk beside the Pope.

In excellent English, he asked for my view of Church politics in China. It was a quiet, under-stated conversation. I had no axe to grind. I presumed the Pope had already heard one point of view from Father Mark Tennien who had been in Rome earlier. At the end of our ten-minute chat, I got up and the Pope blessed my trinkets. As if I didn't have enough of them, he blessed a mother-of-pearl rosary as his personal gift to me. I lost it somewhere years later.

In April, word came that I was booked on a Liberty ship sailing from Naples for New York. During a few days' waiting in Naples, a military chaplain asked me, "Would you like to see a miracle?"

"Ok," I said, "if it doesn't cost too much."

We piled into his jeep and drove a few miles to a convent. Some 100 nuns lived in a large building half-demolished by bombs. When we had coughed up a few lire, a tottering old sister took us to a little chapel where, using three keys in succession, she opened a tiny cupboard in the wall. From it, she took a vial full of dark brown material. The priest explained to me that this was believed to be the dried-up blood of an early Christian martyr. Supposedly, if one recited the Credo with faith, the blood would liquify and turn bright red.

Fortunately, I didn't have to put my faith to that test. Along came an old woman and a child who knelt beside us and rattled off the Credo. Sure enough the substance in the vial turned red. What happened? Search me. Maybe the heat of the sister's hand melted the stuff in the vial.

According to my priest companion, donations associated with this miracle provided most of the nuns' income. I made some remark to him about their living lives of pointless piety when there was much work for the Church to do in places like China. The nun pestered my companion to know what I had said. When he translated my comment for her, the dear old soul looked at me and made that classic Italian gesture — the hand thrusting out from the chin — which could be euphemistically translated today as: "Buzz-off!"

The Liberty ship was jammed with more than 6,000 soldiers who had fought through the Italian campaign. Bunk beds were stacked four high. There were only two meals a day but they were excellent. The sick bay was filled with injured men; a few of them died while we were enroute. What was even sadder was the sight of some men locked in padded cells, their minds completely gone.

Two ships escorted us through the Mediterranean. After Gibraltar, planes covered us for two days. Because of the fear among the men, there was more work for me on board than since I'd left Canada for the missions; the soldiers kept me busy every day hearing their confessions, hundreds of them. It turned out that they were more afraid on the ship than they'd ever been in the thick of battle. The second day on the ocean, a young Catholic officer confided to me that the captain had learned that we had come very close to being hit by a German sub at four o'clock that morning. For the next twelve days, our ship zig-zagged, bringing us to Boston, rather than New York, our intended destination.

Friends met me at Boston and then I went to New York to give my report to Bishop O'Hara (who later became Cardinal Archbishop of Philadelphia). There was an odd circumstance about the ship voyage that I had to explain to him. In Naples, I had not been able to get a mass kit, not knowing my way around church circles in that city. To say mass on the ship, then, I had to use the wine and altar breads supplied by the ship's regular chaplain who was a Lutheran. When I reported this to Bishop O'Hara, he said I'd done the right thing in using the Lutheran's supplies. "But keep quiet about it," he warned me. The days of ecumenical rapprochement were still far off.

At the conclusion of my meeting with O'Hara, my military days were over. Next on my agenda was to buy a black suit and a roman collar. Then I went to Maryknoll at Ossining, New York, for a week of rest. There I received the finest hospitality of my life from Bishop Raymond Lane, superior of the Maryknoll fathers. I gave two talks to the Maryknoll students on co-ops and the Antigonish Movement. Much of my time that week passed in chatting with Michael Williams, a native of Halifax who, like many Maritimers, had migrated to Boston. He had founded *Commonweal* magazine, a major voice of the lay Catholic in the US to this day. Even then, his opinions about the role of the laity in the Church anticipated developments that are still unfolding.

I arrived back in Toronto at Union Station on Easter Sunday morning. What to expect back in my homeland? What would the reception be like from our society? No matter how much I pondered the questions, I could never have imagined what was lying in wait for me. In China, I had slept in some pretty lousy beds but the one given me at Scarboro was worse than any of them. The sheets were stiff with semen stains; even the towels were filthy. Was it a deliberate insult? The superior was in hospital at the time. Perhaps it was simply an oversight. But, given the various reactions to me in the community ever since, I can't help thinking that there may have been some intent to make me feel unwelcome.

Already, there was some open antagonism towards me. An older priest who had returned from China two years earlier told me that one of the authorities in the society believed I had been stealing money in my capacity as procurator. That was the only explanation they could find for my desperate cables asking for more money. The rampant inflation we were dealing with was unimaginable to them. The truth was that far from cheating the society I had saved it thousands of dollars by playing the black market and undertaking those risky flights over the Hump.

Now that all of us China missionaries were back home, there was the question of our futures. Some of my colleagues had been worn away to skin and bone; many would take years to get rid of parasites they'd picked up. But would they ever recover their zeal for the missions? Some had said they would leave the society when they got home. They were fed up with what they saw as the head office's mismanagement of its men in the field, not to mention the consistently bad choice of superiors for China. The missionaries were exasperated by unreasonable demands from men who had little understanding of what our lives in China were like. A few of the more disgruntled did leave the priesthood; a few others returned to work as priests in their home dioceses.

For me, the problem was not so much the conflict between the bosses at home and the workers in the field. I was questioning our whole approach to the missions. It was becoming clear to me that it was bordering on scandalous to dispense the sacraments and a bit of medicine to people without doing anything about the extortion that kept them living at a subhuman level of poverty.

What is the point of trying to win souls for eternal life if you don't give a damn about their misery in this life? It looked to me as though our mission in China, should we ever return to it, was doomed to repeat this pattern of emphasizing the spiritual and ignoring the physical wellbeing.

After just twenty-four hours in Toronto, I left for Cape Breton. On the thirty-six-hour train trip, the scenery of my homeland passed almost unnoticed. I was preoccupied with troubling questions: had I made a mistake in becoming a priest? Certainly my feelings for justice were stronger than ever after seeing the poverty in China and the virulent corruption of every shape and form that caused it. Why, I mused, am I so often under attack? Why is the Hound of Heaven still dogging me?

Then I remembered something that happened at one of the stops on our escape from Lishui. In Kanchow, while staying with the US Vincentian fathers, I was asked to say mass at the convent across the street. The sisters were American Sisters of Charity, the ones the Chinese called *fiji momo* (airplane sisters) because of their big white headdresses. The sisters knew nothing about me except that I was a priest and a Canadian. And yet, when I walked into the dimly lit sacristy, the mother superior clasped my hand and blurted out, "Father, I sense that you are going to go through a lot of suffering for the rest of your life."

That practically knocked me over. Why would she say such a thing on our first meeting? Perhaps she had acquired some special insight through having more experience of life than most sisters; I later learned that, before entering the convent at middle age, she had been an architect. At any rate, when I was eating breakfast after mass, she came in, sat down, and started to sob. "Father, I have no idea why I said that awful thing to you," she said. "I'm very sorry." Whether that was meant as a retraction or not, I don't know, but her prophecy was turning out to be too close to the mark for my comfort.

As the train rolled closer to Nova Scotia, I began to wonder what to expect at home, the home I had run away from. Could the reception be as bad as the one I had just received at Scarboro? I had been cut off from mail from the family for a long time. Dreading to hear the worst and wanting to cling to some hope, I had avoided phoning home on arrival back in North America.

Just before nine in the morning, I came in the kitchen door of my parents' house. My two youngest sisters, Genevieve and Theresa, were getting ready for school. Young teenagers now, they had been just five and six years old respectively when they last saw me.

Confronted by their blank faces, I said, "You don't know who I am, do you?"

One of them looked from me to my ordination picture on the wall and then announced, "It must be Father Harvey."

In a minute, Mother appeared. She had been in bed, having just returned home from a spell in hospital. We had breakfast and talked through most of the day. Things at home, it turned out, were much worse than I'd feared. Naturally, it was too much to hope that Dad would have stayed on the water wagon. He fell off a year after my arrival in China.

So it followed that the business was in disastrous shape. Some years earlier, when I was working with my dad, we had joined a kind of wholesale co-operative. Now the manager was threatening to close the store because the business was on the rocks and many thousands of dollars were owing. He had called Mother several times to find out when I was coming home. A Protestant, he expected me to chuck my roman collar and put the business back on its feet.

Within days of my return, the manager of the wholesale co-op was on my neck, explaining how bad things were. If I did not take responsibility for it all, he threatened, he would have to foreclose. Here I was, the son who had run away from family problems, now immersed in them to the point that I was confronted with the most difficult situation of my life. What made the whole mess so serious was that everything, including the home, was in Dad's name. If the business went under, my mother and the three youngest kids would be out on the street. (Most of the older ones were married by now.) None of our relatives had the means to take them in. There were no social services of any kind to turn to.

The only possible solution that came to mind was a tough one. My brother Angus, five years younger than I and still in the army in England, might be capable of taking over if my dad could be persuaded to sign the business over to him. The war in Europe was just ending, however, and it would take a year or so to get all the soldiers home. Desperate for a quick resolution of our family problem, I turned to a judge of the Supreme Court of Nova Scotia who was something of a big wig in the province and who promised to pull a few strings to bring Angus home earlier. Still, there was a wait of at least three or four months with the wholesaler breathing down our necks.

My brother, on entering the scene, wasn't keen on assuming the responsibility of the family business. He had married before the war. What his preferred way of providing for his own family would have been I really don't know. He didn't say. But he finally agreed to my plan. Then came the most difficult part of the operation — getting Dad to sign over the business. Fortunately, he remained sober for those days of negotiation. I pulled no punches but told him straight: he had no other choice than to turn over the business to Angus, otherwise business, home and all would be lost.

Finally he signed the papers. What a relief when it was done. But there was a price to pay in terms of family harmony. I was already somewhat estranged from the family by my roman collar and my many years away from home. This incident made the gap even wider. The younger ones, the ones who benefited most from my action, were the ones who blamed me most. Such is life.

My dad never showed any resentment towards me, though. After all, he was human and it must have hurt him. I had to admire his humility. He went on working under his son for some years. My brother restored the dying business, paid back the many bills owing and supported my mother and the young members of the family as well as his own wife and children for a good ten years while the business lasted.

In August the war in the Orient ended. Most of the world was at peace again but not China. A new war was beginning: the war between Chiang, the so-called "Strong Man of China" and Mao, the Communist. There was no question in the minds of Westerners but that Chiang would easily win. After all, he had the backing of the most powerful fighting machine and the richest nation in the world. Mao did not have the backing of anybody.

While the war raged on between Mao and Chiang, the world waited. So did Scarboro. All our priests from China were dispatched to their home dioceses to find work, just as we had done while waiting to go to China. Again, the pastor of my home parish in Dominion lost no time in getting me assigned as his helper, so I was stuck once again in the one spot on earth where I did not want to be. Living in the rectory with the pastor's niece and her rambunctious kids was even more difficult the second time around. (The pastor's salvation was his deafness.) Naturally, I was more cynical and less patient than when just ordained.

So, for a year and a half, I threw myself into work, repeating pretty much what I had done seven years earlier: making a visitation of every family in the parish, trying to get people to attend church. As the need for housing was even greater than before, I started another co-op housing group.

Finally it was clear that Mao was the victor in China. To my mind, there were two reasons: one, the destruction of so much of China by the Japanese; and two, the corruption of the Kuonmitang, Chiang's government. It might be added that the discipline of Mao's soldiers had a lot to do with it. They never looted or stole; in fact, they often helped the peasants. Chiang's soldiers, on the other hand, robbed and even killed the peasants. Perhaps it was not simple viciousness that motivated them; the fact that they were getting little pay or food may have helped to brutalize them. Another secret to Mao's success was his promise to the farmers that he would give them land. He kept that promise.

Mao's victory ensured that none of us would be returning for a long time to China, our original mission and the primary focus of our organization. Our society was beginning to branch out to missions in other countries but it occurred to me that I might do more for people by staying in my home diocese of Antigonish and carrying on the work of my mentors Coady and Tompkins. So I went to Bishop James Morrison of Antigonish to tell him of my decision to leave Scarboro and join his diocese. I expected no objections from him because the bishop had been a friend of mine ever since college days when the Rector introduced me to him as the boxer who was going to bring great glory to St. F.X.

Now the bishop grilled me at surprising length about my motives. It wasn't a loss of interest in the missions that was the problem, I explained, but the fact that my views on a missionary's role were so different from those of my colleagues. The bishop said he wanted to think and pray about the situation for a while.

When I went back to see him a few weeks later, he told me his decision. "Stay in the Scarboro Society and return to the missions."

That came as a shock. But another unexpected discovery made up my mind once and for all. Documents arrived from Scarboro conveying Rome's permission for me to leave the society. Included was a copy of the letter from Cardinal Pietro Fumasoni Biondi. The key point in his letter was that I was released from the society because I had lost interest in the missions.

That was not true. In fact, while having tea with Fumasoni Biondi in Rome, I'd explained how my ideas about missionary work were evolving, and now the Cardinal was receiving the false report that I had lost interest in the missions. Refusing to have my departure from the society based on a lie, I wrote to MacRae in Toronto, telling him to cancel my application for permission to leave.

If possible, I decided, I would keep my promise to God to work on the missions. The family situation was resolved so there was no need for me to hang around the Steeles. Then a new challenge came. Father Joe MacDonald, my cousin who had persuaded me to try the seminary, again played a decisive role. During the war years, Joe had become interested in co-ops. In 1944, at the request of the government of Puerto Rico, he had made a survey of the island's Co-op Movement to see what could be done about its shaky state. From there he went to visit some Scarboro priests working in the Dominican Republic. The country's Archbishop, Ricardo Pittini, who was famous for his efforts to help the poor, badgered Joe about getting Scarboro priests to come and help.

On hearing of my intentions, Joe rushed over to dissuade me. "Don't leave Scarboro," he said, "Go to Santo Domingo. It's the challenge of your life."

Soon after, along came a letter from Father Alphonsus Chafe, the Scarboro superior in the Dominican Republic. "There are three million people waiting for you Harvey," he said. "And you will have all the scope to do whatever you want because the Archbishop will back you."

It did not take long to make up my mind.

Chapter Eight

A New Life in the Dominican Republic

In late December, 1946, I was on a slow Norwegian freighter floating down the Gulf Stream to that tiny island where, nearly 500 years earlier, Europeans had founded their first settlement in the New World. Christopher Columbus had said it was the most beautiful land he had ever seen. I couldn't help agreeing with him as our little ship came within sight of the island one morning at sunrise. Floating on the sparkling waters of the Caribbean, it looked like a very large golf course dressed in beautiful green.

Just a few days short of Christmas, our little steamer docked at Ciudad Trujillo, the capital of the Dominican Republic. I was about to begin a life that was almost totally new: a new culture, a new language and a different kind of people. All the faces around me were friendly and smiling, much like the Chinese. But these people were all speaking Spanish, a language I'd never heard. It sounded vaguely like Latin.

The first month or so in the country, I was sent around to meet our men and see their parishes. One of the priests told me that many of the others did not welcome us "Old China Hands" as we were known. When I asked why, the reply was something of a shock: because we were a bunch of trouble-makers, always fighting among ourselves in China.

"Where did you get this idea?" I asked.

"This is what we were told by our teachers in the seminary," he said.

I checked with a couple of other men; they held the same opinion.

It did not seem fair, to my mind. Granted, the early years of our mission in China were, as explained earlier, turbulent. However, by the time our group had reached Lishui, things had settled down somewhat. We had our share of problems but it certainly wasn't just to brand us all as a bunch of trouble-makers. The accusation did not exactly boost my morale in this new assignment.

Just as we had received no preparation in the history, culture or language of the Chinese, I knew nothing about the Dominicans or any other people in South America. Years before, it had often struck me as strange that our Canadian newspapers rarely carried any news about the people living in that continent south of the Rio Grande. Now I was able to find a few books on the history of this little country. And what a sad story it was!

When Columbus landed, there were some 400,000 Tiano Indians on the island that came to be known as Hispaniola. They were a friendly people unlike the war-like Caribes who roamed that part of the world. Less than twenty years later, there were only some 20,000 Tianos alive. Forced labour by the conquistadors and their diseases, such as tuberculosis and others unknown to the natives, quickly spread death. To replace the native Indians, the Spanish brought in blacks from West Africa who were sold on the open market as slaves.

In 1805 the eastern two-thirds of the island came under the control of Toussaint L'Ouverture, an ex-slave who had earlier seized control of Haiti, the western third of the island, from the French. Haiti's control of the eastern two-thirds ended in 1844 when that part of the island was declared the Dominican Republic. In the ensuing chaos, attempts were made at various times by the Spaniards and the Americans to impose order. In 1930, Rafael Trujillo, a young Dominican trained by the Americans in the use of violence and treachery, named himself dictator. His reign of extreme violence and terror was to last for thrity-one years. It was a reign of "peace" under bullets. When he was finally murdered, he had tortured and murdered an estimated 200,000 people.

The population of the country when I arrived was about two million people. Some ten percent of them lived in the capital city. Well over ninety percent of Dominicans were baptized Catholics. Without priests or catechists to teach them, though, they were but nominal Catholics, as is the case in most of Latin America. There were less than a dozen native priests and few of them were living celibate lives. The archbishop for the whole country was Ricardo Pittini, an Italian Salesian who had arrived in 1935 and who was totally blind. One of the first things Pittini did as bishop was to get foreign priests.

The majority of the foreign clergy were Spaniards, mostly belonging to religious orders such as the Jesuits, Franciscans, and Dominicans. Around the time our men arrived, a few American Redemptorists came. Most of the Scarboro parishes had previously been manned by the Missioners of the Sacred Heart, priests from Quebec. About twenty of our men served some ten parishes in the south of the country, the poorest part.

After making a tour of them, I was sent to a small village called Boyá to fill in for a couple of months because the priest there fell sick. After his convalescence, however, he took up another assignment so I stayed in the village for a year and a half. To get there in the first place, I had to learn to ride a horse. Boyá lay in the hills about a half-hour's horseback ride on a rocky path from Monte Plata, the nearest town. The parish stretched twenty miles in all directions, with a total population of about 20,000 people. According to history, Boyá is the burial place of the great Enrequilo, the last Indian to stand up against the Spaniards.

In fact, the village is the Dominican Republic's only remaining example of an aboriginal Indian village. At the heart of the village lies an oval-shaped plaza, about 200 yards long and 100 yards wide, with fifty houses surrounding it. The houses had thatched roofs, bamboo-boarded walls and clay floors. In a typical house, a woman lived with her many kids from various fathers. Only four or five couples were actually married; they were the villagers with Spanish blood. Even so, there was much love in families, even when all dozen kids had different fathers. Abandoned kids were always taken in by somebody. There was no need for orphanages nor, for that matter, old peoples' homes.

The village had no road, no post office, no running water. An electric plant was brought in while I was there, giving lights a few hours a day. There was one merchant who ran the major store in the village; he also controlled a few small candy stores. A small school with the first three grades began a few years prior to my arrival. Most adults were illiterate.

123

Every day the people would plod three or four miles into the countryside to their small farms, called *conucos*. None of the people actually owned the land they farmed. Technically, the whole area was owned by the Church, according to a grant from one of Spain's rulers centuries before. But the Church did not get any income from the land nor did it exercise any rights of ownership. In practice, the land was there for the taking.

A man would just pick an idle piece of land, then clear it and plant corn, rice or yucca. The more prosperous had a wooden plough and oxen or could rent them. But most people just put holes in the ground with a stick. When the fertility of the soil in one area got depleted, the man moved on to another plot. People cut smaller plots to cultivate rice, beans and so on. Most of the villagers had a mule or donkey or horse, along with some hens and pigs. A few might have a duck. Fewer still would have a cow; there was practically no milk in the villagers' lives.

Family life was unstructured, to put it mildly. Boys under ten and girls a few years younger ran naked. A family didn't have regular meals in our sense. When a child was hungry, its mother would offer a piece of corn or a piece of yucca or a mango. Once a day, a meal of some kind would be cooked, but there was no sitting down together. They ate yucca, a starchy vegetable, and other similar vegetables. Most of what people consumed was grown on their own plot. The only meat was pork and it always had to be eaten all at once because there was no way of storing it.

Ironically, the villagers couldn't afford to eat the rice they grew. They had to sell it to buy clothing, medicine, salt and a few other groceries. That's where the *patron* came in. The *patron* in Latin America is the person above you with some access to wealth and power. You turn to him whenever life becomes too complicated to handle yourself. For peasants, the *patron* is usually the merchant. He gives them credit for seeds and for what they buy in his store while the crop is growing. At harvest, they bring the crop to him or he goes to collect it, paying whatever price he likes. Meanwhile, if a family member is seriously ill, the *patron*'s horse takes the patient to hospital. The peasant knows he is being bled, he knows he could get twice the price if he sold the rice himself. "But what can I do?" the peasant will say with a shrug. "The *patron* is my protector. Three years ago he saved my mother's life. Without him we would be lost."

My circumstances in Boyá where much like everybody else's. My house was a little shack with clapboard walls (gaps between the boards letting daylight through) and a palm-thatch floor, no plumbing, glass windows nor electricity. The ancient church was unfit for use as a result of a strong earthquake the previous year, so for a church I had to use a shack with a mud floor and thatched-roof. It could seat forty people. That was plenty of room as few bothered to attend. Two dedicated women looked after my needs for a daily wage of one peso (about $1 US at that time). They washed my clothes, bought and cooked my food. My average Sunday collection was less than 50 centavos (cents). There were always a few baptisms, each bringing me a peso and a half. Marriages were few. To meet my expenses of a peso a day and care for my horse named Indio, our society had to give me some help.

My first task was, of course, to learn Spanish. As in China, I had to adopt a name the people could pronounce. Harvey was out of the question because the letter 'h' is usually dropped in Spanish and 'j' is pronounced as an 'h'. So I became "Padre Pablo" for the next part of my life.

My Spanish teacher was a twelve-year-old boy who was taking grade five in the nearest town. Every day, he'd meet with me after school. Other kids started accompanying him to my shack. At first they were scared of me, never having had any dealings with an outsider. But after about six months, the barriers started to come down and pretty soon all the kids were taking part in my lesson. For backup, there were a dictionary and a grammar. For the best part of each day, I'd sit in a big wicker chair in my shack, with the door open to the breeze, doing my best to master the language. The Spanish I acquired was less than purely classical. It was the language of illiterate Dominicans.

My real task, though, was to get to know the Dominicans themselves. In general Latins are warm, friendly people and excellent diplomats. Their violent history not withstanding, it would be hard to find a more loving people than the Dominicans. They shook hands with you no matter how many times you met in the same day. They always aimed to please — no matter what the cost or how many lies might be needed. This Dominican trait was one of the hardest for plain-speaking Canadians to become accustomed to. Another habit that took some patience — Latin

Americans often take a long road around before coming to the point when they're trying to share something. Perhaps this comes from an inherent quality of their language: it takes many words to say something in Spanish. For instance, a 100-page book in English would come to at least 120 pages if translated into Spanish.

Tropical people around the world are, as is often noted, "children of nature". Their lush climate tends to make them feel relaxed and happy-go-lucky. They enjoy life and are often not fond of hard work. All of this is charming enough to the Northerner among them but another trait is not so easy to accept: their coming late for everything, or not coming at all. They're never in a rush, The word *mañana* which means "tomorrow" explains it all. Another very revealing word usage: in English the clock "runs" while in Spanish it "walks".

One thing about the Dominicans puzzled me. I found that the ones with the blackest skin tended to be the most loving. Yet, it seemed that they wished they could be whiter. Among the mixed blood, for example, the black man with money always wanted a wife whiter than himself. Even children seemed conscious of the distinctions. I recall meeting two little girls all dressed up on a Sunday. When I asked the three-year-old why her face was dusted with white powder, she said, "Because I want to be white."

Surprisingly, some relatively sophisticated adults betrayed similar feelings. A man who was to become a community leader asked me one day if I had seen the famous Harlem Globe Trotters, the black basketball players who were in the country with a team of white college students. After rolling up a margin of points, the Globe Trotters always started performing tricks to make the white kids look ridiculous. My friend was deeply offended; he didn't think it appropriate that black men should mock white men. Astounded, I could only come to the conclusion that racism exists wherever there are people of different colours. It brought to mind the French diplomat's telling me that the people of Indochina had not believed "yellow men" like themselves could build the impressive Japanese navy.

The supposed spokespersons for Christianity were not above blatant racism. One woman who lived in the capital but was visiting her folks in the village told me that when she was a child, a Spanish priest would come to visit every few years. The gist of his sermon always was, "I have pure Spanish blood in my veins; your blood is not pure." What an awful thing to say, I thought, to these poor people.

In the Latin religion, there is tremendous emphasis on externals. Roadside crosses, shrines and saints' pictures were common and no one would pass one of them, or a church, without tipping the hat or making the sign of the cross. For most men, that was about the extent of their religious observance. Religious pictures were everywhere. The Blessed Virgin and the saints took first place, not Christ. And, in remote rural areas, some people believed that the saints actually lived in the statues and pictures. I once saw a twelve-inch wooden carving of a dove in which the people thought the Holy Spirit resided.

This elaborate respect shown to holy things everywhere was largely based on superstition. It usually fills the void where there is only a slight knowledge of religion. Given the lack of priests to teach the Dominican people, it was only natural that superstitious elements of African and indigenous Indian cultures blended into their Catholicism. But such superstition in their background was not to be despised, I believed. The famous Englishman, Cardinal John Henry Newman said, "A people who are not superstitious without the Gospel will not be religious with the Gospel." I was not of the same mind as some of our men in China who would refuse to teach the Gospel in certain villages because the people were "too deeply involved in superstition."

One of my first encounters with Dominican superstition was in Boyá when a woman brought in a ten-year-old boy with long hair. Handing me a pair of scissors, she said, "I want you to cut my son's hair, Padre."

My obvious question was: "Why are you asking me to do it?"

She replied: "I have lost two sons to the devil already. I did not want to lose this one, so to fool the devil, I let his hair grow so that the devil would think it was a girl."

As he was about ten-years-old, he had escaped the death in infancy of her other boys, so she figured it was safe now to declare his true sex. And, being the spiritual man with the direct tie to God, I was the one to do the job. So I did it.

In the Latin culture, priests are showered with respect no matter how hard they try to avoid it. One mark of respect from women was to give the priest a little dip, like a curtsey to royalty. The priest's hand was kissed constantly. That became rather awkward when you were trying to put food in your mouth. Such incidents were not only embarrassing but annoying.

Without religious instruction the people had but a vague idea of sin; therefore great patience was needed to hear confessions. In fact, when I got to understand enough Spanish, I realized that the "penitents" were mostly telling their virtues rather than their sins. Confession, they thought, was a chance to brag about how good they'd been. If I was to give them absolution, they needed a lot of help to admit even the smallest sin.

One time when I had been in the country a bit longer, a call came telling me a very old man was dying. He had been totally blind for years and bed-ridden. Some people said he was the last person with any Indian blood. His family thought he was well over 100 years old. It was a horseback ride of a few hours to get to him. I arrived sweaty and tired but thankful that there was still time to hear his confession. When I broached the subject, he was indignant. Why should he go to confession? He'd never committed any sins, he said. All he wanted was to touch a priest before he died!

Not that there wasn't any real sin among Dominicans. Under all their friendliness, there was an ruthlessly vicious streak in many people. It was as though life was cheap. There was a saying that no *fiesta* is a success unless a few people die. Even outside a *fiesta*, a callousness to life could be demonstrated. One Sunday morning, I saw two men in a knife fight. One survived, the other died. When I spoke to the survivor about sorrow for his sin, he paid no attention to me. All he wanted was revenge.

After about four months in Boyá, two men came to ask me to say mass in their village. It was a four-hour horseback ride up and down hills, crossing the same small river twenty times. Luckily I had with me a former religious brother from Quebec who was married to a local woman. On leaving the professed religious life, Sylvio stayed near the parish doing odd jobs and on this occasion he acted as my guide into the depths of the countryside. For the night we stopped at the home of a man he knew. After supper (rice and beans), I asked where I was to sleep. The man of the house smiled and all of a sudden his three teenaged daughters appeared, parading before us like a fashion show. Then he said, "Take your pick." I wasn't sure I understood but Sylvio made it clear by a sly wink. What a shock! I had thought I was in a Catholic country. Besides, after China, I considered myself shock-proof when it came to sex.

I told Sylvio to ask our host to set up a hammock just for me. The host did so but, on leaving me for the night, he remarked, "You should know, Padre, no man can live alone."

I was learning Latin culture.

The next day I sat for a few hours hearing confessions under a large mango tree. The penitents were mostly old women. Being too poor to afford a mantilla, they often wore a towel over their heads. During confession they would put part of it over the priest's head for privacy. After an hour or so, yet another towel flopped down over my head but this time I felt hot breath on my cheek and a hand rubbing my thigh.

I jumped up and the young girl fled. "You goddamned bitch!" I yelled at her as she ran across the field like a gazelle. She was one of the daughters who had been disappointed by my lack of interest the night before.

Was there any justification for my swearing at her? I had had a bad night, sleepless almost, warding off mosquitoes. My fuse was short. It was the first time those mosquitoes had a chance to drink a different kind of blood. Like humans they like a change of diet and there were more proteins in my blood I guess. In my anger, I had reverted to my native language. This was an escape valve, as it had been for me and other priests in China, when our patience was stretched to the limit in trying to cope with a culture so different from ours. Many times in life, I've had to resort to that tactic.

But I should not have called her a bitch; she wasn't. She was disappointed but still seeking love and probably hoping to catch a foreigner as a husband. For a Dominican woman to bag a white foreigner was a maximum prize for two reasons: he was rich, as she saw it, and he would probably be more faithful than a native man. Apparently, the girl's father too had sized me up as good husband material.

In the eyes of the Dominicans, North American priests put excessive emphasis on sexual sins. Maybe we did and maybe we still do. We take the sexual rulings of the Church seriously; the Latins never have. Unlike us, they don't take laws of any kind seriously. Our concept of Catholicism is therefore very different from that of the Latins. When a new law is promulgated, the non-Latin may not like the law but will say to himself, how can I adjust myself to the law? The Latin looks at it and says to himself, how can I get around this law?

So sexuality among Latins is a matter of doing what comes naturally — even for priests. Several times I met men who boasted to me that their dads were priests. One story a bit hard to credit was of a Spanish priest who was deeply in love with a woman. When, because of this liaison, the priest was transferred by the bishop to another parish, no priest replaced him. That meant she couldn't receive Holy Communion on the First Fridays as was her custom. Out of love for her, her priest friend want to indulge her love of Jesus, so he sent her the consecrated host in the mail every First Friday.

Another story is told of two priests, one Spanish, the other American, discussing their respective values or vices. "A sick call comes," says the Spaniard, "and you cannot get up and go to the dying person because you're drunk. But I can leave my woman in bed a few hours and go to give the sacraments to the dying person."

Without being overly puritanical about it, however, I believe one of the chief causes of the poverty in Latin America is the rampant promiscuity, or, it might be called polygamy, defined as a man having many wives. Call it what you may, the great majority of children did not have parents married either by the state or by the church. In some areas most of the people are, or at least were, illegitimate. The point is that all these children are being produced and men are not taking the responsibility of supporting them.

This is the macho ethic at work. I recall reading a story a few years ago in the newspaper from Puerto Plata, on the north coast of the country. There was a picture of a man reputed to be almost 100 years old. When asked how many children he had, he said, "I lost count when the number passed 100." Next question: how many women did you have? His reply: "God knows." The article portrayed him as a local hero.

Bit by bit, I was getting to know the people and, after about five months, my Spanish vocabulary had grown to a few hundred words. So it was time to try setting up some co-ops, my original purpose in coming to the country. When I started talking about co-ops, the people had never heard of them. But I asked a small group of men to begin their savings, five cents each per week. (They did not want women to be members.) I held the money for them. The idea spread to the hills and, after months, there were nearly 100 names on the list. The savings grew to a couple of hundred pesos.

At that point, most of the men were anxious to know when the loans would start. I kept postponing them to build up more capital. Then people started to withdraw their money. After a few more months, I had to start the loans. No loan was above ten pesos, usually backed by the borrower's savings; a few got backing from a friend. In many cases, those who received the loans never returned to the meetings and those who acted as guarantors lost their money. From nearly 100 men the group was reduced to thirty. Then a few women were allowed to join. But the spirit of the group never revived. It seemed a hopeless job and I thought of giving up and returning to Canada. First, though, I wanted to try a group in the nearby town of Monte Plata where two of our priests lived.

The Monte Plata group started with a bang. Over 100 people attended the first meeting, including town officials. Then attendance dropped to 50 the second meeting, then down to 20. An official of the town began drumming up propaganda and beating the bushes to turn up new members. The most avid co-op member I'd ever seen, he was making loans and paying them back on time. After several months, I got wise to why he liked the credit union. He was the number-one loan shark in town and he was using his loans to lend money to people out in the hills at fifty percent interest per month.

Another loyal member of the group was a woman who looked after cleaning the church. A practising Catholic, she made frequent loans and repaid them. Almost a year passed before I learned what she was doing with the money. She was building an annex to her business, the town's favourite house for "women of the night." I had a good laugh when I thought of it: here I am helping the number-one loan shark in town and the most popular brothel.

Weeks and months passed, broken only by a visit to Monte Plata or by horseback rides to outlying areas. An average trip to the countryside would involve a few days' visiting one or two villages. Longer trips might mean a week or more of constant travelling to the more remote areas of the parish. Sleeping conditions were often unpleasant; the only offering might be a cot or hammock in a school, chapel or small home. Inevitably, the place would be crawling with bugs, rats, lizards and mosquitoes. Usually, the priest experienced the lack of privacy that was inevitable among the poor. It was usually out of the question for a priest to take a bath or even a sponge rub during *campo* trips because of the lack of water or privacy.

A priest's visit to a rural village was a *fiesta*, a time for the village to put on its best face. Days before his arrival the people would be busy cleaning up their church and their homes; even the graveyard was decorated with flowers. The best clothing was washed and ironed. The celebration began on the priest's arrival. Not that it was all religious. Along with the long-standing sins the priest might absolve, many new ones were committed along with the dancing, drinking and fighting that were often part of the *fiesta*.

Among the rural Dominicans, nothing was too good for the priest when he arrived at a village. The faith of the rural people seemed more real than that of the townspeople. The rural people were simple and sincere in showing their appreciation for the priest's visit. Sometimes food might be scarce, but no matter how poor the villagers, they would always provide the very best they could for the priest. People had little money to offer him but he often received gifts of live chickens. Sometimes an old woman would give me a chicken while I was trying to eat and the struggling creature would drop more than feathers into my bowl of rice!

Once, when leaving one of these villages I promised to come back in a couple of months. A pious old woman protested: "Padre, don't come back often. Once a year is enough because it is too much work for us getting things cleaned up, washing clothing and all that."

Routine visits served the purpose of hearing confessions, often for long weary hours. Baptizing children, not just babies, but children up to four years of age, was also demanding work. When one child decided to cry all the others would join the chorus. Some of our priests baptized up to 200 children by themselves in a single ten-hour session, stopping every hour or so to take a drink of the strong local coffee or have a cigarette. The deafening cries of dozens of children, the intense heat under a tin roof and the constant sweating, could, after several hours, wear down even a young man.

The struggle that some of the tiny godmothers had with a squirming, screeching four-year-old was something to behold. By the time the priest poured the water and asked the child's name, the godmother had usually lost the scrap of paper with the name on it. The ceremony had to be delayed while a family member came to the rescue to announce the child's name. If time and patience were running out, the only logical thing to do was pick a couple of potential names and then pull down the diapers to find out whether the child was male or female. One of the Scarboro priests did this just as the baby let loose his fountain, hitting the priest directly in the face.

Marriages can also make heavy demands on endurance. Are the bride and groom related? It's hard to tell because families are so mixed up and there is so much inter-breeding in remote areas. A few cases have been documented where a full brother and sister have married, thinking they were just cousins. I was baffled by my first marriage in the Dominican Republic. When the ceremony was finished, the young couple stared at me. Then they said something I didn't understand. Luckily, a guest who spoke some English told me about an old Spanish custom: the priest had to remove the corona from the bride's head; otherwise the groom was not allowed to take her to bed.

Apart from the minimal collection at mass, the priest's income was from baptisms and "Responses". These were prayers for the dead. People couldn't get enough of them — especially the *Libera* from the burial service. It was thought to have special efficacy. You got 25 cents for saying it, 50 cents for singing it. On All Souls' Day you could hardly keep up with the demand. You'd go to the cemetery, sprinkling holy water on grave after grave, singing the *Libera* until you were hoarse.

On one All Souls' Day, I had been slogging through the night, with candles burning in the cemetery. At two in the morning, people were still waiting. Jokingly, I said to an old lady who wanted to drag me to yet another grave. "I'm old and tired and have a wooden leg. Do you think the blessing will carry if I say it from here?" A little girl put her hand under my cassock and announced indignantly, "They are not wooden." We all laughed, and I had to plod on to the grave to do the right thing.

For Christmas, I wanted to provide the kids of Boyá with some kind of treat and the idea came to mind to make some ice cream. That would be quite novel for them as they'd never experienced anything cold. Hector, my English teacher, could make the horseback ride to Monte Plata in about twenty minutes, so I sent him off to get 100 pounds of ice.

By the time he got back, there were fifty pounds left, enough for my purposes. We used cans of condensed milk, lots of sugar and vanilla flavouring to make the ice cream in an old butter churn. Soon, the naked children began gathering around, using spoons or whatever they could find to scoop up this strange, sweet coldnes that dribbled down their jet black bodies in white rivulets.

One girl was balancing her baby brother on her arm. When a blob of ice cream hit his exposed genitals, he screamed, *"Me Queme! Me Queme!"* (I'm burning).

All the while, I was learning more language. But I was learning something much more important, something that could not be learned in a classroom or with a qualified teacher. I was learning about life among the rural poor. In this respect, my eighteen months' stay in Boyá was the best possible preparation for my later work. I was learning how the rural poor think, what their values are, their hopes, and so on. That's an opportunity not many missionaries get. Most rural places see a priest only on the annual feast of the patron saint of the place. Busy giving the sacraments, the priest has almost no time to get to know the people.

In my later years in the north of the country, many *campesinos* (people who live in the country and work small plots of land) marvelled at my intimate knowledge of rural life. It came from those months in Boyá. At first, mind you, the respect of the people toward the priest prevented me from seeing their lives as they really were. After six months or so, I began to see beyond those barriers that poor people build around their lives. Ashamed of their poverty, they try to bar outsiders from seeing the sadness of their lives. It is the most profound sadness there can be because it stems from knowing that there is simply no hope of their ever escaping their poverty.

Most of the time, though, they hide this sadness with the good humour for which they're renowned. That was revealed to me most forcibly one time when I mentioned to a little girl: "Your mother must be happy because she is singing."

"No," the little girl said, "She sings because she is sad."

Chapter Nine

Beginning Co-ops Among Latinos

My initiation into rural Latin life ended when our superior called me into the capital city, Ciudad Trujillo, as it was then called, to be bursar at our central house. The job was similar to the one I had in China as business manager for our priests. Another part of my work was helping in a nearby parish. In my spare time, I wanted to try my co-op ideas in the big city to see if they worked any better here than in the countryside. I visited city parishes, labour unions, factories and government employees. Local newspapers printed some articles on this Canadian priest's novel idea! After a time, the articles attracted the attention of some high-ranking government people. One of the most interested was Manuel Peña Batlle, a former ambassador and Secretary of State, a man who ranked very high with the dictator.

The old archbishop was delighted. Every month during those years, I would spend time with him and would often do his English letters, as well as drive him to official functions. At a party at the US embassy, Dr. Peña Batlle put his hand on my shoulder and introduced me to the German ambassador. "Mr. Ambassador," he said, "this young priest will do more for our country than any person since Columbus arrived, if..." A silence fell on the crowd as Trujillo, in his glorious uniform, entered. And Dr. Manuel Peña Batlle continued, "...if somebody does not stop him." Saying this, he looked in the direction of the dictator and squeezed my hand.

To my amazement, however, Dr. Peña Batlle told me at one of our many meetings that the dictator was very interested in what I was doing and wanted to help me. I explained that to make the movement grow I needed a building where farmers and workers could take short courses. My friend offered me a lot of his own for the school but it was too far from the city to be useful.

Apparently, he kept putting pressure on Trujillo to help me. The Generalissimo, as he was called, finally asked me to send him a building plan. By now, I had been in the city long enough to make friends with several government officials and professional people. One of them was an architect who made a building plan for me to send to the government. The plan would cost about $35,000 to execute. In a short time, I received a cheque for $10,000 and a promise of the rest in future. I bought a lot in the suburbs to the north of the city and began the building.

But Trujillo broke his promise. No more money for the building came from him. So I went to a rich Spaniard who had made millions of dollars in a US car dealership.

On hearing about my plans, he said, "Look, there at the workers in my yard."

On the lot, there were some 100 black men working on cars. "What is your point?" I asked.

"They're just like animals," he said. "And you think you can make them more human? Padre, I think you're crazy."

I said, "Give them a chance to be humans. After all, you have made your millions on their sweat." Then I walked out, slamming the door.

Next, I went to a rich Dominican family of Italian background; they'd been several generations in the DR and owned three sugar plantations. For an hour I told my story. Their reaction: "This is the first time we have ever heard of a priest wanting to build real Christianity. Come back tomorrow and we will have a cheque for you."

I couldn't believe it. After all I had just met these people. But there was nothing to lose by brashness, so I asked for $10,000.

That's exactly what they gave me — no small amount of money. It would be worth about $100,000 today. Some of my peers said it was a kind of miracle. They'd never heard of rich Dominicans giving like this for a social justice cause. With a few other donations from wealthy US friends, I was able to finish the building.

Now, how was I going to run the place? I thought of the old Chinese story of the foreigner who pulled a drowning man out of the river. The next day the man appeared at the house of the foreigner and said, "You saved my life, now you must support me."

Although Trujillo hadn't come through with the full capital funding, I asked for government help to run the school. My request was for $10,000 per year. After months, the government sent me $7,000 and I was in business. The government cheque continued for the next six years, the same amount every year. I brought in twenty men, mostly farmers from our groups around the country, for three-week courses. I taught the young men six hours a day, five days a week. Lodging and food were free. I also was able to hire two field workers to visit the co-op groups that were starting. The office worker I hired turned out to be a thief. He stole a few thousand dollars before I fired him. That was to be a recurring pattern.

By the time about 100 men had taken the short courses, the word "co-op" was spreading like magic all over the country. I spent more than half my time in the north of the Dominican Republic but I visited every town and most villages in the entire country. Invitations were coming from all over; even branches of government wanted to have a co-op. Three times the government asked me to sit on commissions studying rural problems. Friends in high places in the government passed on the rumour that the dictator was thinking of naming me secretary of agriculture. Not that I knew much about agriculture but maybe I was something of an expert on how farmers' minds worked. My stay in Boyá taught me a lot about that.

What did all this have to do with religion? Not a lot, in the view of many of my colleagues. The standard argument from Scarboro priests was that I was not doing priestly work: I was not giving out sacraments, not preaching sermons and so on. But, in my mind, the co-op work was profoundly religious. It would be foolhardy to claim that I was single-handedly trying to change the face of Catholicism in Latin America, but the comment of an American friend made it clear to me that a change was needed. I had assumed my friend was Catholic, because he was always at mass with his family on Sundays.

I was wrong. "Father," he said one day, "I would never become a Catholic living in this country." He felt that in North America the Catholic Church's effect on society was balanced by the influence of Protestantism. He therefore found Catholicism there dignified and worthy of allegiance. In Latin America, the Church, having a monopoly so to speak, was corrupt and disgraceful. Priests were only concerned about money. "Up north, among the many Protestant Churches, your Church is beautiful," he said, "but here your Church is ugly."

In my way, I was trying to do something about making religion more relevant. In urban areas, religion was generally considered to be something for women and children, but not for big, brawny men. A city man, when asked if he attended church, would usually reply, "I have little time to go myself but I always make sure that my wife and children go." He would consider that quite satisfactory. As somebody said: men played and women prayed. One good man, a former ambassador to France, told me one day, "I will start going to church the day men are going. I would feel like a fool being crushed in a seat with old women." Another comment from a decent-living rich merchant was "How do you expect me to go down on my knees or go to confession with a hundred women watching me."

One day a priest was boasting that he had hundreds of teenaged girls in the "Daughters of Mary" in his parish. I asked him how many young men in his parish came to church. He had to admit there were few. (For many boys all connection to church ends at puberty when their fathers take them to a prostitute to "prove their manhood".) I said to the priest, "If we are here to build Christian families and if we cannot make men moral we are wasting our time."

My work was building Christian families. To that end, I concentrated almost exclusively on men, trying to make them moral. If they were not, neither co-ops nor religion could prosper. Among the members in dozens of our co-op groups in the north of the country, few men ever went to church. Yet, after joining the Co-op Movement, the men often hired somebody to teach them religion. As a result, at the peak of the movement in the 1950s, as many as a thousand men throughout the country got their marriages fixed up each year. Through ordinary parish work, a priest couldn't hope to get one-tenth of that result.

Several times, I had received invitations from the people in a rural village, part of a Scarboro parish, to come and speak to them. Our priests didn't want me there, though. When the priest who looked after the parish was on vacation, the government asked me to go and talk to the people. That Sunday afternoon, I was met by 150 people, all dressed in their finest. None of them had ever seen me before. Standing under a big mango tree, I talked for three hours (with coffee breaks). My talk was the usual mix of co-op philosophy and morality, citing promiscuity as a major cause of poverty in the country.

When I finished, the mayor of the village rose and launched into an oration: "I am sixty years old. Every month when the priest comes, I go to church as part of my duty. But I never pay attention to what the priest is saying. Your priests have been coming here for years but they are so busy all the time baptizing, hearing confessions and so on, they never have time to talk to us. We don't know them and they don't know us. I figure those priests come because it is their duty and because they get money. Padre, you come here when you could be enjoying the day with friends in the capital. I listened to every word you said. I have been living with one woman for years but also pay visits to others. I promise in front of all you people here that I am going to get married soon."

In Santiago, the second largest city, I was giving my monthly talk to the co-op group. A hand rose and a man asked, "What can be done for the many in this city who are too poor to be members?"

My reply was, "I don't know the answer to that."

Another hand. This time it was Eusebio, a man who always had lots to say at meetings. "I disagree that anybody is too poor to be a member. Nobody in this city is poorer than me. I earn a peso a day making furniture. I joined the group almost two years ago. Now I have eighty pesos in savings. I always keep half a peso for myself to get a bottle of rum on Saturdays and then I spend the weekends with one of my eight women. I am fifty years old, never went to church in my life. I never dreamed I could have this much money. Now I am going to build a house and settle down. My big problem is which one of the eight women should I marry? I like them all."

The laughing lasted ten minutes. But Eusebio was serious. He bought a tiny lot, built himself a house and the next year, with twenty-two couples like him, wanted to get married. I got the local bishop to do the group marriage — twenty-two couples. A few years later, I tried to find Eusebio. I was told he then had his own carpentry business and was employing half a dozen helpers and still living with his chosen wife. If these are not spiritual works then there is something lacking in my idea of religion.

The archbishop, at least, liked my approach. "Padre Pablo," he said, "I have been in Latin American over fifty years and here you are, a young man, teaching me something about religion and our people that I never thought of before. God bless you for your work with our poor."

One more story about the connection between co-ops and religion. Manoguayabo was a village of about eighty families, a half-hour drive from Santo Domingo. All the people were black, all were Catholic, and almost all the men were big six-footers, as were some of the women. It seemed to me that about half the people were Guzmans, many of them no doubt family of the future Toronto Blue Jays' star pitcher. Besides seeing the villagers once a month for mass, I met with about sixty men for two hours every Monday night to organize a credit union. They refused to admit women.

The few men who ever showed up for Sunday mass always stood at the back of the church. None ever went to confession or communion. One Monday night as we wrapped up credit union business, I asked some men standing around why they did not receive the sacraments. They looked sheepishly at each other before one spoke. "Padre, you don't understand," he said. "To go down on your knees in a church filled with women looking at you.... Well, it's just too much."

But I persisted. "Will you men go to confession if I come and say mass only for men, no women allowed?"

Slowly, very slowly, their replies came. "Yes, we will."

I added, "Will you also bring all the credit union men?"

"Yes, we will," came the reply.

The men went to work. All women were told they were not allowed at the special mass. The word got around: "Padre Pablo has gone crazy." Despite my edict, a few pious old women came to the men's mass but they had to say their rosaries kneeling on the grass outside the church.

Approximately seventy men showed up. That day, all of them made their first confession — which, in most cases, only took a moment because they had little sense of sin. Many of them, having never before availed themselves of the rare visits by a priest, received their first communion. Some of the men were nearly eighty years old.

They also broke the *machismo* barrier. Many of them continued to come to Sunday mass, to get down on their knees with scores of women looking at them. Many women came to thank me, even though they first thought Padre Pablo was crazy.

One of my most satisfying successes with co-ops was in the largest parish in the north of the country. The monsignor who ran the parish single-handedly was alleged to be the richest priest in the country. The rumour was likely true: with more than 100,000 people in his parish, sacramental fees alone would have made him wealthy. Not surprisingly, the monsignor had banned me from his parish. However, when the good monsignor went to Rome for a visit during the Holy Year (1950), I launched an invasion. The people had often asked to meet with me, so my workers set up a number of meetings. When the pastor returned two months later, I had twenty co-op groups started.

The people were worried about the monsignor's likely reaction. So I told co-op men in the different villages to go to the monsignor with ten-dollar bills asking him to say mass in their villages. Most of the villages had never had mass and $10 was a lot more than the usual stipend. The ploy worked splendidly. When the monsignor realized my work wasn't taking money from him — quite the reverse — he was all for it. At a meeting with the priests in that area, the monsignor was my right-hand man, acting as secretary and praising my work. He even told the old archbishop what a great job Padre Pablo was doing. The archbishop and I had a good laugh over that.

At the peak of the movement, in the mid 1950s, there were more than a hundred groups. Several people warned me to quit. "Trujillo will get you one way or another," they said. "You are too popular, too successful." It was not unusual to arrive in a place for the annual meeting and see a big banner: *"Que Vive Padre Pablo Y Dios!"* (Hurray for Padre Pablo and God!) It was bad enough that God came after me but not to mention Trujillo — that was a capital sin.

When we had one or two leaders in each village with enough knowledge and self-confidence to keep the credit unions going, we encouraged the people to form marketing co-ops. That enabled members to get the market price for their produce, eliminating the middlemen. Also, the consumer co-op could provide sugar, salt, seeds and other essentials at a fair price, thus by-passing the gouging tactics of the *patron*.

Naturally, at this point there was opposition. The first danger sign came when I was talking to the Chamber of Commerce in La Vega, a small town of some 25,000 people. One of the merchants in the audience said, "If this works, you are going to take over the country." I pointed out that even in countries with highly developed co-op movements, this hadn't happened.

But the establishment smelled danger, especially in the new spirit among the *campesinos*. Whenever I called for a meeting in any large town, hundreds of people would appear from surrounding villages to spend an entire day discussing their problems. That was a revolution. Up to that time the poor man had to go hand-in-hand to discuss his problems with the *patron*.

So the word passed among merchants and political cronies and soon harassment of co-op leaders began. I was tailed by spies everywhere; I knew reports were being made to the authorities. Trujillo feared nothing so much as the development of a group which he didn't totally control. However, I felt fairly secure as long as Dr. Peña Batlle was on my side. I kept him fully informed and he backed me one hundred percent. But given the autocratic, arbitrary type of government, I was constantly running the risk of a clash with the ultimate authority.

My success also brought enemies among the clergy. The first was a Spanish Jesuit who denounced me in the local press. His ostensible grounds for attacking me were that I didn't speak Spanish well enough to head up such an organization. But, clearly, the real reason for the opposition was that the Spanish Jesuits were the most powerful group of priests in the country and their superior was a close friend of the dictator. Considering themselves the elite of the priesthood, they naturally thought they should head up a movement that was becoming so important. And yet they'd never heard of co-ops until I arrived!

When the Jesuit priest failed to take over my school, he started a movement in the north of the country where our best groups flourished. Under his influence, several dozen groups broke with the national movement. In total, around 6,000 members departed from the movement. Their independent movement died within two years. A Spanish Franciscan, appointed bishop to the newly-created diocese, publicly threatened to excommunicate those Jesuits who had tried to destroy my work with the poor. Finally the bishop ordered two of the Jesuits out of his diocese.

As if battling this opposition from without was not taxing enough, there were plenty of problems within the co-ops. First, there was the *machismo*: the men, valuing women about as much as cattle, barred them from joining co-ops in most places. Then there was the snobbery of town people. They refused to join a group if the majority of members were *campesinos*. But the bigger and constant problem was theft, or as it was politically called, "mismanagement." Hardly a month passed without a recurrence of this problem and often it meant that a group folded up. And, of course, members lost their money. In most groups, members would not trust any of themselves to look after the money. Nor would they trust some parish priests. A few priests had used the co-op members' money for their own purposes and the news of such abuses spread quickly to other areas.

In Ciudad Trujillo we had two spectacular failures. First, two large labour unions pleaded with me to start a credit union. After a short time, the two highest officers of the unions ran off with all the money. Another group, this one parish-based, consisted mostly of women. After almost three years, when they had a few thousand dollars, we could not find eleven literate people to form a directorate. All the money was returned to the members and the effort ended.

Vital to co-ops is democracy — something about which Dominicans had not the slightest idea. How could they, living as they had for centuries under dictators? Often, a man elected president of a co-op would refuse ever to leave the job. If he could see he was going to be forced out, he would dedicate himself to destroying the group.

I recall a young Spanish priest telling me, "Padre, you are trying to do the impossible. Latins will never accept the democratic idea because it is Protestant and we are Catholics." Almost all the Spanish priests in the country idolized their dictator General Franco, also Trujillo. One day I saw an elderly Spanish priest going down on his knees publicly to kiss the hand of Trujillo. Even one of our Scarboro priests thought highly of the dictator. Because he had funded the building of a church in that priest's parish, the priest saw Trujillo as the great benefactor of the Church, although the priest knew Trujillo was torturing and murdering thousands of people.

In the mid-1950s, I had 7 full-time helpers (office and field workers) and just over 20,000 members in 100 or more places. I was in great need of an honest helper to handle money. My plea to Toronto for a helper went unheeded. I could easily understand why: few people in the society saw what I was doing as the work of a priest. (Shortly before my leaving the country, they did send me a helper.) I was also known as a hard worker and people probably feared I would expect the same of a helper.

On the recommendation of a priest in Antigonish, I took on a young married couple from New Hampshire as helpers. That gave me a look at marriage that wasn't very appealing. The young man was controlled totally by his fiery wife. A few months after they came, she gave birth to her first child. From there on, she sat in a rocking chair and her husband spent his time washing diapers.

Worst of all was the young couple's attitude to the people they had supposedly come to help. Among our employees some were blacker than others. My American helpers always favoured the natives who were less black. The woman wouldn't let any dark black natives touch her baby. In my two weeks' absence every month to visit co-ops, there were battles over the young couple's discrimination against the employees. As a result, several employees wanted to quit. I finally sent the helper couple north. They were ruining my work. Do-gooders without proper training can do great harm.

These were lonely, bitter years. Often months passed without my seeing a Scarboro priest. Except for my *campesino* friends and a few Quebec priests, I had nobody to let down my hair with. My enemies were many: the dictator and his cronies, the Spanish Jesuits, some Scarboro priests. Often the words of the nun in China came back to me: "You are going to suffer a lot."

145

Another thought came to mind, I think it was first articulated by a French priest: "To suffer for the Church is easy; the difficult thing is to suffer at the hands of the Church."

I often wondered how I kept going with so many problems and so few friends. Sometimes it would seem that I should never have been a priest, should never have got myself into this work. Maybe I should forget about the poor, I thought. Why keep trying? Among the different answers that surfaced, one of the key ones was my belief that poor people working together and trusting each other could improve their lives economically and morally. I wanted to prove this to those who thought the sacramental approach was the only one or the best one. The greater my loneliness and sadness, the harder I worked, probably because of my stubborn Scottish nature.

If the temptation to give up got too strong, contact with poor people would usually restore my convictions. In the area of the city near my school was a sort of shanty town that was home for thousands of rural families who had been forced off the land by the government or by wealthy landlords. One day, I was walking through the area, greeting people.

A forty-year-old woman recognized me as I approached her shack. Her family was from a village called La Ceyba where I had started a co-op a few years earlier. She tried to avoid me but I wouldn't be put off. Tears began to flow as we embraced.

Her shack was about ten feet square, made of tin and cardboard, with a straw roof and mud floor. Inside were a bed, a table, a broken chair, a few dishes and pots, rags of clothing hanging on a wire, a kerosene lamp and a makeshift stove to burn charcoal. Living here were four children ages 7 to 15 and the parents. An open sewer, with its pungent odour and swarms of flies was a yard or so from the door.

"Padre," the woman said, through her tears, "I was always so happy to greet you at our home in La Ceyba and we all had such great hope when you started the co-op."

"What happened?" I asked. "Why did you move?"

"The government took over the whole area to plant sugar. Of course we had no title to our farm. An army truck dumped us here at night. It's awful, Padre. We have been here two years. Look at me, Padre, nothing to wear but this one old dress and not even clean water to wash it in. I'm so ashamed. I can't even offer you coffee. Why did God do this to us?"

She continued. "Every day my husband goes to the city with his machete trying to find somebody who wants their grass cut. Some days he returns with a peso or two; other days with nothing, so we don't eat that day. We have not seen Andreas, our eldest boy, for nearly a year. We have heard he is in jail for stealing. I hope it is nothing worse. Dear God, how beautiful was life in La Ceyba. We have lost all hope, my husband is bitter and angry and sometimes comes home drunk, in an awful mood."

"What about the Church?" I asked Mrs. Ramirez.

More tears fell as she stammered: "That too is gone. How can I go to church in these rags among well-dressed people? In La Ceyba it didn't matter. We were all poor and we had water to wash ourselves."

"Does a priest come to the area?"

"Never. They say even the police are afraid to come here."

"Do you mean you really have lost your religion?"

"That's a hard question, Padre. It is not easy anymore to really believe in God. But maybe something remains. (She pointed to a picture of the Sacred Heart of Jesus.) If not, I would have thrown that out. I can't even afford to buy a candle to place before it on First Fridays the way I did in La Ceyba. Will you come again, Padre, to see us? I'm sorry my husband is not here. Do you mind, Padre, if I ask you a question because it is something that keeps bothering me. Is it really a sin to steal at the market when your children are hungry?"

"No, Mrs. Ramirez, it is not a sin for you."

I was convinced then, and still am, that before you can preach morality to people, you have to do something about their poverty.

Chapter Ten

Living Under the Dominican Dictator

Sometimes, my efforts to help the poor involved projects beyond the organizing of co-ops. One of these endeavours was in the north of the country, the Cibao as it is called. That part of the country has the richest soil but the land had been divided among the sons of large families so often that now the plots of land were too small to support a family. Yet few of the young men living there wanted to move their families to other places.

What a great thing it would be, I thought, to buy some land and get some of these young men out on land of their own. During a visit to the US, I told a rich friend of mine about my dream and he gave me $11,000 to make it happen. I bought a large piece of land (average, not rich soil) which had never been cultivated before. Another American friend who was building a highway in the country lent me his heavy machinery and we built a dirt road some five kilometres into the *finca* (farm). I picked twenty-five unmarried young men from several co-ops. We chopped down the trees and built four cabins with the lumber, sank a well, and started planting.

To advise us, I hired one of the two trained agronomists in the country. He was glad to join us for four months as I could pay him more than he was making selling cars, there being little call for his agricultural expertise. Under his direction, the twenty-five men worked together on the farm. Soon they were able to start a little credit union and, in time, a consumer store. Some men quit after a short time but others came to replace them. There were problems of course but the experiment was thriving when I had to leave the country. On a recent visit to the Dominican

Republic, I learned there are now more than 100 families living on that land, each family having carved its own small plot from the larger.

Another attempt to alleviate injustice had to do with rice. Although it's the number-one staple of Dominicans, thousands of rice farmers are too poor to eat it because of the tax on it once it has been processed. I asked the government to grant a special favour to co-op members whereby they would not have to pay the tax. After a long time, the government consented — in writing. Relying on the promise, several co-ops pooled their funds and we bought a small rice factory. Several hundred rice farmers joined co-ops. We waited months, with the factory operating very little. As I should have expected, the government never kept its promise. The operation shut down.

As my rapport with farmers became known widely, American agricultural experts working in what was known as the "Point 4" program asked me to help them demonstrate their modern techniques, especially in growing tobacco, which is one of the chief Dominican exports. I gathered some 400 tobacco farmers for an all-day demonstration of pesticides, fertilizers and other improved procedures that were light years removed from the methods of the local farmers who were still planting the way the Indians had. At the end of the demonstration, the Americans felt they had done a good job, which they had. But I told them it would have no result.

The only way the new methods would catch on, I told them, would be if at least one farmer were given money to buy the fertilizer needed. The American experts couldn't understand that the margin between survival and death for most of these people is too small to allow for experimentation. The traditional way of farming is good enough, they believe; why tamper with it and risk losing everything? So I gave extra money to one of my employees to buy the new fertilizers. After a year, he tripled his income on his tobacco crop. When neighbours saw this, little by little, others agreed to adopt the modern methods.

My renown as an expert on rural problems brought some very surprising callers to my door. One day, who should appear but a Monsignor Luigi Ligutti, a big shot in the Vatican? He lived in Rome and represented Pope Pius XII as the Church's delegate to the United Nations' Food and Agriculture program (FAO).

The Pope had ordered Ligutti to organize a congress to seek ways to help the farmers of Latin America. Ligutti gave me a cheque for travel and expenses and told me to be in Manizales, Colombia, on a certain date and to be ready to give a talk on what I was doing among Dominican farmers.

Attending the six-day conference were over forty bishops, including two cardinals, from all countries south of the Rio Grande. Their governments were represented by ministers of state. Even the president of Colombia and several of his ministers were present. As well, there were observers from several European countries and six bishops from the US. Some two dozen papers were given. The immediate response to my talk was that my *campesino* Spanish got lots of laughs.

But there were other repercussions. Naturally, I mentioned the poverty of the Dominican farmers. A Dominican diplomat attending the conference wired to Trujillo that I had done the unforgivable: I had said there were poor people in his country. When I tried to depart from the country, I was refused re-entry to the Dominican Republic. As I didn't know where to turn now, the papal nuncio in Bogota invited me to his home. He began communicating with the nuncio in Domingo. Three days passed before I was allowed to return. That taught me, if I didn't know it already, that our dictator had eyes and ears all over the continent.

About four years later, in 1955, there was another visit from Monsignor Ligutti. This time he gave me a cheque for $25,000 — the largest amount of money I had ever seen. The Pope had asked him to hold a second rural congress for Latin America, this time in Panama. As the Pope wanted social justice on the program, Ligutti had approached the papal nuncio there for his suggestions. But the nuncio, Paul Bernier a most conservative prelate and the only Québécois ever to hold the position of nuncio in any country, threw up his hands in disgust at the mention of co-ops. That struck me as pretty ironic, given that it was in Quebec that the notion of credit unions first took hold in North America.

Ignoring the nuncio's objections, Ligutti asked me to organize a three-day program at the end of the five-day congress. The large cheque was to cover expenses of as many people as I wished to invite to Panama. Among those I invited were Bishop J.R. McDonald and Monsignor McKinnon from Antigonish; Jerry Voorhis, head of the Co-operative Movement in the US;

several co-op people from Puerto Rico who had studied at Antigonish, and the well-known Jesuit orator Father Foyaca, who was promoting social justice in Cuba. Most of the bishops and ranking government people had departed by the time my mini-congress started. Still, I had an audience of about 200 from all the countries. The three-day meeting was a success in that it sowed the seeds for the beginning of co-ops in several countries. It also prompted some of those present to attend my school in the DR to learn more about co-ops.

Ligutti was delighted with the outcome but our friendship ended because he wanted to throw a big party for the Americans present, excluding the Latins. I disagreed, telling him, "This will undo much of the goodwill created among North and South Americans during the week. Latins are very sensitive in such matters." He blew his top and scolded me for trying to tell him how to behave among Latins. He claimed to understand Latins, being Italian, but the truth was that he was American at heart. In any case, he went ahead and had the party in the newly-built Hilton Hotel. My absence may not have been conspicuous but it was a sincere statement on my part.

I never learned where Ligutti got the many thousands of dollars to run these congresses. The Vatican didn't have that kind of money to throw around. In the long run, I'm reasonably certain that it was US government money, slush funds, I think they are called. Or was it CIA money? Is there a difference?

Before the break with Ligutti, however, he agreed to help with another project. At the 1955 Congress, I proposed forming the Caribbean Confederation of Co-ops (CCC). Both Jerry Voorhis and Monsignor Ligutti promised me funds to organize it. The CCC would not only promote co-ops in the region but would also put pressure on governments of several countries such as Nicaragua which outlawed co-ops. The Puerto Rican government gave money to set up the CCC headquarters in San Juan where it functioned for a few years. After I left Domingo, the CCC was invaded by politicians, opened to the whole continent and renamed the Organization of Co-ops of the Americas. With the US now supplying most of the funds, it became another tool by which Americans controlled that part of the world.

Some time around the mid-1950s, my name appeared on the front page of the leading Dominican paper *El Caribe* in an article about an upcoming International Congress of Co-ops in the English-speaking areas of the Caribbean. According to the article, I was to represent Domingo at the meeting to be held in British Guyana. That was the first I'd heard about it. Days later a cheque arrived from the government for $800. So I went to British Guyana and stayed with the Scarboro fathers.

The government had given me a diplomatic passport for the trip but obviously I didn't know how to live like a diplomat as I had about $400 left when I returned to Domingo. When I spoke to my friend Peña Batlle about returning the money to the government, he smiled and said, "You cannot do that."

I asked, "Why did they give me so much money?"

He replied, with a smile, "You were supposed to give a dinner for the delegates, in honour of Trujillo."

Padre Pablo give a party to honour that criminal? Impossible!

Trujillo's largesse did, however, fund one event that gave me very pleasant memories. Wanting to show the world that he was the benefactor of his people and their Church, Trujillo called for a Catholic Cultural Congress. At the urging of the archbishop, I invited a few Canadian and American friends. Trujillo paid their travel expenses. In all, there were just over 100 participants, many of them intellectuals, from Latin America, Europe and North America, as well as a few from behind the Iron Curtain.

Staying with me for the congress were Monsignor McKinnon from Antigonish and a Jesuit friend, Father Bill Gibbons from Georgetown University, Washington. We invited a few of the outstanding people to a dinner. The evening started at six with drinks, then food, and conversation lasting till midnight. Among those present were: Douglas Woodruff, long-time editor of the prestigious Catholic weekly, *The Tablet*, from London, England; Bruce Marshall, also from London, whose very funny novels with Catholic settings were very popular; Father Cunningham, former president of Notre Dame University; two monsignors who were in charge of Laval University, Quebec City; and, the most intellectual of all, I think, was Georges Delcuve, the Belgian Jesuit who was the director of Lumen Vitae, the internationally known catechetical school in Brussels.

It was a great intellectual evening. Delcuve told us that several of his friends in Europe had been meeting for some years to discuss where the Church was going. In their view, it was not in step with the modern world. He was hoping changes in the Church would come before it was too late. Some changes did come several years later when the beloved Pope John XXIII called for the Second Vatican Council.

In the late 1950s, the minister of agriculture of the Venezuelan government, whom I had met in Panama in 1955, invited me to do a survey of farming in the Andes. I spent a month in an area of the country where farmers were extremely poor. One of the government's concerns was the rampant skin cancer among the farmers. A doctor who worked with them told me that it had to do with the fact that most of them lived in shacks up on the mountainside and worked all day in the valley under the tropical sun. At the end of the day, they had no bathing facilities to rub off the acidic sweat. When the cool night air came into contact with it, the result was skin cancer which often went into other parts of their bodies and became fatal.

Another trip to Venezuela had a very different focus. A young monsignor, a native of the country, wanted me to help him with co-ops. He hoped my involvement would build up the credit union movement in his area, the most devoutly Catholic part of the country. Being very busy with my own work, I didn't want to go but the monsignor pressured my Scarboro superior. Under orders from him, I went and tried to help.

It struck me as odd that the monsignor would not permit me to meet with the farmers in his parish unless he was present. They finally got their chance to speak to me alone on a Sunday morning when the monsignor was saying mass. About 200 of them came. What they poured out was a horror story. The priest was fleecing them and using their money for luxurious vacations. It was obvious why he wanted me to help the movement grow and produce even more money for him!

My problem now was how to escape from my host. There was only one twisting road along the Andes to the nearest town, which happened to be where the bishop lived. Only one bus a day passed through and my host was clearly not going to let me board it. Some German sisters who greatly feared the priest (they thought he was insane) arranged for me to be spirited away on a truck at four o'clock one morning. When I spoke to the bishop, he admitted that he knew what the monsignor was doing. But the monsignor had been appointed to his post when Rome made his predecessor in the parish a bishop. That put the monsignor more or less under the protection of Rome, so the local bishop felt powerless to restrain him.

Back in the Dominican Republic, I was, as usual, helping the old archbishop with his English letters and often driving him to parties. At one of these I met Richard Nixon, Vice-President of the US. He and his wife Patricia stopped in after visits to Lima and Caracas where they had been showered with eggs and tomatoes by anti-US demonstrators. Our dictator made sure this was not going to happen in his country. At a lavish and well-controlled party on the grounds of the US embassy, nearly a thousand people shook hands with Nixon and his wife.

It so happened that, in the past, Nixon's path had crossed that of my friend Gerry Voorhis, head of the Co-operative Movement in the US. Two men more different in character I cannot imagine. Jerry had been a Democrat congressman for his home state of California. The more he spoke about the needs of the poor, however, the more opposition grew against him. A group of wealthy Republicans advertised in California papers for a Republican to oppose Voorhis. The ad brought forward a young man from Whittier College who had a reputation as a good debater — Richard Nixon. Backed by big bucks and by slander that painted Jerry as a virtual communist, Nixon defeated Jerry in the election. Jerry left politics and became head of the US Co-op Movement based in Chicago.

Now here was Nixon being fêted in the Dominican Republic as the second-most important man in the US. Like all VIP's, Nixon was expected to pay his respects to the bones of Christopher Columbus which are kept in an ornate urn at the entrance of the oldest cathedral in the hemisphere. At nine o'clock sharp on the morning after the party, Nixon arrived at the cathedral and saw the bones. Then he came to the adjoining residence where the archbishop awaited him. As I had taken the archbishop to the party the day before, he had asked me to be on hand for Nixon's private visit.

The old archbishop was sitting in his rocking chair, his blind eyes blank as he held the hand of Nixon. "Mr. Vice-President," he said, "I feel in my old bones that some day you will be in the White House."

Nixon, two feet from me, glanced in my direction and I looked into his devious, shifting eyes. The look in them told me his thoughts: "This old patriarch is making a prophecy."

Several times in the following days, I asked the archbishop, "Did you really mean what you said to the vice-president?"

His reply always was, "Of course I meant it."

One day I said to the archbishop, "Monsignor, if you could have looked into Nixon's eyes for those few minutes as I did, I doubt you would have said that."

However, the archbishop's "prophecy" came to pass. But I think my feelings too were borne out by subsequent events.

There never had been strong support among the Scarboro priests for my work but their opposition came to a head over a problem regarding our insurance with the Credit Union National Association of the United States. This organization, established in 1935, included more than 20 million credit union members in the US and had links to credit unions in many other countries. CUNA's insurance program paid handsomely into the estate of a member who died.

Our national co-op organization met CUNA's strict accounting standards to qualify for the insurance. But then we discovered that if we were going to send money out of the country to pay premiums to a US company, the government of the Dominican Republic obliged us to deposit something like half a million dollars with them. Obviously, it would be impossible for us to round up such a deposit. With Peña Batlle's approval, I circumvented this problem by having the Scarboro Society pay the premiums from Canada and I reimbursed Scarboro. But this arrangement was jeopardized by the very first claim. A man in the village of La Torre had been killed one night in his home while leading his family in the rosary. An angry neighbour who had been refused a loan by the village credit union burst in and stuck a knife in him. According to CUNA regulations, a picture of the deceased had to be sent to head office with the insurance claim.

Now one of Trujillo's many quirks was his insistence that the people of the DR were more white than the people of adjoining Haiti. While it is true that there is more white blood in the DR, about seventy percent of the population has an identifiable proportion of African ancestry. But Trujillo did everything he could to hide this fact from the outside world — starting with his own face, which he powdered white to try to hide the traces of a black grandmother. He furthermore refused to allow any picture of a black person to leave the country.

Trujillo had all mail examined, of course, and I received tips from friends that he received reports about my sending out the photograph of the black man. As long as Peña Batlle had been around, I felt secure. But now he was dead. What should I do? I went to my lawyer, Dr. Efraiin Reyes Duluc, who also held a government post, though a less important one than Peña Batlle. "You have to drop the insurance," he said. "You have too many people gunning for you. If they catch you on currency manipulation, they will crucify you." He suggested we start a local insurance program on a small scale.

So now I had to make a major change without explaining why. It wouldn't do to admit that I'd been breaking the law with the connivance of Peña Batlle. The matter was to be decided at the 1958 annual meeting of the Co-op National Federation, which we had set up about four years earlier. Some 150 delegates from all over the country had gathered in the hall when, to our amazement, three men in white cassocks marched up the aisle. They were my superior and two of his friends. I couldn't believe my eyes. Now I knew there was going to be trouble.

Sure enough, they opposed the move I had made about our insurance. The chairman allowed them to offer all their arguments against my action. While they may have had some genuine concerns about Scarboro's involvement in the insurance scheme, their real beef, as I knew, was that my work was not priestly.

When a vote was taken, the delegates gave me total support. The Scarboro priests left the meeting and I did not see a Scarboro priest for more than six months.

Having lost that battle, however, they appealed to a higher court — the number-one boss of our society in Canada. I have no idea what calumnies they heaped on my head but they got immediate action. The superior rushed to Domingo and started to lay me out in lavender.

"Father," I said, "if you believe what these men told you, you are misled. If you want to know what I am doing in this country, speak to the archbishop and the priests from Quebec who have been my loyal friends through the years."

A week later, the superior from Canada called a meeting with me and the Scarboro men who attacked me publicly. In the intervening time, he had consulted with the Quebec priests and the archbishop. The result was that my local superior was roundly chastised. The general superior threatened to remove all my opponents from the country. I learned later that all the trouble was largely due to the fact that one Scarboro priest, a close friend of the local superior, wanted my job.

By now, however, the movement was already in decline. One of the causes was a two-year drought that wrecked the financial prospects of rural people. But the more significant factor was petty persecution of the movement by the dictator. In most groups, a spy was planted to report on my talks. The members knew this and started to run scared. More than a few people told me I should leave the country.

Finally a call came from the colonel who was head of Trujillo's intelligence service. Born in Spain, this man was a graduate of West Point and of Columbia University in New York. The place to which he summoned me was the jail and the torturing centre. Usually, I took my male secretary with me when meeting government people. When he was ordered out of the large office, I knew I was in for a less than pleasant meeting.

Flouting the Dominican custom of respect for a man wearing a soutane, the colonel never addressed me as "Padre". He insisted on calling me "Señor". For that matter, I didn't address him as "Colonel".

The first questions were routine: my name, date of birth, address, and so on. Then, "What are you doing in this country?"

I replied matter-of-factly to all questions.

He now began to move in for the kill. "Do you know Captain So-and-So?"

I acknowledged that I did. The man was retired from the army and was president of a credit union in the city. He used to come to my office with his problems.

The next question, "Was Captain X in your office at nine a.m. on such and such a date?"

I replied that I couldn't be sure of the date and the hour because he came so often. But I suspected my interrogator was referring to one day when my mood was surly. I had just come back from an arduous two-week trip trying to solve co-op problems and I had just heard of two mass murders by Trujillo in the north of the country.

Next question, "At that time you told the captain that it was impossible to help poor Dominicans while Trujillo lived?"

My reply, "It is possible I said something like that. But did I say it on that date? I don't know. I know I have dreamed of saying things like that, as thousands of Dominicans have — many of them dead."

He pulled from his desk a tiny silver pistol in case I had not noticed the .38 calibre revolver on his hip. "You are going to sign this letter admitting that you did say that or you will not leave this office."

I refused. This went on for two hours: his insisting and my refusing. Finally I stood up.

"You sit down," he ordered.

Remaining standing, I said, "Just as you take orders, señor, from your boss, so do I. I am going to see the archbishop."

Then I walked out. It seemed like a mile to the door as I waited for hot lead in my back.

When I told the archbishop about the grilling, he told me not to go out at night and to make sure someone accompanied me in the day. I should return to Canada soon, he said. As it was obvious that my days in the country were coming to an end one way or another, I didn't protest the archbishop's orders.

Nobody in the Dominican Republic, New York or Toronto knew the exact day I was leaving. When I arrived in San Juan, Puerto Rico, my taxi from the airport took me to the American Capuchin fathers' place in old San Juan.

At the entrance, a man accosted me. He said he was a Dominican working on a ship going from Mexico to Venezuela. He needed money, he said, and he was looking for "Padre Pablo who always helps people in need."

Had he ever met Padre Pablo? I asked. He said he hadn't.

Telling him to wait there, I went upstairs and reported this encounter to Father Leon, the superior. He ordered me to remain right where I was. Then he hurried downstairs and told the man he didn't know any Padre Pablo.

Knowing of my trouble with Trujillo, Father Leon insisted on notifying the FBI of this incident. The head of the FBI in Puerto Rico, who was a close friend of the Capuchin fathers, came to get my story. He went away and worked on it for a couple of weeks. In the meantime I was not to leave the house.

It turned out the beggar had been lying. No Dominican ship had docked in San Juan in months. The "beggar" was surely a hit man, possibly a Puerto Rican, sent to get me. The FBI man knew that Trujillo had bumped off people in Puerto Rico, in a New York subway, in Caracas and other places. The point was that Trujillo did not want to kill me on Dominican soil.

After the tense two-week wait in San Juan, I flew to Canada. Three months later, I learned that the colonel who interviewed me had been shot dead shortly after our meeting by orders of Trujillo. True to form, the captain who shot the colonel was killed hours later.

Thirteen years of my life in Domingo had ended. I did not know it then, but more than twenty years later, I would be invited by the government to return. To say the least, I felt sad and wondered if justice was worth fighting for. Monsignor Ivan Illich, a friend who was later to become controversial for his radical views on the Church's role in Latin America, urged me to return to Domingo. "Be a martyr," he said. "The Church needs martyrs." I did not agree, in spite of the well known saying about the persecutions in the Church's early years: "The blood of martyrs is the seed of the Church." At this point in our history, living people who stand for justice may be more important than dead heroes.

A year or so after I left the Dominican Republic, the bishops of the country wrote their first letter condemning Trujillo for his slaughtering of so many people. The letter was read in all churches. An enraged Trujillo opened his big guns against the Church, using every dirty trick: for example, dressing up soldiers in soutanes and sending them out to rape women. Through the years, several plans to kill the dictator had failed but the bishops' letter sparked a new plot and it worked. In 1961 the man was killed. I knew the man who killed him as well as members of his family. Not that it was any secret; he bragged openly about his feat. That, of course, was fatal.

Trujillo's son flew in from Paris and took charge, killing 200 people — everyone in any way related to the killer of his father. In the chaos that followed, many co-ops wilted and died. There were fourteen governments in five years. In a bloody revolution in 1965, a few thousand people died. The revolution was quashed by an invasion of 30,000 or more US marines. There has been relative peace these past years under civilian governments. Behind the rulers, however, is the military and behind them, manning the controls, is the powerful nation to the north.

Harvey Steele, age 3 years. (above)
Fr. Joe Nearing *(left)* and Harvey Steele, after ordination, August 9, 1936.

Fr. Jim McGillivray (left) and Bill McNabb departing for
China, 1931 (above)
Mr. Li (left) who taught Chinese at Lishui, and Fr.
MacIntosh from Nova Scotia with a Chinese boy. (below)

Archbishop Ricardo Pittini, Santo Domingo. (above)
Harvey Steele with two co-op leaders in Santo Domingo.
(below)(Photo courtesy CANAMEDIA)

From the video *Padre Pablo, campesinos* in Panama building a house of
mud and straw. (above) (Photo courtesy CANAMEDIA)
President Marco Robles of Panama swearing Harvey Steele in as an
adviser to his government. (below)

Chapter Eleven

Panama

After leaving the Dominican Republic, I was missioned to British Guyana where some half dozen Scarboro men were serving in parishes. Catholics were but a small fraction of the half-million population of this British colony, located in the highlands in the north of South America. At that time, British Guyana was a very unstable place, politically speaking. England had announced it was going to give the colony its independence the next year. The politician most likely to take over leadership of the new state was Dr. Cheddi Jagan, an avowed communist of Indian descent. The US, unable to tolerate this, was about to ensure that an African leader came to power.

Conflict between the Indian and African people, who made up most of the population, was long-standing. The blacks had been brought in as indentured workers. In the nineteenth century, when they refused to continue working on the old terms, the British imported workers from India to cut the sugar cane. By 1950, their descendants constituted half of the population. They stayed mostly in the country, whereas blacks lived in and around Georgetown, the capital. Although mostly illiterate and poor, the Indians struggled to climb up from the bottom of the social and economic pile.

The friction between the two groups was so intense that it was virtually impossible to have altar boys belonging to the two cultures. Obviously, it was no place for a co-op movement. My stay there was only eight months.

One vivid memory of British Guyana has to do with my first funeral. An old gramophone was playing a jazz tune as I began reading the prayers for the dead. On turning to sprinkle holy water on the coffin, I was startled to see the dead man's wide open eyes staring at me through the glass top of the coffin. Then it occurred to me that maybe he wasn't really dead. After all, he had been delivered to the funeral home just an hour or two before. I had great difficulty concentrating on the prayers. If not dead then, he was soon drowned. As Georgetown is below sea level, the grave was full of water and the coffin made a swishing sound as it sank.

My brief stay in British Guyana was followed by a posting as chaplain to a Catholic hospital in Scarborough run by sisters from Quebec. It wasn't my kind of work. Most of my life had been working with men. What made the sisters unhappy was that my Sunday talks usually concerned justice. A very conservative group, the sisters tended to treat rich patients better than poor ones, I noticed. Also, since their workers were shockingly underpaid, I began talking about starting a union among them. Phone calls from the mother superior to my superior grew in frequency, complaining about my justice talks.

After eighteen months of this, my superior asked me what I really wanted to do. As Trujillo had been killed, it might be possible to go back to Domingo. " Do you want to try it?" he asked. My reply was positive. The superior thought, however, that it might be prudent to see if the five new bishops in the DR would welcome me back. (The old archbishop had died.) He wrote all five bishops. Not one of them agreed to welcome me back. I was a trouble-maker in their books.

Then my boss asked what was my next choice? I wanted to return to work somewhere in Latin America. So the superior gave me the go-ahead to tour Latin America to try to find a place where co-ops might prosper.

Funding for the trip came from a New York friend. I spent eight months travelling to all the Latin countries, from Mexico to Argentina. My objective was to see what the Church was doing in the field of social justice, what kind of co-ops existed, what governments were doing to promote them. A lot of doors were opened by a letter of introduction from Father J. Considine, a Maryknoller who had visited me in the Dominican Republic. He was head of the US bishops' Latin American Bureau. At that time, the American bishops were sending millions of dollars to

Latin America. So my letter from Considine tended to make local hierarchy think US money would be pouring in after my visits. I was able to meet and have dinners with bishops, a few cardinals and several Vatican diplomats.

At the top of the list of interesting people I met on that trip was Dom Helder Camara, then one of the auxiliary bishops of Rio de Janeiro. His thoughts on social justice were much like mine. A man with similar ideas was Eugenio Sales, my host during a two-week rest stop in Natal, Brazil. Then the youngest bishop in the world (he was thirty-three, I think), he wanted me to join his diocese as he was keen on co-ops. Sales is now the cardinal archbishop of Rio and one of the most far-right bishops in Brazil. Helder, however, did not change his thinking and now lives in retirement in his former diocese in north-east Brazil.

In the back of my mind was the possibility of finding a place to begin a school for training lay people in work for social justice. While I had offers to work in Chile and Ecuador, the more attractive location seemed to be Panama. I was encouraged to settle there by Porfirio Gomez, a Panamanian who had worked in Japan for the United Nations, promoting co-ops. The young auxiliary bishop of the archdiocese, Marcos McGrath and a few other Panamanians welcomed the prospect of my establishing the school there. Other reasons why Panama appealed to me were that it was a hub for air travel in that part of the world and it had hard currency — the US dollar — while inflation was galloping in most countries. Also, it had never had a dictatorship but had been ruled for many years by an oligarchy of rich families who rotated the president's job among themselves in a way that was relatively democratic by Latin American standards.

But I came home still uncertain about how to launch my dream of a training centre for lay people. The first question was where to establish my North American base? Having spent only a few years of my adult life in Canada, I knew few people here. My contacts were better in the US. Father Fred McGuire, a Vincentian whom I had known when we were both working in China, was now head of the Mission Secretariat of the US Church. Then there was Father Considine, head of the Latin American bureau. (Both these offices were set up in response to the Vatican's plea that the US Church should give 50,000 missionaries and $50 million to Latin America.) I also had met many people at the annual meeting in the US of CICOP (Catholic Inter-American Cooperation Program), a function that brought together bishops and others from Latin America to meet with the US Church to discuss problems.

So I decided to make my pitch in the US. My first thought was to go to Boston because I had met Archbishop Cushing a few times and knew he was interested in Latin America as he had formed a group of priests called the St. James Society to work there. Another reason: he had been in Antigonish and knew about the co-ops there. He had even brought the St. Martha's Sisters from Antigonish to work in Boston. Not a small point — he was famous for raising money.

However, Father Considine and Monsignor Bill Quinn, his assistant, persuaded me to set up in Chicago. They pointed out that there were many more liberal-minded priests in Chicago than in the Boston area. Monsignor Quinn, a native of Chicago, found me a place to live in the windy city. For the next while, my home was at St. Carthage's rectory with Monsignor John Hayes, a saintly man in poor health, and three other priests. The parish, just south of the Loop, was typical of the Chicago inner-city: populated entirely by poor blacks, crime-infested, without sanitation or street-cleaning services, ignored by police. Every night cars were damaged on the streets and it was dangerous to go out after dark. There was no restaurant within miles but a high school student prepared one meal a day for us. Her repertoire of pork and hamburgers was hard on my ulcer-prone stomach.

Quite unexpectedly, a call came from a priest I had met in Latin America. Father Pancratius Conway, a Franciscan, had been superior in San José, Costa Rica, where the Franciscans ran several parishes and the most prestigious boys' high school in the country. I still remember one of my long night visits with him. His question of conscience was: what am I supposed to do when Catholic friends here at the US embassy keep asking me to give them information about what is going on in the country? Should I help them?

My reply was a firm *NO*. "You came here to work for the local people," I told him. "Your first loyalty should be to them, not to your native country." (I have met many US missionaries, good workers, doing what they thought was right, but always putting loyalty to their native country first.) After a very long talk, Father Conway seemed to come around to my way of thinking.

Having finished his term as superior, he now wanted to work with me even though he had no experience in the field of co-ops or social justice. He came to Chicago and we rented a small office for $50 a month in an old 14-storey building, right on the Loop, that had been donated to the Paulist Fathers. When the time came to install a phone, the question was how to list our office? I decided to name the school the Inter-American Co-operative Institute (ICI). The beauty of that name was that ICI also worked in Spanish (*Instituto Co-operativo Inter-Americano*).

So ICI was born. With a few thousand dollars from my New York friend, we sent out 75,000 pamphlets to members of Catholic organizations and religious orders, outlining the objectives of the institute. There were few replies. We did, however, get some stories into newspapers and magazines about the fledgling ICI. Then, I bought a second-hand car and, with Father Conway, spent three months travelling all over the Midwest giving talks to a score of Catholic organizations, mostly groups of priests. The reactions were almost all negative. After some six months, I received only one donation — $1,000 from a Chicago school teacher.

Father Conway saw the venture as hopeless and left. The prospects didn't look very bright to me either. More than once I was ready to give up, but I took heart from the fact that ICI existed, at least on paper. I was totally convinced that the work of promoting social justice through co-ops or any other tool would never be done by priests. Except for professionals and the rich, we priests are probably the most secure people in the world. Once a man is ordained a priest, he can opt not to do any work for the rest of his life and the Church is bound to support him. It is nearly impossible for a person who has never gone without the needs of life to be totally committed to social justice. That's why the banner of social justice must be carried by lay people who know what it is to struggle to make a living. ICI, a totally independent, self-supporting institute, was to prepare young men and women to do that job.

Just how difficult it was going to be to get funding for such a project was becoming clearer. A friend suggested I go to see

Bishop McNulty of Buffalo, who had been involved in the beginnings of AID, a short-lived Church effort to send young men and women as missionaries to Latin America. " Frankly, Father," McNulty said, "Catholics are not trained to give money to lay peoples' groups. I think you'll have great difficulties trying to get money for your project."

In Chicago at that time I got to know the cream of the liberal priests in the area. Though, in their own way, they believed in justice, not one of them seemed to grasp my Canadian-Antigonish mentality. Another barrier to understanding my dream was the fact that none of them had ever lived in the Third World.

Many times, confronted by the uncomprehending stares of these clerics, I would walk a few blocks over to Gerry Voorhis' office. I felt more at home with him than with most priests. He and his staff understood my ideas and I would return to my priest friends with higher spirits.

Some of them helped me as much as they could. Monsignor Bill Quinn, for example, took me to meet Cardinal Meyers. It was probably thanks to Quinn's putting in a good word for me that the cardinal allowed me to open the office. Significantly, the cardinal never questioned me about my canonical standing in the Church. (According to Church law, a priest must be officially attached to some diocese or fall under the jurisdiction of some religious superior.) That issue didn't arise until Cardinal Cody took over the diocese and wrote Scarboro about my canonical standing.

By now, my contact with Scarboro was minimal. Most of my colleagues in the society had little idea of what I was doing. Those who did were mostly unsympathetic. My boss at Scarboro had more or less bent the law by leaving me free to pursue what he saw as my impossible dream. At Cody's urging, however, he told me to get some kind of Church affiliation. Father Considine suggested attaching me to the American hierarchy's national body in Washington. I refused. I did not want to be linked to a Church body of that kind, and especially not an American one. I continued as a *vagus* (a priest without canonical standing) and heard no more from Canada about that.

Offers to team up with various secular groups and organizations started coming in. Most of them fell through for one of two reasons. Sometimes my would-be partners were frightened off by gossip about my being a communist. More often I sensed that the proposed connection would compromise ICI's integrity. For instance, Sergeant Shriver, John F. Kennedy's brother-in-law and founder of the Peace Corps, told me, "I wish to hell you didn't have that collar on, Father. I'd get you to come and work for us." Suspecting the Peace Corps workers in various countries would be used largely as informers for Washington (which is what happened), I declined to get involved. The head of the labour union AFL-CIO invited me to work with them in training Latin American labour leaders. I refused to have any part of it because his goal was obviously to get control of all Latin American labour unions.

Feeling sorry for me, Father Fred McGuire proposed that his friend John McCormick, the speaker of the US House, should hold a luncheon for me to meet some congressmen in the hope that some government money might come my way. McCormick, a devout Catholic who was interested in China through his friendship with Cardinal Paul Yu Pin, agreed. I sat down with a dozen members of the House in a private dining room in their chambers. McCormick and I were the only Catholics present but, as it was a Friday, the main course was fish. I spoke about my work for nearly two hours.

When the meal ended, a short man who had been sitting at the end of the table called me aside. He was Carl Albert of Oklahoma, who later succeeded McCormick as speaker. "Here in Washington, we have to listen to all kinds of government people from around the world asking for help," he said. " For the first time, your talk gave me an insight into the problems of the Third World. Now I understand a little better how most of the millions we give away does little good because it goes straight into the pockets of corrupt government officials. I would like you to work with us here and help us when we have to deal with these world problems of poverty."

My reply was simple: "I am sorry. I dedicated my life to this collar I'm wearing and will never go to work for any government." That ended that.

It was becoming apparent that trying to get money from the Washington government for my work was impossible. I had three strikes against me: I was not an American citizen; I was too far Left in my thinking; and I was a Catholic priest. About the last point, I had good reason to remember a comment at my three-day course in Panama in 1955. Somebody had asked a USAID worker if it was possible for a priest to get funding from Washington. Although a Catholic himself, the man from USAID smiled and said, " Impossible. Remember, ours is not a Catholic country."

However, one congressman who had been at McCormick's luncheon offered to help round up some money from private sources. Jimmy Roosevelt (son of FDR), who had been sitting on my right at table, promised to phone a rich friend of his. When he did, the friend turned out to be the same man who was already sending me a cheque each year and had given me the money to buy the *finca* in Domingo.

There was another attempt to get money for me from US philanthropists. An elderly convert to Catholicism, who tended to seek out priests, had befriended me. One evening, he invited two dozen of the richest Catholics in New York City to a supper to meet me and hear about my work. Only one donation came in — $4,000. My host, however, continued each year, giving me a cheque for $5,000 until our friendship ended some years later on publication of my book entitled *Who Are the Owners of Latin America?* that criticizes US intervention in Latin America.

At this man's summer home, I spent two days chatting with Father John LaFarge, considered by many the most eminent of all American Jesuits. He was one of the most fascinating men I ever met. One of the first Catholic US leaders calling for civil rights for blacks, he founded the Catholic Interracial Movement. As an author, he promoted social justice all his life. One of the most intriguing moments of our two-day chat occurred when I asked Father LaFarge, why is it that the Catholic church has founded dozens of religious orders and groups to promote charity and not one, to my knowledge, to promote justice?

His reply came with a big smile. " It would take more than a few hours to discuss that. It is something that has bothered me all my life and I don't know the answer but I have some guesses. And I imagine you do too, since you know the Catholic Church as well as I do."

No doubt his guesses, like mine, had to do with the fact that an all-out thrust for social justice would threaten the wealth and prestige of Church leaders, both clerical and lay.

After two years of attempting to raise funds, I was getting nowhere. So I turned to my other rich friend, the one who had funded my tour of Latin America. On hearing about my wanting to put on a pilot course in Panama, he gave me $20,000. I announced a four-month course for January 1964, and through various friends and contacts, I rounded up fifty-three students, mostly *campesinos*.

Then I phoned Father John Kennedy, a Vincentian father working in the Canal Zone with Caritas, a Catholic organization that helped Third World nations develop projects. He made a deal with the Salesian Fathers who agreed, for $1,000 a month, to give me the use of classrooms in their technical school which would be empty for the three-month summer vacation. They would also provide lodging for the foreign students. Food would be extra.

Among the Panamanians I knew were Porfirio Gomez and Oscar Monteza, both of whom had training in the co-op philosophy and were now working in Panama. I phoned them and asked them to hire a secretary for me and a few teachers. They did. Meanwhile, I lined up a place to live and planned that I would eat at restaurants. I was all set to fly to Panama in January with $20,000 in my pocket.

Then, all hell broke loose. Panamanian students stormed the barricades around the Canal Zone. They were protesting the failure of the US to abide by a 1959 agreement to display Panamanian and US flags simultaneously in the zone. The students burnt the US flag and violence continued for several days. About twenty people died, including three US soldiers, and hundreds were injured. I had to postpone the course.

At this point, I was in Chicago at the annual meeting of CICOP, a gathering of Church leaders from Latin America and the US. Vice-President H.H. Humphrey was the key speaker to the crowd of 2,000. I had met him a few years before when he was a senator, in the Prado Hotel in Tegucigalpa, capital of Honduras. We had met in the elevator. I had known he was coming because the local papers ran his picture with an article about his bringing a few million dollars to Honduras. Long before that, he'd won my admiration for his commitment to justice.

Encountering him in the elevator, I said, "How are you, Senator?"

"How did you know me?" he asked.

"From your picture. But I knew you before that. You are the only man who ever put in a good word for co-ops in the laws of the US."

Surprised that I knew this, he asked about me. On hearing about my background, he said, "Antigonish. That is one place I have always wanted to see."

At the end of our elevator ride, we chatted for another five minutes in the lobby while his husky bodyguards ground their teeth, obviously wishing this "damn priest" would quit wasting the senator's time. He invited me to come and see him anytime I was in Washington. Taking his invitation as somewhat less sincere than Mae West's "Come on up and see me some time," I never followed it up. But here he was sitting in the hotel in Chicago, surrounded by the media, waiting to fly back to Washington after his talk to CICOP.

I asked Monsignor Quinn, organizer of the conference, if I should say hello to the VP.

"By all means," he said, taking me in to see Humphrey.

The vice-president said he remembered our meeting in Honduras. That didn't seem very likely to me; the remark was probably just a typical politician's gambit. Still, he seemed genuinely interested in my work. I told him how the incident in Panama had disrupted my plans.

"Father," he said, "What the hell should we do there in Panama?"

I told him, "Your policy for Latin America stinks. Especially for Panama. You should stop treating those people like idiots. Be magnanimous. Quit trying to control them."

He insisted that I fly with him to Washington to tell President Lyndon Johnson exactly what I had said. "Let's go, Father," he said. "My private plane's waiting."

"No thanks," was my reply. "I don't want to get involved in US politics." I never saw him again.

When I arrived in Panama in early February there was still some violence. Anti-US slogans in red paint were splashed everywhere. Long into the night, street-corner orators damned the Yankees. But I decided to follow through on my plan. I rented a small house and took in as housemates a young ex-seminarian from Glace Bay who had offered to help me and a Marist brother from Denver who was taking the course. I had tried to get a priest helper from Antigonish as that diocese had the largest surplus of priests in Canada. No one came forward except the ex-seminarian. When he proved not to be genuinely interested in co-ops, I sent him packing.

How long I was to be here, I had no idea, but it was apparent from the start that the place was very different from the DR. In the nineteenth century, this narrow strip of land separating the two continents of our hemisphere was part of Colombia. It was a French company, though, that began building a canal through Panama to join the Atlantic and the Pacific, to save ships the long trek around Cape Horn. When disease and lack of money forced the French to abandon the project, the Americans took over. In 1903, on paying some $40 million to the French company and another sum to Colombia, the US assumed Panama as a Protectorate and construction of the canal forged ahead under US President Theodore Roosevelt.

Although Panama is no longer a protectorate, the US has retained a strip of land five miles wide on each side of the 51-mile ditch joining the two oceans. As a result of the US involvement, Panama City is probably the most Americanized of Latin American cities. It is a story of love and hate between the two peoples. The outbreak of violence in 1964 was only one of several such incidents through the years. As recently as 1990, the Americans invaded Panama again.

In 1964, Panama had a population of less than two million people, half of them living in the city. Most Panamanians are mulattos with a mix of Spanish and African blood. Other groups in the population include many Asiatics and several tribes of aboriginal Indians. Rubbing shoulders with Yankees made the Panamanians much more sophisticated than Dominicans who had been isolated from most of the world by their dictator.

On arriving in Panama for that 1964 course, I had my plan in my head but not yet on paper. If teachers could be found, I wanted to offer about a dozen subjects to prepare students to work in the field of social justice: leadership, community development, credit unions, co-ops of all kinds, sociology, political science, bookkeeping, business administration, labour unions, group dynamics and field work. The students were expected to attend 500 hours of classes aside from work after hours — a tough program for people in the tropics.

Eventually, I found teachers in Panama for subjects I couldn't teach myself, such as community development and political science. Of the fifty-three students in that first course, about half were Panamanians and the others were from Ecuador, Colombia, the Dominican Republic, El Salvador, Guatemala and Brazil. At the end of three months we had to move out of the Salesian school. For the last month of our course, the government gave me a large hall and the foreign students lived in the homes of local people. Towards the end of the course, the students departed for three weeks of field work with co-ops in different parts of Panama.

Suddenly ICI became national news. But not for any altruistic reason. In one area near the Costa Rican border, seven students were involved in a bar room brawl. One student lost an eye, another had his head split open. Three others had to receive treatment in the local hospital. To get to the site of the fiasco quickly, I had to rent a small plane from Panama City; it landed on a golf course. For three days, the local police brought in a dozen or so local people suspected of attacking our students.

A year or so later, I learned that my students were to blame, not the local people. A burly football player from Honduras had started it all. There was nothing even remotely political about it; it was just a typical brawl between locals and foreigners. But headlines about the incident had trumpeted ICI's name all around the country. Returning to Panama City, we had to make a stopover in David, a city in the middle of the country. The superior of the US Vincentians, our hosts, asked me to speak to a group of local professionals and merchants who had some concerns about ICI. With two of the bandaged students in tow, I met with about forty local people.

One of the most hostile comments came from a young man who was, one of the priests told me, a millionaire. "What kind of a course are you giving, Padre?" he asked. " It sounds to me like communism. I studied ten years in the US at two Catholic colleges. I have taken all the courses given on the social teachings of the Church but I never heard of the stuff you are teaching." Then he pointed to the six American priests and said, " I doubt if they ever learned things like this in the seminary."

"You are right, señor. I'm sure they didn't. Nor did I."

Summoning up all his dignity, he said: " Padre, you cannot carry on this kind of work unless people like me give you money and I wouldn't give you a peso."

"Thank you, señor," was my reply, " and I wouldn't accept your peso on any conditions."

Not all Panamanians were so antagonistic, however. At the end of the course, the president of the country, Roberto Chiari, the archbishop and others came to the closing ceremonies. The president gave me a luncheon in his palace and warmly invited me to return to give more courses. Several Panamanians also urged me to return. With no prospect of further funding, however, I had no idea whether ICI had any future.

Chapter Twelve

Building ICI in Panama

My hopes for justice on a worldwide scale were raised when an invitation came in the early 1960s to an international congress of co-op pioneers in Rome. Various US groups like CUNA were paying our expenses. About eighty people, mostly priests and sisters from the Third World, would be attending. A dozen or more, including an African bishop, had studied at Antigonish.

Almost from the outset the meeting was disheartening to me. While spokespersons for Asia and Africa were highly-educated native people, the spokesperson for Latin America was my gringo friend Herb Wegner, the co-ordinator of CUNA's overseas program. Not that he was happy about taking on the job, as he spoke little Spanish, but it saddened me to see that once again, Latinos looked like second-class humans. Nor did my contacts with other delegates cheer me up. My every attempt to strike up a conversation got the brush-off. Yet I had been working in co-ops years before any of the delegates.

The final straw for me was a papal audience. We were among several thousand crowded around Pope John XXIII who was, in those days before the Second Vatican Council, known as a very conservative prelate. He singled out a group of policemen from San Francisco for special greetings, likewise, firemen from New York. But he ignored us — even though we Catholic missioners were the only international group present. That did it for me! I stomped out and swore never to set foot in the Vatican again.

An enjoyable two weeks' visiting co-op movements in Denmark and Sweden made up somewhat for the disappointment of the congress. I returned to Chicago, still not sure if there was any future for ICI. One person who had strongly urged me to return to Panama was Peggy Jansen, a mother of ten children and a grandmother. A Panamanian whose father was a New York journalist, she had married a prosperous businessman from Sweden. After taking most of my course, she sold one of her summer homes and gave me a cheque for $10,000. It was deposited in a bank in both our names, to be used only if ICI looked viable.

A couple of months after my return to the US, Peggy phoned to say she had found a building suitable for a course. A former convent, it had space for sleeping some forty people, a classroom, kitchen space and so on. My generous New York friend again gave me the money to put on a course. However, having just spent twelve days in hospital with an old sacroiliac complaint, I was almost helpless — supported by a brace and scarcely able to walk. But we scrambled to get ready for the course. By phone and cable, I lined up thirty students from a dozen countries, including four priests, one a monsignor. Along with professors from Panama, I engaged some from Mexico, Colombia and Costa Rica.

I'll never forget that course, mainly because of the cook. Peggy had hired a jovial woman who was a good cook but who kept trying to bed the Ecuadorean priests who were about half her size. Also food was constantly disappearing from the kitchen during her regime. Before I nearly went mad from the hassles, we had to fire her.

After this course, there seemed little hope of another because the building was to be demolished. Then, an offer came to put on a course down country in a small village called San Francisco in the province of Veraguas. The rental charge for use of the building would be $1,000 per month. Lining up students from a dozen countries was no problem. It was another matter persuading teachers to undertake the four-hour car trip from the capital. Some agreed, but I had to do a lot of the teaching myself.

What blighted that course was the physical set-up. We had taken the bishop's word that the facilities would be adequate. It had not occurred to anyone that the local stores might not be able to provide enough food. Nor did anyone suspect that the tiny pond supplying our water might dry up under the tropical sun. It did. And there was no rain. So we sweated through 120 degrees fahrenheit with no air conditioning, not even electric fans. With more than forty kinds of body odour permeating the place, discontent among the under-fed students reached epic proportions. It was a four-month nightmare. I figured this was the end of ICI, at least in Panama.

On return to Chicago, I listened to Monsignor Bill Quinn's tales of the goings-on in Rome at the Second Vatican Council which he had attended as an observer. The thought occurred to me that a visit to Rome would give me a chance to sell my ideas to the Latin American bishops gathered there. Bill arranged for me to live in the same place he had stayed — Villanova House. Living there were twenty-five American bishops, a dozen French and Belgian bishops and a number of *periti* (theological experts or advisors to the bishops), including Hans Küng and John Courtney Murray. Thanks to the reputations of those two men, our house became known as the House of Rebels.

None of us had the slightest inkling of just how much the council was to change our lives down through the decades. One American bishop told me, "I don't accept, let alone understand, all of what's going on here. How in heaven's name am I supposed to communicate the message of the council to my priests and then to my people?"

Even so, it was an impressive show. Over 3,000 bishops from all parts of the world where there, more than fifty internationally renowned *periti*, large numbers of observers from the other world religious groups, hundreds of media people. Feeling a nobody among all these big-wigs, I nevertheless managed to wangle admission to St. Peter's for a day dedicated to the missions. (I relented on my threat never to enter the place again.) That was probably the most colourful day of the whole council. It was also likely the first time African drums sounded off the old walls of St. Peter's. Pope Paul VI, in a rare appearance at a working session, personally intervened in the council just this once when he asked for a vote on the text drafted by the curia-dominated committee. To the curia's astonishment, the council rejected the draft as unduly legalistic, and sent it back to be rewritten.

Every night at Villanova we gathered to re-hash what happened in St. Peter's that day. Bishop Ernest Primeau of Manchester, New Hampshire, acted as chairman for these informal bull sessions. A conservative prelate who'd taught in Rome, he'd usually get the discussion rolling by some sparring with Monsignor George Higgins from Chicago, the labour expert for the Social Action Department of the American Bishops' Conference. Most of the talk in these pow-wow's was about the political infighting and the underhand manoeuvring by which the curia was trying to impose its conservative agenda on the council.

Gradually, though, the more serious issue of how the Church related to the world was beginning to emerge. People were finally talking openly about the Rites Controversy and reaching the same conclusion I had in my talks with Father Aaron Gignac: the curia's refusal to allow the Jesuit missionaries to adapt Christianity to Chinese culture was one of the great blunders of all time. And some Church leaders were admitting publicly that Christian missionaries had often been too closely linked to imperialism. Missionaries would have to show they had broken those ties if there was to be any real spread of the Gospel in the Third World.

One of the prophets of the new way of seeing the relationship between religion and the world was Father John Courtney Murray, the eminent Jesuit theologian, then living at Villanova. We don't know why it is that some people are attracted to each other the first time they meet but he was the person with whom I spent most of my free time. Maybe what drew us together was our common Scottish background. Father Murray had lived under a cloud for a time because the US bishops disapproved of his teaching on the freedom of religion. He was vindicated when the council adopted his ideas, overturning Rome's centuries-old doctrines on the relationship of Church and State. You would never have guessed from his low-key and easy-going manner that he was such a power to be reckoned with.

In the process of moving around to meet bishops, I had a brief reunion with Paul Yu Pin, now a cardinal, and much aged and stooped since we last met in Chungking. Of course, he had left China before Mao took over and was now living mostly in the US. As for the bishops from the Dominican Republic, I gave them as wide a berth as possible. At Domus Maria, Archbishop Angelo Rossi, then Archbishop of Sao Paulo and now a cardinal in Rome, usually made sure I got a drink even though he didn't buy my ideas. But some of the 100 Brazilian bishops living there took an interest. So did a few bishops from Chile and Ecuador. On encountering Bishop Marcos McGrath from Panama, whom I had met years earlier, I little suspected my future close association with him.

Flying back to the US, I wondered what my trip had accomplished. Not many bishops showed any interest in my ideas. A few years later, though, it seemed that maybe my lobbying had borne some fruit. In 1968 at Medellin, Colombia, the Latin American bishops publicly repudiated their traditional alignment with the rich and powerful. At that meeting, Pope Paul VI proclaimed the Church's "fundamental option for the poor." It made me proud to know that my own Archbishop McGrath, along with other sterling leaders like Dom Helder Camara, had a lot to do with putting those words in the Pope's mouth.

During my absences from Chicago, the office was manned by Father John Coffield who had been thrown out of Los Angeles diocese by Cardinal McIntyre because of his radical ideas about justice for the poor. As the years went by, however, it was becoming clearer that raising money in Chicago was impossible. So I closed the office.

Then a long cable arrived from Dr. Ruben D. Carles, minister of agriculture and economics in Panama. He begged me to return, promising that the government would give me a building. Other groups in the country wanted me back, he said.

Give it another try, I told myself. So I flew to Panama. Carles first suggested that I set up on the campus of the National University but I wanted ICI to be independent of Church, government and universities. Then he offered me an old unused government building but we didn't have the money needed to put it in shape.

One day at Carles' office in the agriculture ministry, his secretary introduced me to a man who happened to walk in. His name was Eddy Vallarino. He was the owner of a cargo airline and had just graduated with his MBA from Harvard.

Surprised to see a priest in the government office, he asked, "What are you doing here, Father?"

I told him I was trying to get land to establish a permanent home for ICI. Then I explained a bit about my work.

"No problem," he said, "I'll get land for you."

I didn't believe him. Nobody did. Rarely are Latin promises kept, as past disappointments had shown me. Even Dr. Carles, was sceptical. "You're crazy, Father" he said, "if you think one of the *rabiblancos* is going to give you anything for a program to help the poor." (The *rabiblanco* is a white-tailed bird and its name is applied derisively to the oligarchs of Panama.)

Amazingly, however, Eddy followed through. He found land owned by another Mr. Vallarino, who persuaded his associates to join him in donating the land. It was over 11,000 square metres of bog — but it was mine.

It took many months, though, to clear up the legal matters and get title to the land. Squatters living there were descendants of the people brought in to work on the building of the canal. Dr. Carles helped steer me through these legal hurdles. About $20,000 (from my benefactor in New York) was spent in filling in the bog. Two or three of the largest bulldozers in the country worked on it for two months. It took a lot of sweat with pick and shovel to get a decent road into the place.

Then we started building. Having not yet cottoned on to the full implications of my social justice ideas, the Canal Zone government was only too happy to help this priest whose work with the poor would keep the communists at bay! So various friends dismantled two buildings donated by the government of the Canal Zone and we incorporated the used bricks, the zinc roof, lumber, cement blocks, etc. into our buildings. Also donated were desks, chairs, stoves, refrigerators and other furnishings from the demolished buildings. Meanwhile, Eddy Vallarino's mother and Peggy Jansen spent weeks going around the city begging donations for the new school. An American, just retired from the army, was a great help as a volunteer builder, engineer, electrician and general handyman.

For about eight months of 1967, I spent twelve hours a day with some forty workers. More than 5,000 bags of cement went into the buildings. The total cash outlay, from my New York friend, some other supporters and Peggy Jansen, came to $70,000. Double that amount was donated in materials. All this time, the wonderfully kind American Vincentian priests, my Guardian Angels ever since China, gave me lodging and food.

Because Dr. Carles was my saviour in so many complicated matters such as arranging to bring water and electricity to the site, I was in his office almost every day. The ministry, employing some 500 people, was located in a seven-storey building. In the lobby where I waited for the elevator was the switchboard for the whole building. The operator running it had recently left the Catholic Church to join a fundamental sect. The sight of my roman collar prompted her to talk religion; whether to convert me or to salve her conscience, I don't know. A dozen or more employees would listen to our dialogue on religion while the switchboard went dead for many minutes.

Later I learned from my contacts in the government that the US publication *Time* had wanted to print its Spanish edition in Panama. Negotiations between New York and Panama were stymied because New York complained of not being able to get through to the ministry. That was because my friend on the switchboard preferred chatting with me. The *Time* people in New York finally gave up and made a deal to print the Spanish edition in Venezuela. Panama lost money and jobs for a hundred Panamanians, thanks to the lady's chattiness.

I often told this story to ICI students. Latins are great humanists but how much should humanism mix with business?

A couple of years after the initial construction of ICI, I put up another two-storey building. Because of the steady growth of the city, ICI is now more or less in its centre. So its total value today would be more than a million dollars. It has three large classrooms, bunk beds for some eighty people, full washroom facilities, a kitchen, a library, offices and a soft ball park and basketball court. Facilities make it possible to hold three different courses at the same time. There is nothing luxurious about the place. It is just functional.

Once ICI was operational, I picked friends to constitute a board of directors: two ministers of state, a judge, a lawyer, the archbishop and others. It mattered little to me that few of them knew much about co-ops. Once or twice a year, I called them in for a banquet and a so-called meeting of the board to fulfil the requirements of the law. As legally constituted, ICI is a non-sectarian, self-regulating, non-profit organization. It promotes social justice by offering courses in co-ops and community development. Its goal is thus to bring hope, liberation and better living to the poor throughout the continent. Through their studies, students are prepared to be agents for change.

Basically, the course is modeled on the program at the Coady Institute which stresses adult education as an integral part of the economic process. That makes it particularly useful in Third World countries where the primary need is the formation of men and women who believe in themselves and in their ability to create their own future. The Antigonish approach differs sharply from conventional education which locks pupil and teacher into a hierarchical relationship, with the teacher pouring in vast amounts of knowledge. Mind you, acquiring of facts has its place. But the Antigonish approach starts from the premise that education must be social. Since learning is a two-way process, there must be dialogue between student and teacher. The Antigonish pioneers discovered that in their study circles and kitchen meetings.

Since most of ICI's students, coming from remote villages, have an instinctive resistance to revealing their inmost thoughts publicly, they must learn to express themselves if they're going to provide leadership. To develop that skill in myself, I had signed up for a three-week group dynamics course in Bethel, Maine, back in the 1950s. About 150 of us were put into groups of about fourteen. My group went to a room with a stone-faced moderator who sat there and stared at us. After a while, somebody asked what the hell was going on. Later, somebody else said this was an expensive way to waste time and if we didn't get down to business soon, he was going home. Then someone attacked the moderator for not doing anything. Gradually people began to express their irritations, fears, worries, expectations. From time to time the moderator summed up what each person had said, asking us to weigh it for ourselves.

It was a fascinating process, albeit hard on the nerves. Having thus learned a whole new range of techniques for developing leadership, I managed some such training in my work with co-ops in the Dominican Republic. Once ICI was established, I brought in professionals to do the job properly. At the end of an ICI program, students almost always cite the group dynamics training as one of the most helpful aspects of the course. A typical student's summary of its effects would be, "I am beginning to understand what happens when people work in groups, why groups break up, why they fail to work out their frictions...I am now able to listen to a question and make an attempt to understand what is behind it, instead of going off half-cocked when somebody interrupts."

I have been criticized for not having religion on the program. My policy was that there was no point in forcing students to go to mass when most of them didn't go in their homelands. Besides, they were free on Sundays to attend mass in any of the several churches nearby. As in my work in Domingo, however, I always made the link between morality and the attack on poverty. That wasn't enough for one young priest from Michigan who was helping me at one time. Father Paul Manderfield, a man of enthusiastic faith, wanted to schedule religious discussions among the students. I gave him free reign to do so. For two or three nights, a dwindling number of students showed up for the meetings and then they stopped.

Several students had to be expelled, usually for their sexual conduct or stealing. One forty-year-old woman was making money going to bed with students. Some Dominican students were by far the most difficult to handle; rules relating to hours of rising and retiring, and getting to class on time meant little to them. Given my affection for their country, I bent over backwards to make allowances but sometimes I had no choice but to send them packing.

Then there were staff problems. Theft in the kitchen was chronic. After several break-ins, I hired an armed policeman as night watchman. Of course, the policeman knew a good thing when he saw it. We woke up one morning to find the kitchen almost empty — about $3,000 worth of food and equipment gone. The cupboard was virtually bare.

At various times, helpers from different countries would come to give me a hand for a while. In these first years, two American priests wanted very much to join me. One was Father Jack Catoir whom I had first met in the early 1950s. As a seminarian, he visited the Dominican Republic and joined me on several field trips. Enthusiastic about my work, he tried twice to get released to join me but his bishop refused both times.

The other would-be helper was Monsignor Gino Baroni from Scranton, Pennsylvania, who was *persona non grata* with his bishop because of his commitment to social justice. As ICI's future was at that time still far from certain, however, I couldn't offer him a permanent post. He was later named deputy director of the US federal government's office of health education and welfare, the highest government position ever held by a Catholic priest.

Although training of priests was not a high priority of ICI, some did apply for admission. I decided that, given the great prestige of priests throughout Latin America, they might do something for social justice if properly trained. So I accepted some priests from countries like Colombia, Ecuador, Brazil, Mexico and El Salvador. Some of these priests were the most demanding of all students. Rather than participating at an equal level with other students, they expected to be revered as advisors. This did not endear them to the other students. I had to ask many of these priests to leave. Some lawyers who were equally hard to put up with also had to be shown the door.

With no attachment to Church, state or other institution, raising funds is not easy. People do not consider you legitimate or credible. Throughout those first years, ICI was supported largely by American friends and the German Catholic organization Misereor which responded generously to a letter from me. In Canada, few people believed in what I was doing. In my home province, those who understood the work of Coady and Tompkins were sympathetic to my cause but most Nova Scotians, being extremely conservative Scots, had little interest in anything remotely socialist. In fact, I twice refused to be head of the Coady Institute, knowing that most priests and professors on campus would oppose my socialist ideas.

Nor was the federal government favourably disposed to me. In one of my visits to CIDA (Canadian International Development Agency), I was told their policy was to help natives but not priests, especially foreign priests working in Latin America. Development and Peace, a Catholic organization based in Montreal, also turned me down, though later they did give some help. As I recall, the first donation from Canada came from the United Church — a $2,000 cheque sent by Garth Legge, the director of their outreach ministry who had visited me in Latin America. Later, much to my amazement and without my asking for it, a cheque for $5,000 arrived from Scarboro.

One of my annual stops in New York was at Wall Street to have lunch with an aide of Peter Grace. One of the richest Catholics in the US, Grace had made his fortune in ships and airplanes. Many times his assistant offered me money. He assured me that though it was CIA money, it was well-laundered and nobody would ever know its source. Native and American priests working in Latin America were accepting it, he pointed out. I refused.

In Panama, the local head of USAID, the US federal government agency which was pouring out millions to help local farmers, offered me an open cheque. This offer contradicted the comment of the USAID man who had previously spoken of the impossibility of a Catholic priest's receiving money from Washington. In this case, it turned out that there was a slight proviso: I would have to act as advisor to USAID's program. Naturally, I refused. To follow an independent road and refuse to be bought is not easy.

An invitation to me from the government of El Salvador met with the same response. I was most pressingly urged to set up another ICI there, everything to be paid by the government. I well knew, however, that although El Salvador's government was civilian in name, the real power was in the hands of the military and a few rich families. The independence of ICI there would have been a fiction.

Even in Panama, ICI's independence was coming under threat. One of the reasons I had chosen Panama for the school was that the country had never had a military dictator. That had changed in 1968 when Omar Torrijos took over the government. Having lived under Trujillo in the Dominican Republic for so long, I anticipated trouble. Now, two years after Torrijos seized power, I received word through one of his military people that he would like to meet me. I paid no attention.

Some time later, a captain in his army applied to take the course. I refused to accept him. Months passed; then a captain came to tell me that Omar wanted to give me $25,000 to help the school. I rejected it. On hearing of this, my board of directors said I should have accepted it. I had declined, not for fear that the gift would come with strings attached. From my experience of dictators, I knew there would be ropes attached. Later I heard that had I accepted the gift, the general was going to insist on putting an army man on the board of directors.

Some time in the early 1970s Bishop Marcos McGrath asked me to accompany him to Boston for a three-week course at

Harvard on the rural problems of the world. George Cabot Lodge was the host of the gathering of about fifty American experts who had worked in more than a score of countries around the world. One speaker after another described various failed attempts to eliminate poverty. It angered me to see how often the problem was blamed on the poor people themselves. None of the American experts could see that the real cause of much of the poverty was the exploitation of the poor by foreign multinationals. In most cases, of course, native people in government willingly played the game with the foreigners — for a fee.

This question of America's role in Latin America was becoming a burning issue for me. An American professor at the US-sponsored college in the Canal Zone invited me to his home for dinner. My host was not a Catholic but another guest, a young teacher at the college, was a devout Catholic. After a few drinks I thought it was the perfect milieu in which to pose a question. I asked the young man, "Do you really think Americans are the greatest people on earth?"

Although not a drinker, he blew his top and swore at me. Then he said, "Padre, you better believe it. We have built the greatest country and civilization the world has ever seen."

The rest of the meal passed mostly in silence.

I decided the time had come to write a book about my impressions of US involvement in Latin America. Published in 1972, *Who Are the Owners of Latin America?* was written in Spanish (a Chilean friend helped with the writing) and was something of a summary of my talks at ICI. Exposing the utter ruthlessness of American self-interest in Latin America, the book proposed co-ops as a way for Latin Americans to regain control of their own affairs. Because of customs regulations, separate editions had to be printed in four countries. Without my realizing it at the time, the book prepared my departure from Panama.

In the short term, however, my standing with my US contacts was undamaged. Totally unexpectedly, three Harvard University professors came to see me at ICI in 1973. Drs. Owens, Perry and Velasquez were from the Rockefeller Foundation which promotes, among other things, improvements in agriculture and health programs in poor countries. I could hardly believe my ears when they told me they wanted me to set up another ICI in Cali, Colombia's third largest city. The foundation had, to a great extent, funded Cali University and its affiliated hospital, considered the best medical centre in all Colombia. The idea was that ICI would be established on the university campus, all expenses paid by the foundation.

At the insistence of the three visitors, I went to Cali and spent a week talking with the university's president and deans as well as some of the 15,000 students and professors. While it was an impressive operation, most of the beautiful buildings were splashed with graffiti in red paint saying, "Yankee Go Home." Furthermore, most of the university's leaders were conservative Catholics, as one would expect of one of the most conservative Catholic countries on the continent. One of the deans seemed disgusted at my plan of admitting unwashed farmers among the children of the elite.

I spent an hour with the president of the students' body, an amiable young man who was soon to graduate. "Are you one of the rebels who sprayed the anti-American slogans?" I asked.

He admitted he was. "I would not have been chosen president if I were not anti-American." he said.

"Are you still anti-American?"

"Yes, in my guts I am. But I just got married. I must get a job and my only hope is to get one here at the university, so I guess my days for spreading red paint are over."

When Drs. Owens and Perry visited me again in Panama, I told them honestly how I felt about setting up another ICI in Cali. Obviously, many faculty would be against me, and the prospect of the red-paint treatment from the students didn't appeal to me. Hoping to turn them off, I gave them a copy of *Agent for Change*, a brief story of my life, just published by Maryknoll. The book stated my socialism unequivocally.

Undaunted, they insisted that I visit them at their Manhattan headquarters on my next trip north. There, Dr. Owens told me, "Father, I read every line of your book and it did not make me mad at all. You made some generalizations I may not agree with but I see nothing wrong with calling a spade a spade as you did."

All this he said with a nice smile but I never heard from them again. Likely, they were eventually affected by the general reaction to my book, *Who Are the Owners of Latin America?*

Having made some money on the sale of that book, I decided to travel to Tanzania in the hope of meeting President Julius

Nyerere, and getting a first-hand impression of his great experiment in socialism. When I arrived at the home of some Irish Augustinian priests in Dar es Salaam, the superior demanded to see my clerical credentials. He couldn't believe that anyone interested in socialism could be a bona fide priest.

I moved to a cheap but decent hotel that a Maryknoll priest took me to. Luckily, I was able to spend a whole day with the Irish priest (not at all like the suspicious superior mentioned above) who had been a mentor and friend of Julius Nyerere for years. Julius had become a Catholic on graduating from the high school where this priest taught. The priest helped him get a scholarship to Edinburgh University. At the time, his father was chief of the smallest of 120 tribes in the country of some 15 million people. Young Nyerere returned from Scotland in 1954 when his country was getting its independence from England and became the first president. Except for a gap of a few years, he continued to be re-elected president until his retirement.

After a week's delay, during which Nyerere was busy hosting a meeting of leaders of all the African countries, he agreed to see me. The "palace" where we met was a dilapidated old mansion dating from the days before the First World War when the Germans had control of the country. We had a one-hour chat on dozens of topics — religion, the Church and socialism at the top of the list. Julius was one of the most fascinating people I ever met — honest, intelligent, sincere. Some say his effort to build a socialist state ultimately failed because he was too much of an idealist. The 120 tribes of his country weren't easily converted to his vision of co-operation after long years battling each other. And the Church's attitude didn't help. Although only one quarter of the population was Catholic, most Catholic leaders, including two Maryknoll bishops, disapproved of his socialism.

Back in Panama, antagonism towards me was becoming more open. The label "communist" was applied to me quite regularly. Once, a Guatemalan student at ICI met a priest who told him, "Go back home. This Padre Pablo is a communist." By now *Who Are the Owners of Latin America?* had gone through several editions and was especially popular in universities throughout the continent. Since the book's appearance, many of my American friends saw me as an ungrateful traitor, and the US government was becoming more concerned about me.

At a party in the Canal Zone, a tall man came over, introduced himself as "Joe" and more or less monopolized me over drinks. First, he made it clear that he was a devout Catholic. Born in Hawaii, he spoke several languages. He claimed that he was the new labour attaché at the US embassy. "Joe," I said, "I don't believe you. You are the new chief of the CIA." He laughed. Later I learned from a high-placed churchman who was in a position to know the truth that my guess was accurate.

Although I saw no more of "Joe," the CIA was working to undermine me. My US friends in the Canal Zone told me the authorities informed them not to receive me in their homes. They also let me know that my phone was tapped. Soon I was shunned by all friends. One Yankee friend told me: "Your book was the last straw; they tried to buy you; you refused. The next step in the CIA process is petty persecution and isolation from friends, then more if necessary to push you out."

I was isolated, rarely hearing from my family in the north nor from Scarboro. I began drinking quite heavily. That's never a solution, of course, but it made feeling sorry for myself easier. What a damn fool I was, trying to teach justice and help people, I mused. I stopped praying and began to doubt just about everything, including God. My loss of faith wasn't too conspicuous around ICI as I had made it a policy not to impose my priestly office on the place. Now my private celebration of mass became less and less frequent.

I was at a low ebb in my life. The previous low point had been that dark rainy night when I arrived in Chungking, but that physical suffering had been nothing compared to this spiritual darkness. Eventually, I would find that such an ordeal ultimately proves an elixir to one's faith. In fact, I don't think you can have true faith unless you have grappled with doubts. Ahead of me, however, were a couple of years in the spiritual doldrums before I bounced back.

At the nadir of my depression in Panama, the number-one Scarboro boss dropped in. We talked generalities. I didn't reveal my problems. When he departed, I pondered my fate for a few more days. Then I said, "To hell with this." At sixty-five years old, having had a mild heart attack, I was too old to carry on this battle.

I phoned my superior who was in Bogota now and asked him to drop in on his way north. I proposed turning ICI over to Scarboro. He agreed. The problem was where to find a Scarboro priest willing to take the job. He mentioned a man in Domingo. I flew to Domingo but the priest told me he had no interest in co-ops. That didn't matter, I said. His job would be to get funds and run ICI. He consented.

While I was preparing to depart from Panama, an invitation came to give a talk at a continent-wide meeting of co-op leaders in Buenos Aires. About 200 people attended from all the Latin American countries and some observers came from Europe. In my talk I mentioned that co-ops could only function as they should in a socialist milieu. Among the young men present from Chile were two who had attended ICI. Every time I tried to get their attention, they looked away. Later, one of them confided that they were afraid to greet me lest their companions report them. "Remember, we're living under Pinochet," he said.

Since my arrival in Buenos Aires, the country had been rife with rumours of an expected *golpe* (coup) by the military. Not able to judge the chances of that happening, I accepted an invitation to fly south to give a talk at the university of La Plata, the number-two university of the country. Before leaving Buenos Aires, though, I decided to pay a visit to the Canadian Ambassador, a charming Montrealer (whose name, unfortunately, I can't remember). When I told him about my talk, he panicked. I must get out of the country as fast as possible, he insisted. Predicting that the coup could come any hour, he picked up the phone and made a reservation for me on the next flight to Brazil. Then he sent me to my hotel in one of his cars with an armed guard. Next morning, I flew to Sao Paulo.

It was a close call. Thirty-six hours after my departure, the coup came. General Videla took over the country and in the bloody regime that followed tens of thousands of people with socialist tendencies "disappeared".

After my successor arrived at ICI, I stayed on for a few weeks but it was difficult for him to take full charge with me hanging around. The only thing to do was set a date, pack my bags and go. So I did.

In a few months, word came to Canada that a Panamanian who had worked with me was suing ICI for some $40,000. His complaint was based on lies about overtime due him. Apart from the fact that his son-in-law was a lawyer, I knew that no foreigner could ever win a case against a local person. So I flew to Panama and persuaded him to drop his charge in return for $20,000. Scarboro paid it. Eventually, I learned from various people who knew him that the complainant had wanted to get control of ICI's valuable real estate. A few years later, Scarboro again had to pay out a considerable sum to settle fraudulent claims from employees who had been fired. Such is life in Latin America.

My successor ran ICI for five years. For the next seven years, a layman associated with Scarboro headed up the school. Now another Scarboro priest heads it up. Today, he tells me, most of ICI's funding comes from Europe, largely from ecumenical groups. Some funding comes from Scarboro and other sources in Canada. No help comes from the US.

To date, some 3,000 or more students have taken ICI's fifty major courses. Other thousands have taken shorter ICI courses. Considering the rapid demise of three similar schools founded around the same time as ICI, some say its survival for more than a quarter of a century is something of a miracle.

Chapter Thirteen

Culture Shock in Canada

There is a young lilac bush in a flower bed in front of our headquarters here at 2685 Kingston Road in Scarborough. Someone gave me the lilac a few years ago by way of a birthday present. It sat in a pot by the door for a long time because I couldn't bring myself to plant it on this property. It didn't seem that I had any right to do so; I didn't feel a co-owner of this place. Eventually, a younger priest who was one of the superiors then asked me if he could plant it.

So there it stands and it will probably be blooming long after I have departed the scene. For me, it will always be a symbol of my feeling of not belonging here in my supposed home.

It was May 1976 when I arrived back at Scarboro to stay for the rest of my days. I brought with me from Panama all my worldly belongings — two bags filled mostly with books. Through the years I had been here only for brief visits. My expectations for retirement here were largely negative. Among the twenty-five or so permanent residents, I could not count one as a friend. My reputation had gone before me and fellow members of our society had put many labels on me, few of them complimentary. Maybe I should mention some of them (no doubt some were applied half in jest, half in earnest): I was a communist; a Marxist; I didn't believe in God; I was anti-Church; a radical; I had a one-track mind (justice); I was anti-social; I was anti-woman. The list could go on. Little wonder that I felt ill at ease. Not that there wasn't some truth to some of the charges, at least from the point of view of my colleagues. After all, the majority of them are the old-time conservatives, religiously speaking, so it's understandable that they would be super-sensitive to my radical side.

A major blow came less than twenty-four hours after my arrival. At the dining table, I encountered two young Panamanian university professors who had been on my teaching staff in Panama. They were here to give talks at a Canada-wide congress on social justice. More than 200 people were attending. Naturally I was curious. When I expressed my interest to the Scarboro priest in charge of the congress, he said I was forbidden to attend. Why? Because I had not sent in an application. No invitation had been sent to me, I pointed out. Surely there might be room for one more person among 200? "You cannot attend," he insisted. Right from the start, it was clear that, thanks to my reputation as a rebel, there was going to be opposition to me in my own home.

The next ordeal was a gradual one: trying to understand the Canadian mentality on many scores. After a dozen years, I am still learning things Canadian. What makes the process hard is that most people expect you to see things as they do. They do not realize that you have been away from Canada most of your life, with peoples of other cultures. Going into another culture, you expect things to be different; you try to take them in stride and adjust to them. Frustrations are plentiful, to be sure, but they are easier to cope with than those you meet on re-entering the culture of your birthplace.

One of the things that bewildered me on returning to Canada was the way people were always tossing off casual invitations like, "You must come over to dinner." Thinking that these remarks implied some sort of commitment, I suffered agonies wondering what was supposed to happen next — was I expected to call and make a date or was I just supposed to wait by the phone? As time passed and no confirmation came, I couldn't help wondering if I had inadvertently done something to sour the budding friendship.

Some months after my settling into retirement here at h.q., the superiors asked me to represent the society at meetings with the Church Task Forces, a group of a dozen or more men and women dedicated to studying social justice issues here in Canada and in other parts of the world, especially Latin America. I agreed to give it a try. I had never met any of the people, the great majority of whom were members of Protestant churches. Two Catholic priests were in the group. The funding for the task force came largely from the churches, including money from our society. I was the oldest person in the group and the only person who had worked in the Third World. Most of the others had made short visits to different countries in the Third World. They dealt with bankers, big business people and government people in Canada.

It was the coldest group of people I ever related to. Two or three of them shook hands when I entered the meeting. Nobody asked my name. After attending several meetings, I dared to speak up when someone was giving a report on a visit to a Third World country. I asked a pointed question based on my experience. It soon became apparent I was in hostile company. Probably my age was against me, or, more important, my lifetime of experience in the Third World working for social justice.

Someone told me that a nice young man in the group had been married three times. Coming, as I did, from a culture where one of the primary aims of social justice work was to persuade men to take responsibility by committing themselves to one woman, it seemed incongruous that this man could be a champion of social justice. I am not judging the man, merely pointing out how his situation presented one of many puzzles in my efforts to re-integrate into the North American culture.

After nearly a dozen meetings, I withdrew from the group. Maybe, I mused, I just don't fit into Canadian society. To be fair to these people in the Church Task Forces, I feel sure they are doing effective work trying to bring ethical and moral principles to bear on important groups such as bankers, business people and government. They're to be commended for demanding justice for our native people as well as bringing these same values to peoples in the Third World. It was possibly unfair to expect me to join the group when I was going through cultural shock trying to understand this country and its people. I was not aware of how cold the Canadian people are in comparison to the warm people with whom I had been living.

I also briefly tried to see if I could help in a parish. That too failed. For the homily, I began telling the people in the parish church what I had been doing with my life. After about two minutes, I stopped and asked for questions. One of the first hands raised was that of a young woman with a baby in her arms. "I think you are a communist," she said. "Thank you," was my reply, and I continued saying mass. As far as I can see, affluent Canadians don't want to hear about poor people, their suffering, how they are exploited or anything about social justice. This is probably true of most prosperous people everywhere, including clergy.

The third jolt, perhaps the biggest of all, came a year or so after settling in here. A woman a generation or so younger than I, a Catholic, separated from her husband, and with several kids, saw me saying mass and preaching a few times. She sensed, as women are so apt to do, my frustration in trying to adjust to my new home. She invited me to live with her and her family of three children. This was no gesture of altruistic hospitality. She was clearly looking for a bed-mate. Hard as it was for me to believe, she had picked me.

A brief rundown on this Scarboro family in which I live is in order. A Toronto priest, Monsignor John Mary Fraser, founded our society in 1918. His objective was to train priests exclusively for China. Slightly more than 200 young men have been ordained in the past 74 years.

The following statistics are approximately accurate:

- Present membership — 93
- Members deceased — 54
- Members who left the society (the great majority left the priesthood; a few joined other Church groups) — 58
- Members living in our eight mission areas (a few of them retired) — 43
- The remaining 50 live in North America, some retired
- About 25 permanent residents here at 2685 Kingston Road; about 12 of them are retired or semi-retired because of age or sickness
- One quarter of the living membership is over 70 years old; only two are under 40.

The routine called "community life" works here much as in other religious houses. There are no longer bells to tell you what to do, as in seminary days, but there are necessarily some unwritten rules in order to keep harmony in the family. Priests are free to come and go as they like but most of our time is spent in our "cells" (to use the old monastic term) which are quite comfortable. Our days pass in reading, writing, keeping up with the news on the tube and, for many, a kind of addiction to watching sports. Older priests usually prefer to say their masses privately, while younger men tend to celebrate their masses with others.

There are few close friendships among the men. Though there is no rule against it, few men visit others in their rooms. For the most part, we are loners. The whole community comes together only for food and drink; a happy hour (thirty minutes) precedes supper. At meals, people sit at tables with others to their liking, though all are free to sit where they please. We are blessed with a wonderful staff of employees who serve probably the best institutional food in the country. Through much of the year, our dining room caters to a variety of groups, largely church-related and of different denominations, ranging from twenty up to fifty, who come here for week-end meetings.

After supper, television brings some together to see the news or to watch baseball and hockey. Some go to movies or spend evenings with their friends in the city.

The twenty-five residents here are as varied a group as one could find in any religious house. In fact, there may even be more oddballs here than in most religious communities. Few of us would meet the so-called standard of normalcy. Even among celibate priests, those who choose to go to the missions are generally considered odd. If we weren't a-typical before going to the missions, living with people of other cultures for long years makes us different from the rest of our compatriots.

Among us there are all kinds of addictions. A fondness for alcohol is one addiction that I am tainted with. It came to me in my genes, I guess, if for no other reason. Perhaps it is also a form of compensation. To become a priest in the Church required me to be celibate. I accepted the price tag — a high price indeed — not because I liked the idea of celibacy. After all, I am human. I have kept my vow, paying the price every day of my life. (To be more precise, I kept my promise physically but not mentally. I have broken my promise mentally thousands of times.) Suppressing the physical urge has its effects on one's mind and soul — one seeks compensations. That leads to addictions, substitutes of many kinds. In my own case, it's alcohol.

The media here in North America have been running wild with stories about priests deviating in different ways from their vow of celibacy, some on the score of homosexuality, others by abuse of young people. Some surveys report that as many as fifty percent of priests have slipped from their vow of celibacy but many came back on track. No doubt some of the men in our community have fallen in one way or another. That is their problem and it does not much affect the other members of our community.

To my mind, the addiction that's hardest on others is loquaciousness — talking incessantly. Though perhaps not an addiction in the strict sense, loquaciousness is rampant among us. I admit to indulging in it when sipping my Scotch. Some would explain this trait as the result of our having lived alone on the missions for long years. Others would explain it as the superego asserting itself. In the case of some men, it simply is their nature.

Another irritant among us, especially in the case of the loquacious ones, is the natural tendency of a missionary to talk about his experiences in the country where he worked. If he worked in Japan, he talks about Japan and its people. The men beside him at the table talk about a Latin American country. They probably have no interest in Japan. They may even hate everything about Japan. Those of us who served in China certainly did.

Sycophants usually exist in all religious groups, as in organizations everywhere. Luckily, as I see it, our community has few of them. Irritants to their companions, sometimes even to those holding authority, sycophants ingratiate themselves with authorities by flattery and other means of gaining favours and promotion. Weak superiors tolerate them and even seek them out.

As for the character of superiors, the old adage of Lord Acton that "power tends to corrupt" applies to many but not to all. Through the years a couple of dozen or more of our priests have been placed in authority as general superiors or superiors in regional missions. The great majority of these Scarboro superiors have left office with no scars from having had authority, but a few bear small scars or blemishes.

In my opinion, the ideal superior should be representative of the group, a just person with good common sense. He should not be the brightest person in the group, lest he expect too much of others who do not measure up to his ideas. He should not be a workaholic lest he demand too much work of others since not all priests are fond of work. If he is a person who seeks authority and power over others, he should never be selected as a superior.

Granted, it would be difficult for any leader to suit all of us. Each one of us is different in a variety of ways. Each has his own personality, mannerisms, foibles and so on. Yes, from my viewpoint, we have indeed just about all the types in our society of nearly 100 priests. Each of us has his own ideology, his own interpretation of religion, of vice and virtue and so on. Some have excess male hormones, others excess female hormones; a few have balanced hormones.

"Know thyself" is a fine motto — impossible to practice. As for my place in this myriad of personalities here, my guess is that my companions might give me a five on a scale of ten — average. My score might be higher if I weren't so damn radical. People are put off by my Leftist ideas, my obsession with justice, my failure (unusual in Church circles) to kow-tow to people with conservative ideas, including and especially those wielding power, starting with the Pope. This iconoclasm doesn't sit well with the typically straight-laced members of the community. About one such man, somebody asked, "I wonder if Father So-and-So sleeps with his roman collar on?"

To live in community with other celibates, all of them afflicted with at least some addictions, is not easy. The frustrations stemming from the priestly vows militate against smooth interpersonal relations. To make matters worse, many of the priests are now elderly and suffering from physical and mental ills. Given the difficulties involved, several of our men, including those retired and those still working, refuse to live here.

Ironically, the chronic problem for all of us living in this community is loneliness. The loneliness that comes from a sense of uselessness is probably the hardest thing old priests have to contend with. It is less a problem for lay people who often are consoled by their children and grandchildren. Some cultures, for example that of China, hold elderly people in respect. This is not part of Canadian culture where old people are stored away in "warehouses." Some old priests live out their last years in these places. In general, old priests are, if not ignored, merely tolerated.

Their talents and experiences are not considered of much importance by young superiors.

Some of the issues that divide us here at Scarboro have been mentioned. Still another one is how we see the foreign policy of the nation, and of our neighbour to the south. This issue divides many Canadians, even members of the same family. It especially affects some of our men who have worked in Latin America. For others living here at 2685 Kingston Road, it is not an issue at all. Politics does not interest them. A small number of people here in the house are anti-American like myself. Then there are others who are pro-American even more so, some of them, than they are pro-Canadian.

Unlike the strictly "sacramental" priests, I was brought close to politics by my work in the social economic field. My mission was to liberate people from those who exploited them. I think it to be an inherent right of every person to be free in his quest for his own development, to be the master of his own destiny. With this kind of thinking, logically, I am opposed to the hegemony our southern neighbour has assumed over the continent of peoples living south of the Rio Grande. My sojourn of thirteen years in Panama, the country that divides our two continents, was the ideal opportunity to learn about US control of other places. My eyes were opened after a short time.

Now, with the end of the Cold War and the fall of the other superpower (USSR), it appears from recent events in the Middle East that the US is about to extend its hegemony to that part of the world as well. One of the best expressions of my view of this issue was written several years ago by an eminent American historian, Henry Steele Commager (no relative of mine):

> Because now, as in the past, we are confident that we represent freedom, law, order, justice and the wave of the future...we feel justified in passing policies of intervention, subversion and aggression which we have judged to be reprehensible in others. We have long known that "power tends to corrupt" but we do not think that power corrupts us, or can ever corrupt us because we always wield it for the benefit of mankind. Only a people infatuated with their own moral virtue, their own superiority, their own exemption from the ordinary laws of history and of morality, could so uncritically embrace a double standard of morality

as have the American People. Only a people whose tradition of isolation has made them immune to world opinion could be surprised that they have forfeited the respect of much of mankind by their misuse of power throughout the globe.

Throughout my life, most of my friends have been Americans. To be honest, I prefer them to Canadians. Americans are more friendly, more generous and warmer than Canadians. In their hospitality, Americans are impressively welcoming and considerate. Canadians are offhand, diffident, almost crude. Yet, even with the closest American friends, there was always that hidden barrier; once their nation or government was criticized, the friendship ended. It is a pity that people endowed with many beautiful qualities and blessed in many ways by the Creator are so blind to their country's faults.

Another source of contention here at Scarboro is the decision some dozen years ago to accept lay men and women as associate members of the society. Many of the younger Scarboro priests approve of the program. But few older men like it. Most of the lay people in the program are young women and they often join the priests at their meals and at the happy hour. Although this is accepted Scarboro policy, it's not popular with all clerical members, especially older men. We were not trained to work in close association with young women.

In any case, the plan has been less than successful. Of the sixty young men and women who have been in the program, only six, as far as I know, remain members. This pattern is consistent with the history of the lay missionary movement. Previously I mentioned one of the first programs for sending young lay men and women to the missions. It was called AID, based in Patterson, New Jersey. I was acquainted with the founders and some of the members. It folded after a few years. Next in the US was the program called PAVLA (Papal Volunteers for Latin America). It likewise failed.

In spite of these disappointments, I am in favour of young lay people going to the missions. They can play roles that priests cannot. Native people will open up to lay missionaries in a way that they won't to priests who are still very much regarded with awe and fear in Latin American and other cultures. Standing as proof of my support for lay missioners is the fact, mentioned earlier, that almost forty years ago, I asked a lay married couple from the US to help me in my work in the Dominican Republic. The school I founded in Panama trains lay people to work especially in the field of social justice, a field so few priests see as important.

Yet another issue that can be divisive is social justice. A small number of our men are firmly committed to it; most are indifferent or opposed. Liberation theology, born in Latin America, has formed a basis for social justice work in many parts of the world. However, it is not popular with many in our group — nor with many in the Vatican, starting with the Pope. Our society has a strong reputation nationally for social justice, largely because our monthly magazine runs many articles on it. On this score we are, as a group, over-rated, as I see it. Most of our men are what may be called "sacramental priests." They're more interested in providing the mass and the sacraments than in working for more humane living conditions for their people.

Not long ago, an item in *The Tablet* reported the recommendation of a Vatican relief agency, Caritas International, that student priests should be directly involved in working with the poor. The Vatican said: "Direct involvement with the underprivileged and marginalized leads to a deeper appreciation of the gifts of life and to personal maturity, deep joy and constant hope." The statement added, "In order to be effective a priest's formation must concentrate on the social welfare field and consider it as an '*integral part of evangelization.*'"

"Social welfare", as the Vatican calls it, is one thing but social justice is another. It is rare, very rare indeed, that the words "social justice" appear in any documents emanating from the Vatican. A few years ago, in one of the reports from the synod of bishops, the words did appear. The statement said, as best I can recall, that "social justice should be a constitutive part of evangelization."

In my old age, it is consoling to see that social justice and concern for the poor are finally getting a hearing, at least in a small way, among some Church people. It's very gratifying to see a few brave souls spreading this gospel. At the top of that list, I put the great Brazilian Archbishop Helder Camara. In 1962, when I first met him, he was one of the auxiliary bishops of Rio. At that time, I asked how he felt about the Vatican's call for North

America to send 50,000 missionaries and $50 million to the Latin American Church. Camara's reply was something to the effect that, "We don't want that kind of help. What we want is that the north treat us with justice, give us fair prices for the goods we ship them."

St. Thomas Aquinas tells us that justice is the chief of all the virtues. He defines justice as "the strong and firm will to give to each his due." From my point of view, charity and justice must go together — they make a marriage. One without the other will be neither justice nor charity. It is good to feed the poor (charity) but it is much more important to eradicate the causes of poverty (justice). And yet, priority could be given to charity since it leads one to justice: if you don't first have some love for people, you won't care about obtaining justice for them. Charity should, then, act as a catalyst. All too often, unfortunately, the charitable impulse stops with warm feelings that can stifle justice. Charity is comforting; it soothes the conscience. Justice, on the other hand, challenges it.

The first pope to speak out on justice was Leo XIII, who reigned just a century ago. Few people in high or low levels of the Church paid much attention to his teachings on social justice. In a way, it's understandable that social justice was ignored for so long. After all, the Church was ruled by Europeans who, in large numbers, thought that God made two kinds of people — those who ruled and those who obeyed. For centuries, the Church accepted slavery. A gross injustice, slavery was a denial of human dignity and the rights of the human. If the Church took so long to see the sinfulness of that, it's no wonder that justice still isn't a very high priority for many.

At one time, I dreamed of founding a secular institute (a group of clerics and lay people working together with Church approval) to promote justice. When I mentioned the plan to Bishop McNulty of Buffalo, he told me the difficulties Cardinal Cushing of Boston had in getting approval for his group of priests, the St. James Society, who work in Latin America. If Rome moved so slowly even for a Cardinal, there wasn't much chance of my making any headway. Bishop McGrath of Panama liked my idea and was willing to help but I dropped the plan and ended up laughing at my presumption. Who was I to start a religious group? One has to have a certain degree of holiness. That lets me out.

I want to tell a story, little known in Church circles, about the power of justice in drawing people to God. I learned this story while living a few months in Calcutta with Belgian Jesuits. Around the end of the nineteenth century, their men had been working among the Indians for several years without attracting many to the Church. But then, Father Constant Lievens, a young priest, got to the root of the tragic plight of the people: they had been losing their land. They were exploited by merchants, government authorities and especially the local policemen. Lievens made an in-depth study of the land laws of the country. He travelled by horseback all over the area telling the people, most of whom were illiterate, about the laws and about ways to defend themselves and hold on to their land. He was known to spend entire nights with villagers explaining these matters.

As his fame spread throughout northeastern India, whole villages of people came to him wanting to enter the Church. Within a few years Ranchi became a diocese with over 300,000 new Christians. After only six years, worn out by work, Father Lievens was called back to his homeland where he died before reaching forty years of age. He was succeeded by another Belgian Jesuit, Father Hoffman, who organized co-ops among the people. In the small town near Brussels where Father Lievens was born, there is now a life-sized statue of him on horseback.

Lievens' story shows how social justice can lead people to religion. Recently, people have started asking me, "Do you still believe in socialism after what has happened to the USSR and Eastern Europe?" My answer is affirmative. I never believed in the kind of socialism that prevailed in those countries. It was not democratic and might better have been described as state capitalism controlled by dictators.

Several times the world media has reported the story of the meeting of Lenin, the leader of the Russian revolution of 1917, and A. Hammer, his wealthy American friend (who just died, well into his nineties). Lenin admitted to Hammer that communism would not succeed economically. The question might then be asked, why did Lenin promote the revolution? The obvious answer is that he wanted power over other people.

The fall of the communist regimes does not, however, make capitalism of the west more acceptable. Western capitalism is immoral, anti-human and anti-Christian to a great extent. It is built on greed and selfishness, human vices which, unfortunately, are stronger in most of us than the opposite virtues.

Granted, socialist systems based on an appeal to the finer human qualities have almost always failed. Sweden, probably the best example of an exception, has one of the highest living standards in the world, with an economy built largely on co-ops. This kind of democratic socialism has much in common with Christianity. Both aim for high ideals and demand much from their adherents. Why, then, hasn't Christianity had more impact on social structures — given the fact that almost one quarter of all peoples are Christians? Perhaps because many are so in name only.

Some biblical scholars, Christians and Jews, believe that God chose the Jewish people under Abraham because they, in contrast to their neighbours, were inclined toward a socialist way of life. This may have had something to do with the fact that the Jews were poorer than many of their neighbours. Certainly there were other peoples in that part of the ancient world who had higher civilizations. Several Old Testament texts promote social democracy against private ownership of land:

> Leviticus, 23: The land shall not be sold in perpetuity, for the land is mine and you are but aliens who have become my tenants...

> Deuteronomy, 15: At the end of every seven years, you shall have a relaxation of debts...every creditor shall relax his claim on what he has lent to his neighbour...if your kinsmen in any community is in need in the land which the Lord is giving you, you shall open your hand to him and freely lend him enough to meet his need.

> Leviticus, 15: During the seventh year, the land shall have a complete rest...a sabbath of the land...while the land has its sabbath, all its produce will be equally divided for you yourself, for your hired help and the tenants that live with you.

Certainly, socialism was the way of life of the first Christians,
who were mostly Jews. Scripture shows that they had virtual
credit unions and co-ops, sharing their possessions with each
other. This underground socialism enabled them to survive
under the cruel Roman emperors.

Many of the Fathers of the early Church favoured socialism.
St. John Chrysostom wrote:

> The community of goods is far more suitable to us and is
> better grounded in nature than private property...the rich
> are in possession of the goods of the poor, even if they have
> acquired them legally...all the wealth of the world belongs
> to you and to others in common, as the sun, air, earth and all
> the rest.

From St. Ambrose came this searing indictment:

> Think you that you commit no injustice by keeping to
> yourself alone what would be the means of life to many? It
> is the bread of the hungry that you cling to; it is the clothing
> of the naked that you lock up; the money you bury is the
> redemption of the poor.

Saint Gregory of Nissa and the well known St. Augustine were in
favour of socialism. The latter said that people had a right to
property they needed but any surplus should be given to those in
need.

As a footnote to this subject, it strikes me as odd that, in spite
of these strong endorsements of socialism from the early fathers,
the Church has opposed its application to society at large. Yet the
Church imposes it on the million and a half members of religious
orders — priests, brothers and sisters — who live a kind of
enforced socialism in their communities.

The liberal-conservative split that has erupted in all ranks of
the Church since the Second Vatican Council in the 1960s is, of
course, reflected in our family here at Scarboro. Those on the
right want to stick with the old time religion and refuse to accept
change. Those on the left accept the changes called for by Vatican
Council II and want even more.

Before the council, Catholics, especially priests, were a pretty
smug crowd. We held all the truths for salvation in our hip
pockets. Indeed, 100 years ago at the First Vatican Council, popes
were said to be infallible under certain conditions. Though that

council did not declare priests and bishops to be infallible, many of us really thought we were in a way. Rarely in history has the hierarchy of the Catholic Church admitted mistakes. However, twenty-five years ago the council announced that it was time to update the Church, to get rid of much of its medieval thinking. That opened up a Pandora's box. Large and vociferous groups of people are pushing for ever greater reforms in keeping with the spirit of the council. On the other hand, much that the council called for has been ignored by Catholics at all levels including, as I see it, the present pope. While such debate rages within Catholic ranks, millions of people, including priests, have left those ranks.

With change occurring in our world at a pace never before known in history, I think it is time to call another council to thoroughly revamp the Church. To put it another way, we are in another Reformation, but one very different from the one four centuries ago when Martin Luther broke away and started a new religion. We need a Catholicism that thoroughly addresses itself to the "Signs of the Times", to use the phrase coined at Vatican II. If the Church is not relevant to the world and its people, there is no point in its existence. The days of an Imperial Vatican and of a pope issuing decrees from his ivory tower are passed. That worked for centuries while most lay people had little or no education and blind obedience seemed appropriate. Not any more.

Yet Rome remains intransigent. Look at the celibacy issue. Tens of thousands of parishes in the world are priestless today and the number is increasing. To cope with this shortage, two solutions are being proposed: the ordaining of married men and of women. We know that the requirement of celibacy is not based on scripture and only became an obligation in the Roman rite in the twelfth century. Furthermore, imposing celibacy as a condition of being a priest is contrary to the cultures of many peoples throughout the world — in Africa, Asia, and, to some degree, Latin America, wherever *machismo* is part of the culture. It has been said, for example, that in Zaire celibate men are seen as less than males and are, therefore, not respected, but seen as suspect.

But Rome refuses to alter the status quo. This Vatican obsession with a celibate, male priesthood could destroy our religion. Will Rome ever admit that celibacy is not working and never did in many places? Not likely. Given the imperialistic style of the Pope and the curia, they're impervious to pressures from former priests, to arguments based on studies by sociologists and psychologists, and to Gallup poles.

The Rites Controversy in China was an example of how hard it is to move Rome. That's why we need another Council in which the whole Church, not just the curia, can argue for necessary reforms. One of the most significant, I feel, will be the approach to the priesthood. In the future, a candidate for the priesthood might be chosen by the people of the community where he (assuming we're still talking about a male priesthood) lives, by the people who know him and his family, rather than by far away celibate academics. The latter, of course, with their expertise will prepare the candidate for his vocation.

Such a process of selection of future priests might help screen out those with unworthy motives. While one might assume, without undue naïveté, that the primary motive of most candidates for the priesthood has usually been praiseworthy — to serve God and his people — there may be various secondary reasons: a life of prestige, a comfortable home, food and economic security, work that is not hard, power over people, the chance of becoming a bishop. Also, there are clergy benefits — discounts and so on. There are sops to one's vanity: the roman collar attracts respect and, often, love (sometimes, hate too). There is an old story which says: if you put a roman collar on a broom stick and march it down Fifth Avenue, women will follow in droves.

As for the selection of bishops, they should be chosen by the clergy and the lay people of the diocese, not by bureaucrats in Rome. This is not a new nor a radical idea. Centuries ago, the great bishop of Milan, St. Ambrose, was acclaimed as bishop after the people heard his powerful sermons. Ambrose had not even been baptized yet.

Bishops are priests in technicolour, who wear chains, rings, pectoral crosses and high mitres. It would seem that the Church has ordained that bishops be so dressed to engender respect and perhaps fear in lesser mortals. This ploy has probably worked well in the past. As the faithful become more sophisticated, ring-kissing and genuflecting to a bishop are disappearing. This, I think, is a good thing for the bishops. Unless a bishop is a man with super humility, all this adulation naturally tends to make him feel like a small god.

Having known many priests who became bishops, I find it remarkable how many of these good men did change with the office. The adulation got to them. But it may not be just the adulation that brought the change; it may be the power they wielded, power over people. What a frightening thing power is. The power of the natural world, whether it comes from an earthquake or a hydrogen bomb, rivets people with fear. Maybe spiritual power, if misused, is even more frightening.

So, the picture of our family life here at Scarboro is not one of unmitigated harmony. Lay people who have never lived in a religious community may think my observations on Scarboro harsh. Men and women living in other religious groups will, I think, agree for the most part, that the picture I have painted is accurate. Despite all, perhaps there is, down underneath, more caring for each other than we admit. After all, we are males and many of us have lived in cultures where *machismo* is strong. Some of it rubs off after years. While Latin machos demonstrate affection easily, we don't.

For those who are willing to try it, this is a model milieu to practise charity. That's the glue that holds us together — the queen of virtues, the most difficult one to practise. How profound the wisdom of the Bible when it speaks of charity and the beam and mote in one's eyes. (Matthew 7: 3-5) How often the irritating defect we see in the other is the same defect we have in ourselves.

I do my best to get along with my fellow priests. Often it falls short. For me, it is only a few more years. But I dread the thought that I might have to spend eternity with many of my companions from 2685 Kingston Road and I'm sure many of them feel the same about me.

Chapter Fourteen

The Home Stretch

In my first year in retirement, I was asked to give a talk at the Sunday mass at the Newman Club (the site of my career as a wallflower at student tea parties). My brief talk was my usual *spiel* on the work I had been doing in Latin America. A teacher in the audience, someone I never met before or since, phoned a freelance producer of CBC radio shows to tell him about my talk. The young freelancer, Dave Tarnow, phoned me and we met. His background, though he was born in Toronto, was different from that of the other young people I had met. A Jew, he had lived in Israel several years and also in Paris. He had a feeling for the poor, for justice. Our thinking on many things was similar.

Dave began taping our informal talks. The next thing I knew, he had finished making a one-hour documentary about me. It played on CBC radio across the country. Then he wanted to do more — to make a TV documentary of my life. For several years, he tried to sell the idea to film makers. Finally, in 1989 he succeeded.

The company that made the film "Padre Pablo: Fighter for Justice" is CANAMEDIA. Its owner is Les Harris. Working with him is Andrew Johnson. They have produced more than two dozen documentaries. Les came to Canada from England fourteen years ago, having previously worked with London's BBC. Andrew was born here in Toronto. They both told me that they have some Jewish blood. Neither is Catholic but we got along famously.

These three, along with a camera man and an audio man, took me to Latin America where we spent eight days filming in

Panama, then another eight in the Dominican Republic. The camera and audio men were excellent companions and experts at their jobs. Both had worked in Russia and China with the well-known Peter Ustinov, making his television series on those countries. The five young men in our crew treated me better than a favourite grandfather. We had to live together in the same hotels because each night the film taken during the day had to be reviewed and plans for the following day made.

The completed one-hour film played on the air from coast to coast in Canada as well as in several other countries. Almost all the feedback, some sixty letters and phone calls as well as visits from people, was positive. Most of it came from Ontario. Very few people in Cape Breton saw the documentary because of blackouts due to storms. Similarly, there was a blackout in Toronto when an abridged version of the film appeared on CBC's "Man Alive". (Later the full version was shown on Vision TV, a religious cable channel.) There has been no response from the several million Canadians who are members of credit unions and co-ops. To my surprise, however, eight communications came from cousins, nephews and nieces whom I had never met even though they have been living in the Toronto area for decades. It sounded from some of their remarks as if they saw me, "Padre Pablo", as a hero. That's hard to believe because Canadians hate heroes, in contrast to Americans who adore them, as demonstrated by the way Hollywood makes millions creating them. Most of my companions living here in the house made no comment on the film; a few said they liked it.

For the past ten years or so, Dave Tarnow has been closer to me than any of my priest companions. We agree on many things; religion rarely enters our conversation. A special quality of his, one which I so admire, is his persistence. He never gave up seeking his goal of making that documentary. I guess he and I are alike in that quality. If the documentary has done some good, and the feedback tells me it did, the credit must go to Dave.

Apart from him, I have had few friends. The book of Sirach says, "A faithful friend is a sturdy shelter; he who finds one, finds a treasure. A faithful friend is beyond price." But I am not good at making friends. Maybe I am timid in this respect. For the most part, those who have been closest to me have been people who, in a sense, latched on to me. On the missions, of course, loneliness is inevitable. While the missionary has lots of contact with his parishioners, often more than he wishes, true friendship is not easy to achieve among people of another culture. Trying to cope here in our Scarboro family, my policy is to try and get along with everybody. Having a really close friend might militate against this policy.

Nor have friendships attempted outside the community worked very well for me. Not long after I moved in here at Scarboro, one of our young priests began having a Sunday mass for young men and women who were not comfortable attending their local parish churches. Not the typical Canadian Catholics, many of these young people were interested in social issues. Most of them, around the age of forty, were teachers. I was asked a few times to say mass for them and to talk about my work on the missions. In time, several of them picked me up to take in some talks in different places in the city. I also went to the homes of a few of them. Contacts with these people gave me better insights into things Canadian and I am grateful for that. However, both the age gap and my background often proved, in time, obstacles to any close relationships. Unlike many of our priests, I found visiting homes boring. I suspect my visits were tedious for my hosts too.

Two years or so after retiring here, I had my second heart attack. The first, a mild one, had occurred in Panama a few years before. This second one occurred here at headquarters early in the morning. It was a Sunday morning. I had been sitting in the chapel and felt chilled when I went to say mass. But I carried on. Walking to my room after breakfast, I was accosted in the corridor by one of our young priests, Father Bill Smith. (He recently died of a heart attack.) "Harvey, you are dying," he said.

What did he see? I was not feeling any pain or discomfort. Perhaps my face was ashen. At any rate, he told me later, "I saw death written in your face." Strange how others can read our faces and we cannot see our own. He rushed me to the hospital where a young doctor confirmed what Bill had said. When the doctor left the room for a moment, I heard him tell a nurse "Call a priest if that old man is a Catholic." After nearly two weeks, half the time in intensive care, I returned home.

A couple of months after that heart attack, I received a surprising invitation to return to the Dominican Republic. The government representative in charge of co-ops wanted me to visit various groups to bolster the movement. The government promised to pay all my expenses. And it kept its promise. So I was back doing the kind of work I had done twenty years before — travelling the country, meeting old friends and new ones, talking to groups. Now there were over 100 people in the government office for co-ops, although few of them had much knowledge of the co-op philosophy. Twice, the president of the country asked me to give talks to his cabinet, a group of over eighty people.

Little by little, though, I began to realize that I was being used by the director of the national federation. When farmers saw us together, they concluded that we were friends. To them, that meant things in the federation were going well, which was far from the case. Money was being badly managed and used to pay off "yes" men. So I went home to Canada.

A year later I weakened and accepted another invitation to the Dominican Republic but found myself caught in the crossfire between two groups struggling for control of the co-op movement. Former students of mine were in both groups. To live in this warring zone without anyone's accepting my advice was too much of a strain, not to mention the fact that I wasn't helping anybody. Again, I packed it in.

A couple of years later, the whole mess blew up. The government and an international funding organization took over the co-op centre I had built years earlier. Though the national federation almost ceased to exist, a number of co-ops continued to function and still do. Sadly, though, on my last visit to the country, I discovered that the school I had built nearly forty years earlier had been torn down and replaced by some high-rise buildings. The national directors who had taken over the movement had sold the property and run off with the money. The land alone would have been worth millions of dollars. I left with an empty feeling, never wanting to see the place again.

Then, in 1982, came a different sort of invitation. Father Bill Smith was project director for the Canadian Catholic Office of Development and Peace (CCODP). As much of their funding went to support co-ops in the Third World, Father Smith suggested I make a trip, paid for by CCODP, to evaluate co-ops in the Central Americas and the countries of the Caribbean Basin.

Because of the constant turmoil in Latin America, the story of the co-ops in the sixteen countries I visited was a sad one—many more failures than successes. Not all the blame could be put on political and economic chaos, though. Mismanagement and stealing of funds by co-op members and directors were chronic.

Two exceptions were the co-op movements in Puerto Rico and Jamaica. In the case of Puerto Rico, the movement had been started among the upper middle class by government employees and university professors. Archbishop Jim Davis of San Juan had asked me to train four of his priests at my school in the Dominican Republic. One of them, who became known as "Father Dynamite", founded about fifty co-ops among rural people in less than a year.

In its early years, though, the co-op movement in Puerto Rico had barely touched the rural population. My cousin, Father Joe MacDonald from Antigonish, had played a prominent role at that time. It astonished me to discover his long-lasting bitterness towards my work. While attending a co-op conference in Puerto Rico, I visited him where he was in retirement in an old people's home. He threatened me saying, "If you ever come to this island again I will kill you." How does one explain such animosity? Although he had battled alcoholism, he was not drinking at the time so I don't think his threat can be attributed to the bottle. Bishop Davis told me he thought my cousin was virtually a schizophrenic by the time of his death a couple of years after that.

In Jamaica, credit unions were begun by a Boston Jesuit, Father John Sullivan. When I asked the leaders of the co-ops in Jamaica why they had been so successful, they answered: "We don't have any special love for the British but we have to admit that they gave us some worthwhile things. They taught us to respect laws—an attitude not common among Latins. They also gave us a good educational system and taught us the importance of education. Almost all members of our co-ops are literate and even in the early years directors of our co-ops were well qualified. Money was never stolen or mismanaged. Only recently, have we had to deal with that."

Respect for law and order, as demonstrated by the Jamaicans, not only makes co-ops possible but is vital to democracy. More than a few Latins told me that involvement in co-ops was their first experience of what democracy really meant. The kind of democracy that prevailed in Latin American countries not under dictatorships was more like oligarchy. I personally knew a man who had been selected by the rich to represent their party in presidential elections of his country. Naturally, with their backing, he won. But when he suggested reforms not congenial to the wealthy, they told the man he must either back down or resign or something worse would happen to him. In other words, he had to play their game. On finishing his term of office, he went to live in exile a very rich man.

These comments about the difficulty of finding honesty in Latin America might seem harsh. In my early years there, however, I was comparing politics in that part of the world with the Canada I had known as a young man. Now I am learning that Canada is much changed. Honesty is fast disappearing here too. Only a few years ago in Toronto, directors of a large credit union were charged with theft of $11 million. The media are constantly reporting on bribery and fraud among our political leaders — occurrences that seemed very rare when I was young. Is the situation really that much worse? Or could it be that the media are now more truthful whereas, in the past, they were bought off by politicians to prevent exposure of their misdeeds?

On the subject of integrity in our political leaders, I am reminded of an encounter with some young people in Venezuela. Aristides Calvani, the Venezuelan foreign minister under the Social Christian government of Rafael Caldera, was a friend I had first met at one of the CICOP meetings in Chicago. When I was passing through Caracas a few years later he invited me to stop over an extra day to give a talk to about sixty young men from every country on the continent. They were being groomed to be future leaders of the Social Christian Party. Also present were six professors from different Social Christian parties in Europe.

When I finished my talk a big young man from Brazil led off the discussion. "The problem we have in Latin America," he said, "is that our leaders are not honest people."

I asked him, "Who do you mean by your leaders?"

He replied, "All of them — the politicians, the leaders of governments, the rich people and all the rest."

"Do you include leaders of the Church as well?"

"Yes, I do," he answered.

"So you are demanding honesty of all leaders. May I ask you, are you an honest person?" To justify my blunt question, I added, "None of us can demand of others what we ourselves do not have."

Silence.

As I left, the European professors warmly congratulated me. One of them said, "You know this problem is much worse than we thought it was. You hit the nail on the head. That was great."

What the professor was referring to was the Latin *machismo* that makes a mockery of honesty. A common example of the hypocrisy or moral double standard among Latins is that the men, although considering themselves free to play the field, demand that their brides be virgins. I have encountered cases where the man threw his wife out when he learned the first night of their honeymoon that she was not a virgin.

It's not likely that my remarks to the conference effected any lasting change in the morals of the men of Latin America. I do think, however, that when we're criticizing the all-too-obvious flaws of our leaders, we would do well to see whether our own moral houses are in order.

In my retirement here at Scarboro, health continues to be a problem. I have had a prostate operation and two serious operations on my legs to improve blood circulation. In June 1990, my third heart attack struck. I was "out of the world" briefly. My first awareness on returning to the land of the living was the smell of metal burning. Electric shocks had been applied to get my heart going again. Hearing about that experience, people often ask, "How does it feel to die? Did you see a tunnel and lights?" No, I did not. The experience showed me how easy it is to die. There was no fear, no worry about my sins, no thought of praying — nothing at all but total emptiness.

As a result of the attack, I have slowed up considerably, staying alive by consuming lots of pills every day. My walking pace is slower and the distances covered are shorter. Neither my mind nor my memory seem to have been affected, though. My list of interests, however, is decreasing. For example, I have little interest in travel, less in food, clothing, going to shows, movies and the like.

Much to my amazement, not long ago I received an invitation to speak to a huge gathering of high school students at an

Ash Wednesday service in a suburb of Toronto. Of course, everybody expected me to talk about justice but I soon moved on to the topic of sexuality. The teachers had told me that these were basically good kids — no problems with drugs or violence — but that they were all obsessed with sex. So I talked about how your body is your most precious possession and if you start giving it away, you'll never respect yourself. The kids lapped up my talk, according to the teachers. Since then, I have received a couple more invitations to speak to teen groups.

Is this the start of a new phase of my priesthood at this late stage? Not likely. It does show, though, that even when you think your life story is finished, interesting new experiences may come along.

In any case, I am drawing near the end of this saga. I have done my best to be truthful. No doubt a few people may be hurt by my bluntness. Probably, I too will be hurt. No doubt I will be criticized for name dropping, also for omitting names. Most of the names in the first category were those of people well known and therefore unlikely to object. As for the names omitted, charity was the reason. I should mention that I am grateful to a few people who believed in me and my work. One person in particular, an American, who was my greatest benefactor, wishes to remain anonymous.

Reaching the end of these memoirs, I feel much as I did when Dave Tarnow was convincing me to make the film. Several times I wanted to call the whole thing off. I am now wondering if maybe I should cancel the publishing of these writings. It seems to me, however, that the film did some good, judging from the feedback, so maybe this book will too.

Now, some final thoughts on this unique institution called the Catholic priesthood, so rapidly disappearing in many places. Several times I have been asked whether I would do the same work if I had my life to live over. My answer is *yes*. I am grateful for the gift of the priesthood, without which I would not have been able to do a fraction of what I did.

One of the most beautiful things written on the priesthood is by a French Dominican priest, Father Jean Baptiste Henri Lacordaire:

To live in the midst of the world
without wishing its pleasures; to be
a member of each family, yet belonging
to none; to share all sufferings; to
penetrate all secrets; to heal all wounds;
to go to men from God and offer Him
their prayers; to return from God to men
to bring pardon and hope; to have a heart of
fire for charity and a heart of bronze
for chastity; to teach and to pardon,
console and bless always. My God,
what a life! And it is yours, O priest of Jesus Christ.

The "heart of bronze for chastity" is the weak link in the priests' armour of today. But to say young men have weaker characters than formerly is inaccurate. It is the conditions of life that have changed. Certainly, a "bronze heart" is necessary in a world like ours where sex permeates all of life. To keep my vow, I built a bronze shield around me; otherwise, my vow would have been broken a thousand times. That shield has led to accusations of my being anti-woman. In any case, I do not think priests of the future will have such problems. Obligatory celibacy for parish priests will soon be a thing of the past, I hope. It is not impossible for monks to live good, celibate lives in monasteries but it is hardly a viable way of life for the active parish priest.

What were the saddest and gladdest events of my priesthood? The saddest, I think, were the two occasions, some years ago, when my parents were celebrating their sixtieth and seventieth wedding anniversaries and I was not invited to either. Both times, I had been home a few months earlier and was assured they would let me know the date of the official celebrations. Back in Panama, I waited, bag packed, ready to fly home. Being the only priest in the family, I thought it might be my privilege to offer the anniversary masses. I was not informed of the date nor invited on either occasion.

It is not easy to choose a few happy moments from a life that included so many. But two, perhaps, stand out. They were when I completed the building of the schools in Santo Domingo and in Panama. Both occasions were the culmination of long gruelling months — getting the money and materials for putting up the buildings, then the much more exasperating negotiations with government, all the red tape involved in getting so many permissions to connect water, lights and so on. It took four months to finish the job in Santo Domingo, eight months in Panama.

The goal of every priest is to bring people to God and, of course, to bring Him to the people. Few missionaries working in foreign fields ever have the consolation of seeing great results from their work. I think of the time, a few years ago in the Dominican Republic, when I was visiting a Quebec priest whom I knew well. He had worked almost forty years in the same parish and he was one of the hardest workers I ever knew. Much of his work consisted of visiting more than three dozen outlying villages by horseback. I asked him how he felt about his life. What results did he see for his long years of work?

He began by saying that the parish had more than doubled in population. The poverty of the people had worsened dramatically. The rate of promiscuity had at least tripled and despite the increase in population, even fewer were going to church than when he first came to the parish. Probably this story is typical of what most missionaries can see at the end of their lives.

Without faith, of course, the priest could not go on. Belief in God and love for Him are the forces motivating the priest to be a man of prayer and a worker for God's kingdom. Can a priest be dedicated to his work without prayer and faith? Most experts on the spiritual life would reply in the negative.

But there are exceptions. I recall reading, some years ago, a story by Bernanos about a model parish priest, as he was seen, in a rural parish in France. His diary, discovered after his death, revealed that he did not believe in God. Maybe the story is not true. A few years ago, however, I made my annual spiritual retreat with a retreat master whose content and delivery were excellent. My companions at the retreat agreed that this man gave one of the best retreats we had made in years. Only a short time later, the retreat master walked out of his monastery, leaving a note explaining that he was leaving the priesthood because he did not believe in God and never did. Mind you, he had fallen in love with a woman. Was that the real reason for his departure or was it that he had never truly believed?

To sum up my own belief as simply as possible: I believe, first of all, in God, the Creator, in His infinity, and in the Trinity. I believe He loves me, otherwise He would not have created me.

For that reason I should love Him. I do this by keeping faith and hope in Him and the means to this end is prayer. The supreme prayer, the core of our religion, is the mass, or the eucharist. It is the precious gift Christ gave us a few hours before He died, when He told us, "Do this in my memory."

I feel sure that whatever real religion is, it should express the greatest gifts that God gave us humans — joyfulness, for example. Another essential feature of religion, is that in bringing us closer to God, it should bring us closer to one another. Sometimes what passes for religion separates us from God and each other. The fact that I spent my life working for the poor was the natural expression of religion for me.

Furthermore, I believe there are truths in the beliefs of peoples who never heard of God. The way was paved for recognition of this when Vatican Council II scrapped the old adage "outside the Church there is no salvation." One of the truths we should recognize is the aboriginal peoples' belief in the sacredness of our planet. The story has been told of an Indian chief dealing with a white man who wanted to buy land. The Indian thought the white man crazy because only the Creator is the owner of land. Perhaps the chief in that story was the great Seattle.

Another story tells about his comments to Governor Stevens. "Your religion," Seattle told the governor, "was written on tablets of stone by the iron finger of an angry god...Our religion is the tradition of our ancestors...The dream of our old men given to them in solemn hours of the night by the Great Spirit...and is written in the hearts of our people."

As we get closer to destroying this beautiful planet, we should confess a sin few of us ever acknowledged: how we hurt God by our greed and lack of respect for a planet He loves. The fact that He created it is proof that He loves it. The book of Genesis tells us how, when He finished creation, He saw it as "good". Surely if we love Him we should also love what He loves.

Part of old age is looking back on one's life as I am doing in this writing. Often I think of Thompson's poem "The Hound of Heaven" cited earlier. For years I fought the idea of being a priest. When I finally accepted the idea, one of the reasons I chose China was to get away from my family situation. Then I had to work almost three years in the one place in the world I did not want to be — my home parish. The Hound of Heaven forced me to face the very things I was running away from. In retrospect, it may be possible to get some glimpse of purpose in the divine plan. Certainly one great blessing as a result of my time in that parish was my getting to know Father Jimmy Tompkins. His passion for justice influenced all the rest of my life.

My ideal in becoming a priest was to be like the Man from Galilee. I saw Him as a reformer, a radical, who turned the world upside down. He opted for the poor. He condemned the religious leaders and called them "hypocrites". I often wonder if He returned now to earth, would He possibly call our Church leaders by the same name?

My favourite scripture passage about Him is Luke 4: 16-20. In the scene described, Jesus stands up in the synagogue and reads from Isaiah: "The Spirit of the Lord is upon me, because He has anointed me to preach the good news to the poor. He has sent me to proclaim release to the captives and recovering sight to the blind, to set at liberty those who are oppressed, to proclaim the acceptable year of the Lord." When He closed the book, He added, "Today this scripture has been fulfilled in your hearing." As this was happening in His home town where His reception was less than enthusiastic, He later said: (v. 24) "No prophet is accepted in his own country."

Well, I know what it feels like to be rejected by your own people. But I'm not complaining. Support and acceptance have come my way too. A few days ago I received a letter from a long-time friend, a priest in New York, Father John Catoir, Director of the Christophers. He told me he had lent the film "Padre Pablo" to a mutual friend of ours. The friend wrote in response, "We loved Harvey's film. He did so much. It brought tears to our eyes remembering that dear old rebel."